BUT AS FOR ME . . .

365 Daily Devotionals

Obieray Rogers

But As For Me . . . 365 Daily Devotionals. Copyright © 2018 by Obieray Rogers

Editor: Cynthia Donaldson

ISBN 9781724003126

Printed in the United States of America

ANTICIPATION

The reason I can still find hope is that I keep this one thing in mind: The LORD's mercy. We were not completely wiped out. His compassion is never limited. It is new every morning. His faithfulness is great. (Lamentations 3:21-23, GWT)

As we embark on a new day and a new year, let's do so with a greater sense of anticipation. If you think back over the past year, you'll realize that every day brought a new set of circumstances that were sometimes unexpected and out of our control. That's okay because it added to the sense of adventure. If you knew everything that was going to happen and how it would happen and who would be involved, you'd soon be bored. You'd have nothing to expect.

As the new year begins, let's vow to ask God to keep us in the palm of His hand. That way, no matter what happens, we're covered by the Almighty. And, since the Almighty covers us, no weapon formed against us can prosper. That doesn't mean the weapon won't be formed; it means that since we're in God's hands, nothing can harm us. I don't know about you, but I'll take that assurance any day.

God continually amazes me, and I'm on tiptoes looking forward to what's going to happen within the upcoming year. Won't you join me in the anticipation?

God, we thank You that You're willing to partner
with us in this adventure called life.
Help us to hold tightly to Your unchanging hand.

I HAVE THE POWER

Look to the Lord and ask for His strength. Look to Him all the time. (1 Chronicles 16:11, NLV)

Growing up reading comic books—and before Women's Lib was a reality—I'd often see advertisements for the Charles Atlas bodybuilding program, which promised to turn scrawny men into muscle-bound machines, if followed correctly. Also, during this time, Popeye cartoons were shown daily, geared toward men (again) who would miraculously gain muscles, if they ate spinach. The goal was to gain enough strength to take care of any problem that came your way.

Fortunately, I don't have to change genders, increase my muscles, or eat spinach to get strength. God has promised to give me His strength—and everything else I need—if I but ask for it. He's willing to do the same for you.

The LORD is my strength and my shield;
in him my heart trusts,
and I am helped; my heart exults, and with my song
I give thanks to him.
(Psalm 28:7, ESV)

IS THAT YOUR FINAL ANSWER?

Then he told them: "Go and preach the good news to everyone in the world." (Mark 16:15, CEV)

I enjoy watching the game show *Who Wants to be a Millionaire*. It's a fun and entertaining way to learn something new. I especially like watching the thought process of the contestants as they work through the multiple choices to (hopefully) arrive at the correct answer. Once they give their answer the host always asks, "Is that your final answer?" allowing them an opportunity to think things over one more time before committing to their choice.

When we incorporate today's Scripture in our everyday lives, we are going to encounter those who will be like the contestants working their way to (hopefully) the correct answer—yes to accepting Jesus Christ as their Lord and Savior. Although we would like to, we can't make anyone say yes. That is not our responsibility. All we can do is present the Good News and pray they are receptive. "So then neither he who plants is anything, nor he who waters, but God who gives the increase" (1 Corinthians 3:7, NKJV). However, if those we witness to choose not to accept our offer, they will never be able to stand before God and say that no one ever told them they didn't have to be lost. And, please don't let their refusal deter you from sharing the Good News with everyone you encounter.

Be sure . . . 'cause forever is a
long, long, long, long time.
Be Sure. Kenny Gamble and Leon Huff. 1977.

BUSINESS AS USUAL

"But as the days of Noah were, so also will the coming of the Son of Man be. For as in the days before the flood, they were eating and drinking, marrying and giving in marriage, until the day that Noah entered the ark, and did not know until the flood came and took them all away, so also will the coming of the Son of Man be." (Matthew 24:37-39, NKJV)

Only God knows why He's delayed the Second Coming. We need to be ready spiritually for that day when "in a moment, in the twinkling of an eye, we're going to be changed" (1 Corinthians 15:52).

Don't get caught unaware. Be ready spiritually for Jesus' return. Don't assume you'll have time to get it right. And, please don't think that because God hasn't stopped the negative things you do that He's okay with what you're doing. There are no levels of sin, and only you know what in your life is displeasing to God. Perhaps He's giving you time to get it right. Perhaps He's using this devotional as another warning. You've seen in your own life how God has kept His Word. Jesus said He would return and take back with Him those who belong to Him.

The people of Noah's time didn't believe Noah's warning either until it started raining. By then it was too late. Don't let that be said of you.

It was not long afterwards that he rose into the sky and disappeared into a cloud, leaving them staring after him. As they were straining their eyes for another glimpse, suddenly two white-robed men were standing there among them, and said, "Men of Galilee, why are you standing here staring at the sky? Jesus has gone away to heaven, and some day, just as he went, he will return!" (Acts 1:9-11, TLB)

DOING WHAT I DO

Work willingly at whatever you do, as though you were working for the Lord rather than for people. Remember that the Lord will give you an inheritance as your reward, and that the Master you are serving is Christ. (Colossians 3:23-24, NLT)

Some people erroneously assume that a person who cooks also bakes, but that is not true. Baking requires a lot of patience. It is confining in the sense that you're forced to follow the recipe exactly, or the taste of the final product will be off.

Although I do not consider myself a baker, there are four cakes I know I make better than most. That's not a conceited statement, just a fact, based on the amount of time I've spent perfecting these four desserts: (1) A whipped cream pound cake with a pecan and cashew crust; (2) A carrot cake topped with a perfect cream cheese frosting; (3) A buttermilk mint chocolate chip cake with a mint chocolate chip whipped cream frosting; and (4) A made-from-scratch yellow cake with a hint of orange zest topped with pineapple, whipped cream, pecans, and fresh strawberries.

I refined these cakes because of my former catering business. But, God didn't call me to be a baker. My "real job" is to build up the Kingdom of God through words. Someone else's job is to do it with baking. God hasn't called me to do everything; He expects me to be faithful over what He's anointed and appointed me to do.

Thank You, Lord, for making our calling clear.
Help us to open our ears to hear, our mouths to say yes, and our eyes to see those who need what we have to offer.

A BEAUTIFUL DUET

"Ask me and I will tell you remarkable secrets you do not know about things to come." (Jeremiah 33:3, NLT)

During funerals, my pastor (Bishop Timothy J. Clarke) quotes several Scriptures as he and the other ministers enter the sanctuary and walk to the pulpit. He does this to start the celebration of life service and to reassure those in attendance that God is still in control, even when it's a sad occasion.

You may wonder why I call this devotional a duet when I only provide one Scripture. Well, wonder no more! Like a great singer who partners with another great singer to produce beautiful music, the prophet Jeremiah partnered with himself to create a beautiful promise.

We often quote Jeremiah 29:11—"For I know the plans I have for you," says the LORD. "They are plans for good and not for disaster, to give you a future and a hope" (NLT)—and receive comfort from the words, and rightly so. They are profound in their simplicity. However, I suggest that if we couple Jeremiah 29:11 with today's Scripture, it will make you sit down, take a deep breath and absorb the enormity of the statements. God has plans for us, tells us to ask Him what they are, and lets us know He'll respond. So many Christians are walking through life wondering what they're to do and how to do it when all they need do is ask God. Now, He may not immediately answer every question or tell you every single detail. However, He will point you in the right direction and put you on the right path to achieve His promise. God said, "I know . . ." which tells me you need to ask Him directly what His plans are for you. Go ahead and pray and stand ready to be amazed at His response. I know you won't be disappointed.

We thank You, God, for the direct line we have to You.
Thank You for the assurance that if we ask, You will respond.
Help us to seek Your face for direction.

DARE TO BE DIFFERENT

Two of the men who had explored the land, Joshua son of Nun and Caleb son of Jephunneh, tore their clothing. They said to all the people of Israel, "The land we traveled through and explored is a wonderful land! And if the LORD is pleased with us, he will bring us safely into that land and give it to us. It is a rich land flowing with milk and honey. Do not rebel against the LORD, and don't be afraid of the people of the land. They are only helpless prey to us! They have no protection, but the LORD is with us! Don't be afraid of them!" (Numbers 14:6-9, NLT)

It is challenging to take a stand for something in the face of opposition, especially when it comes from people who should be on your side. The children of Israel had been given instructions to spy out the land. Ten returned with a negative report of what couldn't happen. However, Joshua and Caleb reported what could happen. See, Joshua and Caleb didn't worry about the size of the inhabitants occupying the land they were going to conquer. After experiencing the Red Sea crossing, any doubts they may have had about God were erased. Their faith was firmly rooted and grounded in the belief that God could do anything; and because they were His children, Joshua and Caleb believed they could do anything, too.

Just because something has never been done doesn't mean it can't happen. Most times God is waiting on someone to line up with what He has already said. There was nothing wrong with either Joshua's or Caleb's memory and they were just crazy enough to believe that if God said it, they could do it. Why don't you ask God to give you a Red Sea crossing type of faith so that you, too, can dare to be different!

Fear not, I am with thee, oh, be not dismayed,
For I am thy God and will still give thee aid.
I'll strengthen thee, help thee, and cause thee to stand,
upheld by my gracious, omnipotent hand.
How Firm A Foundation. John Rippon. 1787.

KEEP IT TO YOURSELF

I set out during the night with a few others. I had not told anyone what my God had put in my heart to do . . . The officials did not know where I had gone or what I was doing, because as yet I had said nothing to the Jews or the priests or nobles or officials or any others who would be doing the work. (Nehemiah 2:12, 16, NIV)

There are some lessons you can only learn the hard way. One such lesson for me was not sharing what God is doing in my life with everyone. I discovered that people can't always relate to what God is saying to me, especially if it's something they wouldn't do. And since it's something they wouldn't do, they can't always understand why I would even consider doing it. We must be careful not to let people—especially those we respect—talk us out of our blessing. We don't disregard or dismiss their advice; we filter it through the Holy Spirit and we stand firm on what God has said.

Nehemiah had a desire to rebuild the walls of Jerusalem, which was going to be a monumental task. He was almost immediately met with opposition but pressed on anyway. He assembled a team of people committed to the process and passed out assignments. When the threats from Sanballat and Tobias started coming fast and furious, Nehemiah prayed harder (Nehemiah 5:4-5).

Nehemiah's strategy for success should be ours as well: get clear directions from God about what to do and how to do it, follow it up with prayer and work, stay focused, and give God the glory for His accomplishments.

So the wall was completed on the twenty-fifth of Elul, in fifty-two days. (Nehemiah 6:15, NIV)

DUE UPON RECEIPT

For this is the love of God, that we keep His commandments. And His commandments are not burdensome. (1 John 5:3, NKJV)

Some bills arrive with a specific date when payment is due, usually at least ten days from the date of the invoice. Then, there are those bills that are payable upon receipt; there is no grace period. Those are the ones you can't ignore because doing so will involve adverse results.

God has been good to all of us. Every morning we awake means that a bill is due upon receipt. What's the payment, you ask? Thankfulness, praise, and worship to God; love and peace for others; demonstrating the faithfulness of God to everyone you meet.

Unlike our money, which frequently runs out before the month is over, the payment God requires is never-ending. I don't know about you, but every time I think of it, I'm humbled and awed.

Lord, thank You for giving us the privilege of knowing You.
Help us to embrace everything You have for us,
and be willing to share with everyone we encounter.

I'VE PITCHED MY TENT
IN A LAND CALLED HOPE

I saw God before me for all time. Nothing can shake me; he's right by my side. I'm glad from the inside out, ecstatic; I've pitched my tent in the land of hope. I know you'll never dump me in Hades; I'll never even smell the stench of death. You've got my feet on the life-path, with your face shining sun-joy all around. (Acts 2:25-26, MSG)

According to the American Institute of Stress, stress has many different causes, which can vary from person to person. A situation or condition that bothers one person might not worry another person at all. Some individuals get stressed easily, while others need several different stressful events before they begin to feel the physical or psychological effects.

One of the things I find most stressful is moving. I've moved several times in my life, and hopefully this last one is the final one before I go to Heaven.

People in the Old Testament instituted the original mobile homes because they lived in tents that they transported from place to place. I like that idea. No, I'm not going to sell my home and live in a tent, but, I am going to adopt a mindset of hope. *The NAS New Testament Greek Lexicon* says that the word hope is translated "elpis," meaning to be an expectation of good. This is my new philosophy in every situation and every circumstance: I *hope* that things will get better. I *hope* that things will change. I *hope* that I will be able to accept whatever comes. I *hope* that my patience will increase, and my stubbornness will decrease. I *hope* that my love for people will grow to a phenomenal size. I *hope* that in everything and with everything God will be glorified.

That's where I'm moving my tent: To a land of hope. There's plenty of room, if you'd like to join me.

Those who trust in the Lord are like Mount Zion,
which cannot be moved,
but abides forever. (Psalm 125:1, NKJV)

EXIT STAGE LEFT

The Lord is near to those who have a broken heart. And He saves those who are broken in spirit. (Psalm 34:18, NLV)

Ending a relationship is hard. Sometimes, God requires us to break an association because the person has fulfilled their purpose in our life. It's not easy; matter of fact, most of the time we're reluctant to move to obedience, especially if the connection was positive. Yet, we must trust that God knows what He's doing. We often quote Jeremiah 29:11 (NLV), "For I know the plans I have for you," says the Lord, "plans for well-being and not for trouble, to give you a future and a hope." We believe what the prophet wrote until God puts it to the test. Then, we try to circumvent God's command, so we can "have our cake and eat it too."

The next time God ends a relationship through death, distance, or deceit, it's okay to shed tears over the loss. Every person we encounter leaves an imprint, so it's only natural to be emotional when they're no longer around. But, after the tears, we must ask God to help us move forward. He still has something for us to do.

My body and my heart may grow weak,
but God is the strength of my heart
and all I need forever. (Psalm 73:26, NLV)

KEEP THE FAITH, BABY

Don't be weary in prayer; keep at it; watch for God's answers and remember to be thankful when they come. (Colossians 4:2, TLB)

I think we all can admit that some of our days are busier than others. Some events that take place are planned; others are unexpected. I submit that our lives will be less stressful when we stay in an attitude of prayer.

Our Scripture reminds us not to grow tired of praying, to be persistent, and to be thankful. That's good advice, especially as it pertains to something we've been praying for a while. God's timing isn't like ours. We have the blessed assurance that He hears and will respond at the appropriate time. Our job is to stay faithful in prayer and wait for the manifestation. That isn't always easy, but God never said it would be.

Each morning You listen to my prayer, as I bring my requests to You and wait for Your reply.
(Psalm 5:3, CEV)

YOU MIGHT AS WELL GET COMFORTABLE

But you must not forget this one thing, dear friends: A day is like a thousand years to the Lord, and a thousand years is like a day. (2 Peter 3:8, NLT)

The last time I was in Chicago, we were on the Dan Ryan Expressway. As is often the case, traffic was at a standstill. It was a beautiful day, so several of the drivers had gotten out of their cars. They knew traffic wasn't going to move anytime soon, so rather than sit frustrated in the car, they took advantage of the weather. Eventually, traffic began to move, but it was at such a snail's pace that I'm sure some drivers would have preferred it to return to the standstill.

My point is, there are circumstances beyond our control. It's frustrating and irritating, and we may be prone to throw a temper tantrum. But, when we're finished, we're still in the situation and nothing has changed. Then, when things do begin to change, it's so minuscule that the frustration continues. The reality is that even when things move slowly, we need to remind ourselves they *are* moving. If we keep moving forward, we'll eventually reach our destination.

> *"We must keep moving. If you can't fly, run;*
> *if you can't run, walk; if you can't walk, crawl;*
> *but by all means, keep moving."*
> —Dr. Martin Luther King, Jr.

USE WHAT YOU HAVE

For even if I should boast somewhat more about our authority, which the Lord gave us for edification and not for your destruction, I shall not be ashamed—lest I seem to terrify you by letters. "For his letters," they say, "are weighty and powerful, but his bodily presence is weak, and his speech contemptible." (2 Corinthians 10:8-10, NKJV)

I love to read, and when I do, I *never* think about the author's appearance or their speaking voice. It's incredible that the apostle who wrote a large portion of the New Testament was allegedly not the most effective speaker.

Paul didn't stop preaching because of what some perceived as lack. "Seated in a window was a young man named Eutychus, who was sinking into a deep sleep as Paul talked on and on. When he was sound asleep, he fell to the ground from the third story and was picked up dead" (Acts 20:9, NIV). That incident didn't deter Paul. "Paul went down, threw himself on the young man and put his arms around him. 'Don't be alarmed,' he said. 'He's alive!' Then he went upstairs again and broke bread and ate. After talking until daylight, he left. The people took the young man home alive and were greatly comforted" (Acts 20:9-12, NIV).

Perhaps Paul wasn't the most eloquent of speakers. There are no audio recordings to confirm one way or the other. Regardless, Paul kept going forward in his assignment to spread the Gospel. His speaking may have been weak, but we know without a doubt that his writing was flawless. The words are just as powerful today as they were then.

Let the one who boasts boast in the Lord. For it is not the one who commends himself who is approved, but the one whom the Lord commends. (2 Corinthians 10:17-18, NIV)

TODAY IS A GREAT DAY

But then I think about this, and I have hope: We are still alive because the LORD's faithful love never ends. Every morning he shows it in new ways! You are so very true and loyal! I say to myself, "The LORD is my God, and I trust him." (Lamentations 3:21-24, ERV)

In the movie *The Wiz*, there's a song close to the end of the film where the people are freed from the torment of the wicked witch. They dance and sing and rejoice because a brand-new day has come for them. It's out with the old and in with the new.

That's the way we should look at each day we're blessed to wake. Whatever happened the previous day is over, and there's nothing we can do about it, whether it was good or bad. If we train ourselves to see every day as one we've never experienced before, we'll open ourselves to the adventure of living. When we get complacent—oh, it's Monday again—we miss out on the joy God has for us. Yes, Monday comes every seven days; however, every Monday is different because you've never experienced it before. You may do routine things such as going to work or school, but these are things you've never done on *this* day. It's fresh. It's new. It's exciting!

When you wake up every morning, tell God "Thank You" and then remind yourself, "Today is going to be a great day!" It doesn't matter if there's snow on the ground or the sun is shining; the bills still need to be paid, and the kids are again acting crazy. You have the gift of a new day. Dance, sing, rejoice in the fact you're alive. That's reason enough to celebrate!

Lord, this morning when I woke up, I didn't have any doubt that it was because of Your mercy. Thank You for loving me enough to give me another day to enjoy Your beauty and creation. Help me to remember to tell somebody about Your goodness.

MAKE IT SO, NUMBER ONE

People from many nations will go there and say, "Come, let's go up to the mountain of the LORD, to the Temple of the God of Jacob. Then God will teach us his way of living, and we will follow him." His teaching, the LORD's message, will begin in Jerusalem on Mount Zion and will go out to all the world. Then God will act as judge to end arguments between people in many places. He will decide what is right for great nations far and near. They will stop using their weapons for war. They will hammer their swords into plows and use their spears to make tools for harvesting. All fighting between nations will end. They will never again train for war. They will sit under their own grapevine and fig tree. No one will make them afraid. That is because the LORD All-Powerful said it would happen like that. All the people from other nations follow their own gods, but we will follow the LORD our God forever and ever! (Micah 4:2-5, ERV)

On the television show *Star Trek: The Next Generation*, Captain Jean-Luc Picard made numerous decisions as the leader of the starship. Commander William T. Riker was given the instructions to carry out Captain Picard's orders with a familiar phrase: "Make it so, Number One."

Whenever I read today's Scripture, I say a variation of Captain Picard's phrase. Anyone reading the headlines or listening to the news knows that if ever unity was needed in this world, it's now. I'm encouraging you to adopt Captain Picard's phrase, knowing that the Number One who can help isn't a fictional character on a television show, but the Number One of all existence! God alone is the only One who can stop the madness and bring peace. We need only to agree in prayer with what He has already said.

"If My people who are called by My name will humble themselves, and pray and seek My face, and turn from their wicked ways, then I will hear from heaven, and will forgive their sin and heal their land."
(2 Chronicles 7:14, NKJV)

PREPARE YOUR FIELD

Get ready; be prepared! (Ezekiel 38:7, NLT)

Whenever I watch the DVD of the Kendrick Brothers' 2006 movie, *Facing the Giants,* there's a scene that always grabs my attention. It's the one where Coach Grant interacts with Mr. Bridges. Coach Grant has been praying for direction; Mr. Bridges stops by his office and reads Revelation 3:7-8 about having an open door set before us. When Coach Grant asks for clarification, Mr. Bridges tells him the story of two farmers who desperately needed rain, but only one prepared his field. Mr. Bridges then asks: "Which one do you think trusted God to send the rain?" Coach Grant replies, "The one who prepared his field." Mr. Bridges then asks, "Which one are you?" and goes on to say that, "God will send the rain when He's ready. You need to prepare your field to receive it." That is one of my favorite scenes out of the entire movie.

When God gives us a promise, it is our responsibility to prepare for it to come to fruition. How? I'm glad you asked! After determining the purpose for the field, there are steps necessary to make our field (us) receptive to what God has:

The first thing is to smooth out the ground (our lives) by getting rid of all the unnecessary things that prevent us from moving forward in God.

The second thing is to keep our ground (our lives) well-fed and hydrated, by reading and absorbing the Word of God as a steady diet.

The third thing is to accept only good seed in our ground (our lives). We have choices as to what we will and will not receive.

After we've prepared, we then wait for God's timing. Whatever God has promised will come to pass. In the words of singer/composer Dottie Peoples, He's an on-time God, yes, He is!

So watch out and be ready! You don't know when
the time will come. (Mark 13:33, CEV)

SUPERMAN OR CLARK KENT?

For by You I can run against a troop, by my God I can leap over a wall. As for God, His way is perfect; The word of the LORD is proven; He is a shield to all who trust in Him. For who is God, except the LORD? And who is a rock, except our God? It is God who arms me with strength and makes my way perfect. (Psalm 18:28-31, NKJV)

The Adventures of Superman, a television show from the 1950s, was based on characters created by Jerry Siegel and Joe Shuster. George Reeves played the roles of Superman (a visitor from another planet) and his alter-ego, Clark Kent (a mild-mannered reporter for a great metropolitan newspaper). While reading Psalm 18, the thought came to me that if *The Adventures of Superman* had been set in biblical times, the ideal person for the job would have been King David.

The same man who penned, "For by You I can run against a troop, by my God I can leap over a wall" (Psalm 18:29, NKJV) is the same one who penned, "The Lord is my shepherd; I shall not want" (Psalm 23:1, NKJV). David knew where his help came from and was never shy about tapping into his source of power: God.

David knew what each of us needs to learn and embrace. We all have a dual personality: There's our Superman persona who, when the need arises, finds strength we didn't know we possessed to do the seemingly impossible. And then there's our Clark Kent persona, who turns the other cheek, loves our neighbors as we love ourselves, and goes the extra mile. Both personas are required for us to do the work of the Kingdom, and both personas need God to empower us.

Lord, help us to tap into Your power and strength
to accomplish Your will and work.

WHAT ARE YOU GOING TO DO WITH THE GIFT?

And when they came together, he gave them this order: "Do not leave Jerusalem, but wait for the gift I told you about, the gift my Father promised. John baptized with water, but in a few days you will be baptized with the Holy Spirit." (Acts 1:4-5, GNT)

Gift-*giving* is an art. There are: (1) those who take the time to find out what you need and give appropriately; (2) those who give you what they would want if they were receiving the gift; (3) those who provide you with something because they want something in return; and (4) those who give you something merely for the sheer enjoyment of seeing a smile on your face. You're the only one who knows which category you fall into and why, but it is something to ponder.

Gift-*receiving* is also an art. There are: (1) those who receive the gift and gratefully use it; (2) those who receive the gift and put it away until a special occasion arises; and (3) those who receive the gift and discard it as insignificant. Again, only you know which category you fall into and why.

God has graciously given us His Son, Jesus Christ, to bring us into right relationship with Him. He further gave us the gift of the Holy Spirit to provide us with power for the journey called life. I thank God daily for thinking enough of me to *gift* me with His Son and the Holy Spirit. God's gifts are from everlasting to everlasting.

You don't have to save God's gifts only for company.
They are meant to be used daily for
both you and God's people to enjoy.

GO AHEAD AND ASK FOR WHAT YOU WANT

Elisha talked to the woman whose son he had brought back to life. He said, "You and your family should move to another country, because the LORD has decided that there will be a famine here. It will last for seven years." After seven years she returned from the land of the Philistines. She went to speak with the king to ask him to help her get back her house and land. The king was talking with Gehazi, the servant of the man of God. Gehazi was telling the king about Elisha bringing a dead person back to life. At that same time the woman whose son Elisha brought back to life went to the king . . . . Gehazi said, "My lord and king, this is the woman, and this is the son who Elisha brought back to life." The king asked the woman what she wanted, and she told him. The king said, "Give to the woman all that belongs to her. And give her all the harvest of her land from the day she left the country until now." (2 Kings 8:1-6, ERV)

There are times when it seems like what we need is impossible to obtain. The thought of merely asking for the object we need from whoever has it isn't in our realm of possibilities, but it is what's necessary for our desire to be fulfilled.

God had orchestrated events so that the Shunammite woman would be in the right place at the right time. She had seen God move on her behalf before. She gave birth to a son she didn't anticipate because she took care of Elisha, the man of God. When her son died, she watched God return him to her, whole and healthy. Surviving a seven-year famine was no big deal. She needed her property back and went to someone who could restore it to her. She may have been physically speaking with the king, but God responded.

It's okay to ask humans for what we need
so long as we recognize God as our source.
People are okay, but God is far greater!

LESSONS LEARNED

"I have always been God. When I do something, no one can change what I have done. And no one can save people from my power. . . So, don't remember what happened in earlier times. Don't think about what happened a long time ago, because I am doing something new! Now you will grow like a new plant. Surely you know this is true. I will even make a road in the desert, and rivers will flow through that dry land." (Isaiah 43:13[b], 18-19, ERV)

When I got saved, there were people who told me I wouldn't make it as a Christian and, to be honest, there were days I wondered about it myself.

I haven't done everything perfectly (who has?), and I've always tried to learn from my mistakes. That doesn't mean I don't have regrets. I would love to have the opportunity to do a lot of things over. There are people who still take pleasure in reminding me of the mistakes I've made. Nevertheless, one thing I've learned while walking with the Lord is that His memory is the only one that counts. People may try to hold me to what I used to do or how I used to be, but God has clearly said that is not the way it's going to be.

It doesn't matter whether you've crossed every "t" and dotted every "i" during your spiritual lifetime. What matters is that you've learned from your mistakes and have put the past in perspective. Don't dwell on it. Don't allow your past to keep you in bondage. And, whatever you do, don't allow people to keep you from pursuing the things God has for you.

Lord, let me learn my lessons quickly,
so I can continue to move up in You.

WATCH OVER ME, LORD

I will both lie down in peace, and sleep; For You alone, O LORD, make me dwell in safety. (Psalm 4:8, NKJV)

As a child, my mother taught me this prayer: "Now I lay me down to sleep. I pray the Lord my soul to keep. If I should die before I wake. I pray the Lord my soul to take." And, I must confess, it's the prayer I prayed every night until I received Jesus as Lord and Savior at the age of 34, because it was the only one I knew.

I'm not sure who wrote this 18th Century children's prayer, but I believe the theology behind it is simply a desire for God to watch over and protect us while we sleep. This was not a new desire, since King David penned Psalm 4:8 years before the Incarnation of Christ. The words allowed David to put the cares of the day behind him and go to sleep, knowing that God would watch over him. I have that same confidence.

In the years since accepting Jesus Christ, I've learned a lot, cried a lot, and grown a lot. One thing that has been consistent is my belief that God would and will watch over me. At the close of the day when I shut down for the night, the last thing I say to God before turning my face into my pillow is, "Watch over me, Lord." My prayer life has significantly evolved from "Now I lay me down to sleep." I no longer cite a childhood prayer, but I still have sense enough to continue to ask for God's protection while I slumber. How about you?

Lord, whether it's a request from a child or an adult,
You provide peace, sleep, and protection.
For this, I give You praise.

CUT ... THAT'S A WRAP

Therefore, if anyone is in Christ, he is a new creation; old things have passed away; behold, all things have become new. (2 Corinthians 5:17, NKJV)

When the final scene of a movie is shot, the director calls out "Cut! That's a wrap!" meaning the film is finished, although it's not yet ready for public viewing. The movie needs to be edited. Some scenes will be deleted, others may have to be re-shot, and sometimes new scenes are added. Those who work in the industry realize it's all a process.

Before we accepted Jesus Christ as Lord and Savior, our lives could have been compared to the unedited version of a movie. All the scenes were in place, and we thought that it was complete. But, then, Jesus comes into our lives, and He, the Father, and the Holy Spirit begin the editing process. Some scenes are deleted, some changed, and some new ones are added. It's all a process. When we realize Who is in control, we're not likely to get upset at how long the process takes.

Don't be impatient. Wait for the Lord, and he will come and save you!
Be brave, stouthearted, and courageous.
Yes, wait and he will help you.
(Psalm 27:14, TLB)

JUST A LITTLE BUMP IN THE ROAD

So, we're not giving up. How could we! Even though on the outside it often looks like things are falling apart on us, on the inside, where God is making new life, not a day goes by without his unfolding grace. These hard times are small potatoes compared to the coming good times, the lavish celebration prepared for us. There's far more here than meets the eye. The things we see now are here today, gone tomorrow. But the things we can't see now will last forever. (2 Corinthians 4:16-18, MSG)

The streets in my neighborhood were being re-paved. The workers had taken care of the main street, but the side streets still had an indentation between the old and the new portions. Some of the indentations were quite deep, causing you to really feel the bumps. On the way to work the other day, we went over a stretch of road that had not yet been completed, and it was quite jolting. Just when we thought it would never end, we suddenly hit the portion of the street that had already been paved. The difference was like night and day.

I thought about that in terms of the experiences we go through. There are times when we're right in the eye of the hurricane, being tossed to and fro, and wondering if it's ever going to stop. Then, just when we think we can't take much more, we suddenly hit a smooth patch and realize that what we went through was only temporary.

For our present troubles are small and won't last very long. Yet they produce for us a glory that vastly outweighs them and will last forever!
(2 Corinthians 4:17, NLT)

FREE!

As he stepped out onto land, a madman from town met him; he was a victim of demons. He hadn't worn clothes for a long time, nor lived at home; he lived in the cemetery. When he saw Jesus he screamed, fell before him, and bellowed, "What business do you have messing with me? You're Jesus, Son of the High God, but don't give me a hard time!" (The man said this because Jesus had started to order the unclean spirit out of him). Time after time the demon threw the man into convulsions. He had been placed under constant guard and tied with chains and shackles, but crazed and driven wild by the demon, he would shatter the bonds. Jesus asked him, "What is your name?" "Mob. My name is Mob," he said, because many demons afflicted him. (Luke 8:26-30, MSG)

According to *Webster's New World College Dictionary, 4th Edition* (1999), the word "free" has several definitions, including: (1) not under the control of some other person or some arbitrary power; (2) able to move in any direction; not held, as in chains; not kept from motion; loose; and (3) released or removed from. The man in the above Scripture embodies these definitions, and so do we who were once held captive and are now free in the power of Jesus Christ.

Can you remember the day you met Jesus? Do you remember how you felt? If you're like me, you felt awe, amazement, gratefulness, and humility all at the same time. I look back at the way I was living and wonder how I survived! But, when God enters your life, you realize how bound you are.

Like the man in today's Scripture, God wants you free because He has something for you to do. The man in the Scripture was told "Return to your own house and tell what great things God has done for you." And he went his way and proclaimed throughout the whole city what great things Jesus had done for him (Luke 8:39, NKJV). God would have you to do the same.

Therefore, if the Son makes you free,
you shall be free indeed. (John 8:36, NKJV)

DOING THE NECESSARY

Humble yourselves, therefore, under God's mighty hand, that he may lift you up in due time. Cast all your anxiety on him because he cares for you. (1 Peter 5:6-7, NIV)

I've heard people say, "I prayed, and God didn't answer, so I had to take matters into my own hands." I wonder why they bothered to pray at all if they weren't going to allow God time to move. However, I believe if we follow the admonition in today's Scripture, our lives will become less stressful. Verse seven begins with six words that, if embraced, will change our perspective:

Cast. This means to throw off, discard. Follow the example of professional fishers who "fling" their nets out as far as possible. We need to "fling" our problems in God's direction.

All. The first two words of verse six are essential: Humble yourselves. I believe part of the problem with worrying is that we think we can handle things on our own. Humbling yourself requires standing naked before God, telling Him "I can't do this!" and then stepping aside so He can work. It doesn't mean turning things over to God and then taking them back to "help" Him.

Your Anxiety. We are a community of those connected to us, so the things that concern you may involve other people. Psalm 138:8 (NKJV) is a verse to stand on: "The LORD will perfect that which concerns me" and that means anything and everything.

On Him. No one else can help you. People can give you advice and perhaps a temporary solution to the problem. But, if you want the problem fixed once and for all, you're going to need God!

Don't fret or worry. Instead of worrying, pray. Let petitions and praises shape your worries into prayers, letting God know your concerns. Before you know it, a sense of God's wholeness, everything coming together for good, will come and settle you down. It's wonderful what happens when Christ displaces worry at the center of your life.
(Philippians 4:6-7, MSG)

IT REALLY IS ALL ABOUT YOU

I, therefore, the prisoner of the Lord, beseech you to walk worthy of the calling with which you were called, with all lowliness and gentleness, with longsuffering, bearing with one another in love, endeavoring to keep the unity of the Spirit in the bond of peace. (Ephesians 4:1-3, NKJV)

Have you heard the expression, "It's not you, but me?" It's usually said regarding a breakup, to let the other person down gently, although the other person may well be causing the need for the separation. Usually, hearing the words manifests some level of pain, depending on how involved one was in the relationship.

Regardless of the pain level, if we can look at it from the other person's point of view, we may see things differently. It is *you* who can take the high road. It is *you* who can reach past the hurt and pain for a possible resolution. It is *you* who can tap into God's Spirit so profoundly that you can forget and release and move on.

We must make every effort to keep the bond of peace. You won't have exhausted every effort until God says "done," and you won't hear Him speak if you don't stay in touch. So, see, it really is about you!

"My peace is the legacy I leave to you.
I don't give gifts like those of this world.
Do not let your heart be troubled or fearful."
(John 14:27, VOICE)

IN THE BEGINNING

The faithful love of the LORD never ends! His mercies never cease. Great is his faithfulness; his mercies begin afresh each morning. (Lamentations 3:22-23, NLT)

The first few days of a new year bring a sense of excitement and unbridled enthusiasm for all that will occur between now and this time next year. We hope for the best. We pray for the best. We anticipate the best. We make plans for vacations and holidays, birthdays and anniversaries. We set goals for ourselves and our families. We celebrate the old year and eagerly await the new.

The beginning of a new year can also be the beginning of a new you. Ask God to take you higher so you're not satisfied with what you have and where you are. God will give you more than you can imagine and is waiting on you to ask. No, I'm not necessarily talking about more stuff. Some of us have more stuff than we know what to do with. I'm talking about asking for more of Him . . . the One you can never have too much of.

God alone knows the mountains and valleys you'll travel this year. Why not commit this moment to partner with Him as your travel guide so that no matter whether you're up or down, you know you're in good hands? A reputable insurance company may want you to believe you're in good hands with them, but God's hands are a lot more capable of taking care of you.

Wealth and honor come from You alone, for You rule over everything.
Power and might are in Your hand, and at Your discretion
people are made great and given strength.
(1 Chronicles 29:12, NLT)

BRAGGING RIGHTS

Five times I received from the Jews the forty lashes minus one. Three times I was beaten with rods, once I was pelted with stones, three times I was shipwrecked, I spent a night and a day in the open sea, I have been constantly on the move. I have been in danger from rivers, in danger from bandits, in danger from my fellow Jews, in danger from Gentiles; in danger in the city, in danger in the country, in danger at sea; and in danger from false believers. I have labored and toiled and have often gone without sleep; I have known hunger and thirst and have often gone without food; I have been cold and naked. Besides everything else, I face daily the pressure of my concern for all the churches. Who is weak, and I do not feel weak? Who is led into sin, and I do not inwardly burn? If I must boast, I will boast of the things that show my weakness. (2 Corinthians 11:24-31, NIV)

Ecclesiastes 3:7 says there is "a time to be quiet and a time to speak," suggesting that timing is everything. The apostle Paul's primary goal was to spread the gospel of Jesus Christ, and he was willing to be transparent to accomplish it.

In our Scripture today, Paul was dealing with false prophets and those he called "super-apostles" (2 Corinthians 10:5-7). He had been put in the position of having to defend his authority. It's an interesting story and you should read Chapters 10 and 11 of 2 Corinthians to get the full picture. In response to the accusations against him, Paul shared all that he had experienced for the sake of bringing the gospel to God's people. It sounded unbelievable and amazing. Paul ended his dissertation with a final comment: "The God and Father of the Lord Jesus, who is to be praised forever, knows that I am not lying" (v. 31).

"Truth is stranger than fiction, but it is because
fiction is obliged to stick to possibilities; truth isn't."
—Mark Twain

YOU'LL ONLY NEED A TASTE

Taste and see that the Lord is good. . . (Psalm 34:8, NIV)

In my parents' house, we weren't allowed to turn our nose up at any food without at least tasting it first. It didn't have to be a large bite, but we had to taste it to determine whether we'd like whatever we were trying to avoid eating. My mother's motto was, "If you try it, you might like it." I discovered some great tasting food that way.

When we offer Jesus to sinners, we need to persuade them to at least take a taste before turning their nose up at the idea of salvation. I don't know of anyone who has tried Jesus and didn't like Him, although they may not have liked the stuff "church folks" tried to impose on them in Jesus' name.

If sinners can see past the people to Jesus, they'd hang around long enough to get filled with the Holy Spirit. As Christians we need to ensure that our words and actions positively reflect who Jesus is so that those watching will want what we have.

Let's fully embrace the fruit of the spirit: love, joy, peace, forbearance, kindness, goodness, faithfulness, gentleness and self-control.
(Galatians 5:22-23, NIV)

SEASONS

"For I am the LORD, I do not change. . . " (Malachi 3:6, NKJV)

When I was a child, I thought that some people were old because of their age, the way they acted, or the color of their hair. What can I say? I was a kid, so chalk it up to ignorance.

Those of us who reside in the Midwest experience summer, fall, winter, and spring, and may prefer one over the other. Like the four seasons we experience annually, I've also experienced a lot of seasons and learned a lot of lessons. Some were fun and some not so much so. Some lessons I learned quickly; others took a few repeat performances before I got it. And, while God doesn't change, my relationship with Him has. As a new Christian I often wondered if what the Bible and other Christians said about God was true. As a mature Christian, I know that it is.

We can have the relationship with God that we desire. Some Christians keep God at arm's-length; others want Him up close and personal. Since we're in the season of winter, isn't this a good time to re-evaluate your relationship with God? In the words of Chef Emeril Lagasse, let's "kick it (our relationship) up a notch!"

God is so much God that
He allows you to set the parameters.
How awesome is that? How awesome is God?

NO INTERRUPTION

Then God said, "Let the land sprout with vegetation—every sort of seed-bearing plant, and trees that grow seed-bearing fruit. These seeds will then produce the kinds of plants and trees from which they came." (Genesis 1:11, NLT)

Growing up in the Baby Boomer era, I ate very little processed food. My mother canned fresh fruits and vegetables that my siblings and I picked from an aunt's farm. (She wasn't really an aunt, but in my generation, we put a handle on grown folks' names.) This aunt lived in Grove City, Ohio. Today, according to www.areavibes.com, Grove City is a growing suburb of approximately 39,000 people; then, it was a handful of farms.

Going to my aunt's house was an adventure because there were no highways. It took close to an hour to get from our home to where she lived. Once there, we had ample room to run and play in between picking peaches, cherries, grapes, strawberries, pears, apples, green beans, collard greens, squash, tomatoes, and corn. I distinctly remember picking strawberries, wiping off the dirt, and popping them in my mouth. I wasn't concerned about pesticides, because none were used. The berries were always sweet. And the peaches—well, let's just say your face was a mess when you finished eating one! When we got home, we washed, peeled, froze, or canned our bounty, after my mother put aside fruit for a cobbler or two.

I relay this story not to make you hungry—although fresh fruits and vegetables are never a bad thing—but to remind you that just as there was no interruption between picking the fruits and vegetables and eating them, there is no interruption in our access to God. We have a direct line to Heaven; isn't that amazing? So, when was the last time you talked to God?

"To pray is to let God into our lives. He knocks and seeks admittance, not only in the solemn hours of secret prayer. He knocks in the midst of your daily work, your daily struggles, your daily grind.
That is when you need Him most."
—Ole Kristian Hallesby (1879-1961)

INCOMPARABLE

All of them depend on you to give them food when they need it. You give it to them, and they eat it; you provide food, and they are satisfied. When you turn away, they are afraid; when you take away your breath, they die and go back to the dust from which they came. But when you give them breath, they are created; you give new life to the earth. (Psalm 104:27-30, GNT)

Rich Little, an impressionist of Hollywood actors, was a staple on talk shows during the 1960s through the 1980s. I remember seeing him frequently on the Ed Sullivan Show when I was a child. He was funny and accurate in his portrayals.

Recently, I was watching a talk show, and one of the guests was also an impressionist. He was funny, bringing to life people of this era. When interviewed, he explained that a lot of people attempt to do impersonations before they're ready, but he isn't willing to reveal a new character until he has the persona as close to perfect as he can get.

Aren't you glad that no matter how long someone practices, they will never be able to imitate God? They may try, but they won't succeed. It's a futile effort; they need to stop and focus their energy on something doable.

Thus says the LORD, the King of Israel, And his Redeemer, the LORD of hosts: "I am the First and I am the Last; Besides Me there is no God. And who can proclaim as I do? Then let him declare it and set it in order for Me, Since I appointed the ancient people. And the things that are coming and shall come, Let them show these to them. Do not fear, nor be afraid; Have I not told you from that time, and declared it? You are My witnesses. Is there a God besides Me? Indeed there is no other Rock; I know not one."
(Isaiah 44:6-8, NKJV)

SNAP OUT OF IT

Some of God's people were prisoners, locked behind bars in dark prisons. That was because they had fought against what God said. They refused to listen to the advice of God Most High. God made life hard for those people because of what they did. They stumbled and fell, and there was no one to help them. They were in trouble, so they called to the LORD for help, and he saved them from their troubles. He took them out of their dark prisons. He broke the ropes that held them. Thank the LORD for his faithful love and for the amazing things he does for people. (Psalm 107:10-15, ERV)

Can you admit that before salvation, you were in darkness, sometimes to the point of wondering if you'd ever see the light again? You were in prison, with or without bars, because you weren't free. You might have believed you had everything together until something happened. You realized that what you thought was an illusion. And, then, you heard a universal truth: God loves you. Warts and all, inconsistent and erratic, the least of the least. The chains began to fall, the darkness became dimmer, and you were on the path to freedom.

In a world seemingly gone mad, where you're not sure if you're liked, let alone loved, the assurance of God's willingness to bring us into the light is all we need to make it.

Jesus is able! To you who are driv'n
Farther and farther from God and from Heav'n,
Helpless and hopeless, o'erwhelmed by the wave,
We throw out the lifeline—'tis, "Jesus can save."
Throw Out the Lifeline. Edwin S. Ufford. 1888.
Public Domain.

DECISION TIME

Then Joshua commanded the officers of the people, saying, "Pass through the camp and command the people, saying, 'Prepare provisions for yourselves, for within three days you will cross over this Jordan, to go in to possess the land which the LORD your God is giving you to possess.'" (Joshua 1:10-11, NKJV)

Daily we're confronted with issues that require a decision. What to eat? What to wear? What to say? Do we do this or that? Go here or there? If we're not careful, we'll spend more time deciding what to do than doing something.

The children of Israel spent 40 years in the desert under the leadership of Moses. When he died, and Joshua took charge, the Israelites immediately discovered the difference in leadership style. Moses was a kinder, gentler leader who interceded for them on a regular basis. Joshua was a warrior who had a warrior's mentality to fight for what you want. While he admired and loved Moses, Joshua was tired of walking in circles! It was time to get the show on the road and possess what God said they could have. The long wait was over.

God is still in the adventure business. He's willing to give you new territories. Sometimes it comes without a struggle; other times you'll need to roll up your sleeves and fight. When God presents something to us, we need to decide if it's worth expending our energy. If we choose to fight, we need to remember the words God gave Joshua:

"This Book of the Law shall not depart from your mouth, but you shall meditate in it day and night, that you may observe to do according to all that is written in it. For then you will make your way prosperous, and then you will have good success. Have I not commanded you? Be strong and of good courage; do not be afraid, nor be dismayed, for the LORD your God is with you wherever you go." (Joshua 1:8-9, NKJV)

IT'S IN YOUR DNA

In the beginning God created the heavens and the earth. . . . So, God created human beings in his own image. In the image of God, he created them; male and female he created them. (Genesis 1:1, 27, NLT)

The fall of man caused a temporary disruption in God's plan to fellowship with His creation. When the sacrifice of animals didn't fill the void, He sent His Son, Jesus Christ, to help us reconnect with God.

If you ever get a chance, read *Sacred Pathways: Discover Your Soul's Path to God* by Gary Thomas. In the book, he shows various ways Christians connect with God, from the naturalists (outdoors) to the traditionalists (ritual and symbols) to the contemplatives (adoration) to the intellectuals (mind). There are nine pathways altogether, and each one is carefully examined. When I was in graduate school, it was my favorite book. You may not agree with everything the author writes, but it will cause you to examine why you do what you do to celebrate God.

People spend time and money tracing their ancestry; Christians should do the same. We're made in the image of God, and we have His DNA inside us. It's only natural that we would want to know as much about Him as possible.

Then God looked over all he had made,
and he saw that it was very good!
(Genesis 1:31, NLT)

YAKETY, YAK, YAK

To everything there is a season, A time for every purpose under heaven: . . . A time to keep silence, and a time to speak. (Ecclesiastes 3:1, 7[b], NKJV)

There are some people who just love to talk and talk and talk. After a while, my ears get tired of listening and all I want is silence. My sister Joyce was one of those people. She's in Heaven now, but I remember through most of her schooling the box "talks too much" was always checked on her report card. She was a good student who just liked to talk during class, which obviously wasn't acceptable. I have an acquaintance at church who also talks a lot, so much so that I told her she probably talks in her sleep. She laughed, but I noticed she didn't deny the accusation!

I don't understand people who talk all the time. I would think at some point they'd run out of words. I've always lived by the thought that God gave us two ears and one mouth for a reason; meaning, we're to listen more than we talk.

However, unlike me, God doesn't have a problem listening to our talking (which is why He's God and I'm not). He doesn't mind excessive wordage, especially when it's directed to Him. He loves the sound of our voices, whether we say a little or a lot. And, He doesn't even mind when we keep repeating the same thing!

If just a little talk with Jesus makes everything alright,
have you had a conversation with God today?

DO YOU LOVE ME ENOUGH?

When they were finished eating, Jesus said to Simon Peter, "Simon, son of John, do you love Me more than these?" Peter answered Jesus, "Yes, Lord, You know that I love You." Jesus said to him, "Feed My lambs." Jesus said to Peter the second time, "Simon, son of John, do you love Me?" He answered Jesus, "Yes, Lord, You know that I love You." Jesus said to him, "Take care of My sheep." Jesus said to Peter the third time, "Simon, son of John, do you love Me?" Peter felt bad because Jesus asked him the third time, "Do you love Me?" He answered Jesus, "Lord, You know everything. You know I love You." Jesus said to him, "Feed My sheep." (John 21:15-17, NLV)

I had a conversation with a man who was speaking of his long-time girlfriend. After he had gone on for a while about her many virtues and what she meant to him, I inquired as to when they would get married. He responded, "Oh, I don't love her enough to marry her!" I was shocked and surprised by his answer. It did get me to thinking, though, about the many levels of love we experience. After a while I began to see what he meant. I also realized we do the same thing with Jesus.

If Jesus is married to the Church and we're the Church, doesn't that suggest a reciprocal relationship is required? Jesus doesn't just give lip service to loving us. He demonstrated His love on the cross. What have we demonstrated in return? That's a rhetorical question for you to think about in your devotional time. Fortunately, we can grow in love and get to a point where we can emphatically answer with both our mouth and our heart "Yes!" when asked, "Do you love me enough?"

"How do I love thee? Let me count the ways."
—Elizabeth Barrett Browning (1845)

"Oh, how I love Jesus. Because He first loved me."
—Frederick Whitfield (1855)

I'VE GOT TO SEE THIS FOR MYSELF

On the first day of the week, very early in the morning, the women took the spices they had prepared and went to the tomb. They found the stone rolled away from the tomb, but when they entered, they did not find the body of the Lord Jesus. While they were wondering about this, suddenly two men in clothes that gleamed like lightning stood beside them. In their fright the women bowed down with their faces to the ground, but the men said to them, "Why do you look for the living among the dead? He is not here; he has risen! Remember how he told you, while he was still with you in Galilee: The Son of Man must be delivered over to the hands of sinners, be crucified and on the third day be raised again.'" Then they remembered his words. When they came back from the tomb, they told all these things to the Eleven and to all the others. It was Mary Magdalene, Joanna, Mary the mother of James, and the others with them who told this to the apostles. But they did not believe the women, because their words seemed to them like nonsense. Peter, however, got up and ran to the tomb. Bending over, he saw the strips of linen lying by themselves, and he went away, wondering to himself what had happened. (Luke 24:1-12, NIV)

When the apostles and others heard the report of the women, they assumed they were joking (or worse, that they were being hysterical) and dismissed their statements. However, I think something in Peter knew that they were telling the truth. After all, why would they concoct a story like that, even including dialogue with angels, if there wasn't some semblance of truth to it? Peter went to the tomb because he was the type of person who needed to see things for himself. He wasn't so quick to take other people's word, especially for something as important as the missing body of Jesus.

Let's not waste time looking for the living among the dead. Jesus is alive. Invite Him into your life so you can see for yourself.

TOO GOOD TO BE TRUE

When Jesus rose early on the first day of the week, he appeared first to Mary Magdalene, out of whom he had driven seven demons. She went and told those who had been with him and who were mourning and weeping. When they heard that Jesus was alive and that she had seen him, they did not believe it. Afterward Jesus appeared in a different form to two of them while they were walking in the country. These returned and reported it to the rest; but they did not believe them either. (Mark 16:9-13, NIV)

I don't believe people were intentionally disregarding the reports of Jesus' resurrection. I think they just couldn't figure out how it was possible, so they probably assumed that those reporting seeing Jesus were suffering from a case of wishful thinking. They knew Jesus had been crucified and buried. But, when Jesus appeared to His disciples He rebuked their unbelief (Mark 16:14). They should have remembered what they had seen and heard during the time He was with them.

This is an invaluable lesson to us. God can be taken at His Word despite what it sounds like, looks like, or feels like. All we need do is believe!

We bless You, Lord, for Your trustworthiness.
We may not be able to depend on people,
but we can certainly depend on You.
Thank You, Lord.

THAT'S HOW MUCH I LOVE YOU

For God so loved the world, that he gave his only begotten Son, that whosoever believeth in him should not perish, but have everlasting life. (John 3:16, KJV)

I ran into Becca, a former co-worker, who shared that she and her husband, Theo, were about to move across the country to take care of her parents. Unfortunately, both were diagnosed with pre-dementia. As an only child, Becca, along with Theo, agreed to disrupt their lives to take on the responsibility. Becca shared that her parents weren't happy with the move because they knew Becca and Theo had worked hard to find positions in corporate America that allowed them to become financially stable. Although thankful they were willing to make the sacrifice, Becca's parents didn't want them to quit good paying jobs with the hope of obtaining another one in a different state. Becca assured her parents that she believed God would work all the details out in their favor. She loved her parents and knew she was loved in return. There was no doubt in Becca's mind that if the situation were reversed, her parents would do the same for her. She was appreciative of having a spouse who was willing to partner with her in this endeavor.

We can't begin to comprehend precisely how large of a sacrifice Jesus made for us. He willingly left Heaven to come to Earth for you and me. Those of us who have accepted the gift of salvation are eternally grateful for the love He's shown us.

You may not be asked to leave a job and move across the country or to leave an idyllic environment, but all of us can show love to each other in an assortment of ways. Everything doesn't have to be a big production; it only needs to be sincere. When was the last time you demonstrated your love for a fellow human being? Are you overdue for an exhibition?

Beloved, let us love one another: for love is of God; and every one that loveth is born of God, and knoweth God.
(1 John 4:7, KJV)

A CONVERSATION WITH A FRENCH FRY

"You did not choose Me, but I chose you. . ." (John 15:16[a], NKJV)

"Hey, welcome to the group! When did you arrive?"

"I just got off the truck. I was picked from the patch, washed, dried, and put in a crate with other potatoes. Then, they put me in a separate truck with a few other potatoes and drove us here, although I don't know where we are. Nobody told us where we were going or what was happening."

"That's great news! What's happening is you've been chosen to become a French fry. But, not just *any* French fry. You have the privilege of being among the elite. The Picker must have seen something special in you."

"I don't know what that could have been. I'm just a potato."

"No, you're not! Every potato has the potential to be chosen, but not all of them have the privilege.

"Why not?"

"Well, some growers look only at the outward appearance. You know, the size and shape of us; any blemishes . . . that type of thing. The Picker looks at the inside of us. Our heart, if you will."

"The Picker? Who's that?"

"The Picker is the One who takes care of us. He knows all about everything—things that happened even before we were placed in the ground to grow. It's amazing."

"Yeah, but, we're going to become a French fry, which means our lives will be over!"

"Uh-huh. That's right. But, you're being used by the Picker to make someone else's life better. Isn't that worth a little suffering?"

The moral of this story is to be available
for God's use, to be obedient to what God says,
and to become what God wants.

SCHOOL IS NEVER OUT

Train up a child in the way he should go, and when he is old he will not depart from it. (Proverbs 22:6, NKJV)

Today's Scripture is often quoted regarding training children in the ways of God at an early age, so that it is instilled in their nature. However, I want to examine it from a different angle. New Christians—those who are accepting Jesus for the first time—are like children in that they, too, need to be trained in the ways of God.

New Christians already feel like fish out of water. Most churches, including mine, have foundational classes for new members and new Christians. But, the most effective teaching isn't going to take place in a formalized setting. It's going to take place in the pews.

When I was a newly saved Christian, I had no idea of what to do or when to do certain things at church. So, since I've always been an observer, I chose a few people who looked like they knew what they were doing and imitated them. Fortunately, they were doing the right thing!

If someone watched you during the church service, what would he or she see? Do you come in late? Do you spend the entire time talking or texting? Do you participate in the congregational singing? Are you paying attention when the Word is being shared? Are you praying during the altar call or checking messages on your phone? Do you always have to slip out at offering time and never return? Do you stay for the benediction?

I think if we asked new Christians what they observed, we would be surprised. So, let's vow to do this: Come to church on time, participate in all aspects of the service, stay until the end, and lead by example.

Every Christian is unknowingly a teacher in Your classroom, Lord.
Help us to show by example what it means to serve You.

FOLLOW THE LEADER

The LORD is my shepherd; I shall not want. He makes me lie down in green pastures. He leads me beside still waters. He restores my soul. He leads me in paths of righteousness for his name's sake. Even though I walk through the valley of the shadow of death, I will fear no evil, for you are with me; your rod and your staff, they comfort me. You prepare a table before me in the presence of my enemies; you anoint my head with oil; my cup overflows. Surely goodness and mercy shall follow me all the days of my life, and I shall dwell in the house of the LORD forever. (Psalm 23:1-6, ESV)

Psalm 23 is one of the first Scriptures most of us were taught. As a child, I quoted it without fully understanding the meaning. As I grew up, I realized that there is only One who is qualified to lead and guide us. Jesus is the Shepherd; we're the sheep. Let's not get confused.

"To him the gatekeeper opens. The sheep hear his voice,
and he calls his own sheep by name and leads them out.
When he has brought out all his own, he goes before them, and the
sheep follow him, for they know his voice.
A stranger they will not follow, but they will flee from him, for they do
not know the voice of strangers."
(John 10:3-5, ESV)

NOBODY CAN LOVE YOU BETTER

But now, GOD's Message, the God who made you in the first place, Jacob the One who got you started, Israel: "Don't be afraid, I've redeemed you. I've called your name. You're mine. When you're in over your head, I'll be there with you. When you're in rough waters, you will not go down. When you're between a rock and a hard place it won't be a dead end—Because I am GOD, your personal God, The Holy of Israel, your Savior. I paid a huge price for you: all of Egypt, with rich Cush and Seba thrown in! That's how much you mean to me! That's how much I love you! I'd sell off the whole world to get you back, trade the creation just for you." (Isaiah 43:1-4, MSG)

Have you ever said, "I love you to the moon and back," or responded, "I love you more," when someone said, "I love you"? Or, how about stretching your arms out wide to indicate how much you love someone? I'm sure we're sincere when we say or make the gesture to express love. We feel better around certain people and think that's love. We marry spouses and grow in love with our limited ability. We show love to family and friends, but only God knows what love is and only God demonstrates true love for us.

The best we can do is imitate what God shows us—compassion, kindness, sensitivity. It may take a few attempts before we get it right. The important thing is to move in the direction of perfection. As we do, we'll become more Christ-like, and the people we encounter will benefit from our growth.

And I pray that you and all God's holy people will have the power to understand the greatness of Christ's love—how wide, how long, how high, and how deep that love is. Christ's love is greater than anyone can ever know, but I pray that you will be able to know that love. Then you can be filled with everything God has for you.
(Ephesians 3:18-19, ERV)

CALORIE-FREE

Jesus responded, "The real significance of that Scripture is not that Moses gave you bread from heaven but that my Father is right now offering you bread from heaven, the real bread. The Bread of God came down out of heaven and is giving life to the world." They jumped at that: "Master, give us this bread, now and forever!" Jesus said, "I am the Bread of Life. The person who aligns with me hungers no more and thirsts no more, ever. I have told you this explicitly because even though you have seen me in action, you don't really believe me. Every person the Father gives me eventually comes running to me. And once that person is with me, I hold on and don't let go. I came down from heaven not to follow my own whim but to accomplish the will of the One who sent me. This, in a nutshell, is that will: that everything handed over to me by the Father be completed—not a single detail missed—and at the wrap-up of time I have everything, and everyone put together, upright and whole. This is what my Father wants: that anyone who sees the Son and trusts who he is and what he does and then aligns with him will enter real life, eternal life. My part is to put them on their feet alive and whole at the completion of time." (John 6:32-40, MSG)

If asked, nine out of ten people would tell you that the consumption of bread in any of its varieties is a weakness. Restaurants understand this, which is why so many of them make it available during your meal. Some go so far as to bake fresh bread throughout the day, so you're constantly bombarded with the aroma. People trying to count carbs and watch calories are sorely tested to discipline themselves against overindulging.

However, there is one bread that has zero carbs, zero calories, and zero guilt. We can have as much of the Bread of Life as we want without gaining a pound of flesh. Instead, we will gain a pound of the Spirit, and that's a good thing.

"Bread of heaven feed me 'till I want no more!"
—Richard Blanchard (1925-2004)

CHANGED

Do you not know that the unrighteous will not inherit the kingdom of God? Do not be deceived. Neither fornicators, nor idolaters, nor adulterers, nor homosexuals, nor sodomites, nor thieves, nor covetous, nor drunkards, nor revilers, nor extortioners will inherit the kingdom of God. And such were some of you. But you were washed, but you were sanctified, but you were justified in the name of the Lord Jesus and by the Spirit of our God. (1 Corinthians 6:9-11, NKJV)

The air conditioning in my office is very high, so I don't dress for the outside; I dress for the inside, which usually involves something with long sleeves. While changing tops for the third time before leaving for work the other day, I had to pause for a praise break to thank God for choices. I am not a clotheshorse by any means, but I have ample clothes to wear. However, I can remember a time when there weren't as many choices, and that's why I had to thank God. And, while thanking Him for clothes, I had to thank Him for allowing me into the Kingdom despite all the crazy and unholy things I did before salvation.

It is not God's will that anyone is lost, but it is our choice as to whether we'll accept the gift of salvation and all that comes with it. Take a moment to thank God for the change He made in your life when you said yes. Pray for those who have yet to respond. Then, realize there's one more change coming:

Behold, I tell you a mystery: We shall not all sleep, but we shall all be changed—in a moment, in the twinkling of an eye, at the last trumpet. For the trumpet will sound, and the dead will be raised incorruptible, and we shall be changed. For this corruptible must put on incorruption, and this mortal must put on immortality. So, when this corruptible has put on incorruption, and this mortal has put on immortality, then shall be brought to pass the saying that is written: "Death is swallowed up in victory. O Death, where is your sting? O Hades, where is your victory?"
(1 Corinthians 15:51-55, NKJV)

WITH THIS RING

Let us be glad and rejoice and give Him glory, for the marriage of the Lamb has come, and His wife has made herself ready. (Revelation 19:7, NKJV)

Movies often show a man in a public setting getting down on one knee to propose to his girlfriend. The people around them become fascinated with the scene (whether they know the couple or not) and anxiously look on as the man waits for an answer. Sometimes, the woman responds before the man can get the question out! At other times, the woman is so busy crying that she can't even speak, only nod. And, sadly, there are times when the man has misjudged the woman's feelings, and she responds with a flat-out no or a not yet, allowing the door to stay open.

Jesus Christ is married to the Church—those who are shapened in iniquity and conceived in sin (Psalm 51:5, paraphrased), and have accepted the gift of the Savior of the world. For some of us, saying yes was immediately after hearing the proposal; others (like me) took a lot longer to get to yes. The good news is that God is patient, but don't keep Him waiting. He's ready to slip the ring on your finger the moment you say yes.

"Light, so low upon earth, you send a flash to the sun.
Here is the golden close of love, all my wooing is done."
Marriage Morning. Alfred Lord Tennyson (1809-1892)

WHEN IT'S ALL SAID AND DONE

This is the kind of God I have and I'm telling the world! (Exodus 15:2 (b), MSG)

Have you ever wanted to be a spectator at your own funeral, just to hear what is said about you? Well, you don't have to die for your obituary to be read. You're writing it every day. Only you can decide what people will say about you when it's all said and done. Will people celebrate that "Ding-dong the witch is dead" or "I'm going to miss her?" Will people say, "Good riddance" or "I can't believe she's gone?"

I want people to miss me. I want them to realize the legacy I've left behind: the birth of my son and then the addition of a daughter-in-law and grandchildren; the books God has allowed me to write, friends He's placed in my life, good familial relationships, college degrees. . .all those things are important. Yet, when anyone asks what was *most* important, I want someone to say that it was having Jesus in my life because that changed everything. I want someone to say that I strove to make Him an integral part of my life, leading and guiding me in the way I should go. I want someone to say that I was a woman of faith who strongly believed in the power of prayer. I want someone to say that I may not have crossed every "t" and dotted every "I" and that every day may not have been sunny, but every day was good because I was alive to experience it. I don't know about you, but I want someone to say that I loved the Lord with all my heart, soul, and mind (Deuteronomy 6:5).

GOD is my strength, GOD is my song,
and, yes! GOD is my salvation. (Exodus 15:2[a], MSG)

WHO WILL YOU TRUST?

I have declared to both Jews and Greeks that they must turn to God in repentance and have faith in our Lord Jesus. And now, compelled by the Spirit, I am going to Jerusalem, not knowing what will happen to me there. I only know that in every city the Holy Spirit warns me that prison and hardships are facing me. However, I consider my life worth nothing to me; my only aim is to finish the race and complete the task the Lord Jesus has given me—the task of testifying to the good news of God's grace. (Acts 20:21-24, NIV)

When faced with a decision as to whom to trust, we must deal with our dual personality. We have the logical side which says, "If you do *this*, then *that* will happen. You have no control over the outcome or the circumstances. Perhaps this might not be the wisest move to make." Then, there's our spiritual side which says, "I'm going to trust that God knows what He's doing. I'm sure this is what I heard Him say. Therefore, regardless of what does or doesn't happen, I'm going to be obedient to the word of the Lord."

If you've ever been in a situation where you feel "compelled" to do something for God, Paul shows us the importance of finishing what we start. God often places a burden on us for a specific group, people, or place. There is usually an uneasiness that won't lift until we've done what God has asked. Paul felt the need to go to Jerusalem despite what he knew awaited him. He trusted that God would finish what He started. We can too.

Some people trust the power of chariots or horses, but we trust you,
LORD God. (Psalm 20:7, CEV)

HOLD ONTO THE PROMISE

But the following night the Lord stood by him and said, "Be of good cheer, Paul; for as you have testified for Me in Jerusalem, so you must also bear witness at Rome." (Acts 23:11, NKJV)

When it was decided that we would sail for Italy, Paul and some other prisoners were handed over to a centurion named Julius, who belonged to the Imperial Regiment. . . The ship was caught by the storm and couldn't head into the wind; so, we gave way to it and were driven along. . .When neither sun nor stars appeared for many days and the storm continued raging, we finally gave up all hope of being saved. After they had gone a long time without food, Paul stood up before them and said. . . "I urge you to keep up your courage, because not one of you will be lost; only the ship will be destroyed. Last night an angel of the God to whom I belong and whom I serve stood beside me and said, 'Do not be afraid, Paul. You must stand trial before Caesar; and God has graciously given you the lives of all who sail with you.' So, keep up your courage, men, for I have faith in God that it will happen just as he told me." (Acts 27:1, 15, 20-21[a], 22-25, NIV)

Sometimes when you're in the period between promise and fulfillment, so much happens that you might think that God has forgotten what He said. That's the time you must call to your remembrance the things God has already done for you. It's during those times that you remind yourself that God is not a liar; whatever He's said will come to pass. It may not be a stroll in the park; matter of fact, it may be more like a hike through rough, uneven terrain. Nevertheless, keep going forward.

Lord, when You give us a promise, please provide
tunnel vision so that all we focus on is the path
You have us on.

ALMOST DOESN'T MEAN NO

Then Agrippa said to Paul, "You are permitted to speak for yourself." So, Paul stretched out his hand and answered for himself: "I think myself happy, King Agrippa, because today I shall answer for myself before you concerning all the things of which I am accused by the Jews, especially because you are expert in all customs and questions which have to do with the Jews. Therefore, I beg you to hear me patiently." (Acts 26:1-4, NKJV)

When witnessing for Christ, we often encounter people who appear to not be interested in what we're saying; but you can't take it personally. The devil's job is to make people believe their immoral lifestyle is okay; when they are confronted with the truth, it is sometimes difficult to digest. I know from personal experience that sinners hear every word being said.

While Paul stated his argument, they couldn't say he was a mad man, because they knew he wasn't. He made his case point by point and then directly asked Agrippa, "Do you believe the prophets?" Paul didn't bother to wait for an answer because he already knew it: "I know that you do believe." Agrippa then confessed, "You almost persuaded me to become a Christian" (Acts 26:27-28, NKJV).

Paul realized that everything he experienced before and after his conversion was to bring him to this point. He didn't ignore what he used to be; he used it to his advantage. That's what we need to do. So many times, we want to sugarcoat what we did before salvation. I'm not saying you need to tell everything; but sometimes, people need to know you can relate to what they're going through.

Just because someone says, "I was almost persuaded," doesn't mean they didn't hear you. At the appropriate time, God will bring the conversation back to their remembrance. We don't know why people hesitate to accept Jesus the first time they hear of Him. We can only pray that God gives them enough time to get it right before death and judgment. My prayer is that we won't give up on them. After all, God didn't give up on us.

Lord, help us to tell our story.
We don't know who will respond either now or later, but You do.

SURROUNDED

Surely goodness and mercy shall follow me all the days of my life. (Psalm 23:6, NKJV)

When I was a child, my father controlled the television and we were the remote. Other than sports, my father watched westerns and so did anyone else wanting to watch TV in our home. I still love westerns and anything to do with cowboys to this day.

In the westerns, the good guys always won but first had to deal with some dastardly individuals. And usually, before the victims of the plot were destroyed, one of the good guys came to the rescue with guns drawn yelling, "Put your hands up. You're surrounded!" The story would end with everybody happily riding off into the sunset.

It would be wonderful if our lives were like the movies; however, that's not the case as most of us well know. Yet, I submit there are times when we are surrounded. The Psalmist said that goodness and mercy follow us, but I suggest that there are times when goodness and mercy are ahead of us. God sends these twins to cut the enemy off at the pass so that when we arrive at our destination, there are no obstructions. In other words, we're surrounded!

Lord, we thank You for constantly and consistently watching over us,
protecting us from hurt, harm, and dangers seen and unseen.
We bless You for the loving care You direct toward us.

COMING OUT WITH YOUR HANDS UP

Coming out, He went to the Mount of Olives, as He was accustomed, and His disciples also followed Him. When He came to the place, He said to them, "Pray that you may not enter into temptation." And He was withdrawn from them about a stone's throw, and He knelt down and prayed, saying, "Father, if it is Your will, take this cup away from Me; nevertheless, not My will, but Yours, be done." Then an angel appeared to Him from heaven, strengthening Him. (Luke 22:39-43, NKJV)

While it is true that raised hands may symbolize surrender, it is equally true that they symbolize praise. Jesus shows us it is impossible to pray without praising and the praising leads to surrender. Luke chapter 22 tells us the events that led to Jesus' arrest in the garden: (1) He had chosen Judas as a disciple, knowing he would betray him; (2) He ate the Passover with His disciples, knowing it would be the last time; (3) He instituted the Lord's Supper, knowing it would be continually celebrated until the end of time; (4) He settled yet another petty argument among His disciples, knowing what the future held for them; (5) He predicted Peter's denial, knowing Peter would be restored soon thereafter; and (6) He left the garden knowing we would be reconciled back to God.

And with all that was weighing so heavily on Jesus that night, He knew He needed to have a talk with His Father in preparation for what was about to happen. To fulfill His assignment, Jesus had to bring His flesh under subjection. He needed to pray. The Bible records that His prayers were so intense that, "His sweat became like great drops of blood falling down to the ground" (v. 44[b]). This was *after* He had surrendered His will to God's.

Jesus finished praying, fully confident that no matter what happened in the next few days, He was doing the will of the Father. He walked out of the garden with His hands up in praise. We, too, can have that same confidence when we go into prayer, settle who is in control, and then come out praising God.

Thank You, God, for the privilege of surrender. Help me to get to the point of quickly saying ". . . nevertheless not my will, but Your will be done."

ONE AND DONE

So when Christ came into the world he said, "You don't want sacrifices and offerings, but you have prepared a body for me. You are not pleased with the sacrifices of animals killed and burned or with offerings to take away sins. Then I said, 'Here I am, God. It is written about me in the book of the law. I have come to do what you want.'" (Hebrews 10:5-14, ERV)

There are things we do daily, weekly, monthly, and annually. Some of them are pleasant; some, not so much. Some we look forward to; others we dread.

I don't know how you feel about it, but I'm forever grateful that Jesus came to Earth to die for me. Unlike the animal sacrifices that were annually offered, Jesus' visit was a one-time event. It will never be duplicated because it's not necessary. His death was final. When He uttered the words, "It is finished," He was talking about the assignment He accepted when He left Heaven: to save us from our sin. Hallelujah! Jesus finished His assignment; we're still working on ours. Don't confuse the two.

There is only one God, and there is only one way that people can reach God. That way is through Christ Jesus, who as a man gave himself to pay for everyone to be free. This is the message that was given to us at just the right time. (1 Timothy 2:5-6, ERV)

CONFIDENCE

Meanwhile, the boat was far out to sea when the wind came up against them and they were battered by the waves. At about four o'clock in the morning, Jesus came toward them walking on the water. They were scared out of their wits. "A ghost!" they said, crying out in terror. But Jesus was quick to comfort them. "Courage, it's me. Don't be afraid." Peter, suddenly bold, said, "Master, if it's really you, call me to come to you on the water." He said, "Come ahead." Jumping out of the boat, Peter walked on the water to Jesus. But when he looked down at the waves churning beneath his feet, he lost his nerve and started to sink. He cried, "Master, save me!" (Matthew 14:24-30, MSG)

I admire Peter's boldness and confidence in getting out of a boat that was secure to walk on a surface not designed for walking. It took a lot of courage. Peter was successful until he realized he was doing the impossible and fear raised its head.

We're all called to do what seems impossible until we do it. When I look at my adult son and realize that it was only God who helped me raise a productive man, I am amazed. While in the process, there were too many times to count where I doubted that I was doing the right thing. That doesn't mean I didn't make mistakes, but it means that God didn't allow the blunders to destroy my son or me.

Is there anything too hard for God? Of course, the answer is no! Even when it seems that what you're facing is impossible, trust that God has your back, front, and sides. Partner with Him to accomplish whatever the task is before you. You won't be disappointed.

But as the Scriptures say, "No one has ever seen, no one has ever heard, no one has ever imagined what God has prepared for those who love him."
(1 Corinthians 2:9, ERV)

BEFORE AND AFTER

For I am the least worthy of all the apostles, and I shouldn't even be called an apostle at all after the way I treated the church of God. But whatever I am now it is all because God poured out such kindness and grace upon me—and not without results: for I have worked harder than all the other apostles, yet actually I wasn't doing it, but God working in me, to bless me. (1 Corinthians 15:9-10, TLB)

We all have regrets about things done before salvation. Merriam-Webster defines *regret* as "sorrow aroused by circumstances beyond one's control or power to repair." There is nothing that will erase the memory of negative behavior *except* the grace of God.

Paul teaches us to put our past in perspective, use it to build up the Kingdom, and remind people to focus on the *message* and not the *messenger*.

Then I heard the Lord asking,
"Whom shall I send as a messenger to my people? Who will go?"
And I said, "Lord, I'll go! Send me."
(Isaiah 6:8, TLB)

FORGET ABOUT IT!

I'm not saying that I have this all together, that I have it made. But I am well on my way, reaching out for Christ, who has so wondrously reached out for me. Friends don't get me wrong: By no means do I count myself an expert in all of this, but I've got my eye on the goal, where God is beckoning us onward—to Jesus. I'm off and running and I'm not turning back. (Philippians 3:12-14, MSG)

Whenever God shines His spotlight on an area of my life that needs some work, the Word comes to me in several ways in a short period. It may be through a devotional I'm reading, a Word from the pulpit, a sentence that jumps off the page of a book, a tossed-out phrase from one of the saints, or the lyrics of a song. Recently, God decided to spotlight an area I've neglected for years: my love affair with food.

I watched a reality show featuring a group of sisters who were struggling with their weight. I could relate to their stories on several levels, and at one point I said aloud, "God, I don't want to do this anymore!" God knew what my spoken phrase meant and had been waiting for me to get to the point of surrender.

So, the journey begins, although I know it won't be easy. After all, if it were easy, I would have dealt with it years ago. Once I made the decision, the enemy immediately began to do what he does: bring doubt about being able to finish what's started. But, I believe the Word: "God has not given us a spirit of fear; but of power, and of love, and of a sound mind" (2 Timothy 1:7, KJV).

When I'm tempted to go back to the familiar, I remind myself that God has great things in store for me. I choose to be at my best to enjoy them.

Lord, I thank You that You give us time to catch up with Your plans for us. "The Lord says, 'I will guide you along the best pathway for your life. I will advise you and watch over you.'" (Psalm 32:8, NLT).

RIVER PRAISE

Let the rivers clap their hands and the mountains sing joyfully.
(Psalm 98:8, GWT)

A river is a large natural stream of water emptying into an ocean, lake, or other body of water and usually fed along its course by converging tributaries (www.answers.com).

A river is fluid; it's alive. It has ebb and flow, movement and stagnation. Despite what stage a river is in, it's in constant touch with its surroundings. Because of that, the river affects everything around it. If it's moving, it's flowing with other water. If it's stagnant, it's touching additional water or the ground.

John Donne told us, "No man is an island, entire of itself" (*Devotions Upon Emergent Occasions*, 1624). Although we may be self-sufficient, we were created to interact with other humans. Similar to the fluidity of a river, our lives are also fluid, allowing for arrivals and departures that make our lives fuller, richer, deeper. "Iron sharpens iron" (Proverbs 27:17, NKJV), but the sharpening only happens with connectivity to others of a like mind.

An enemy might be able to defeat one person,
but two people can stand back-to-back to defend each other. And three
people are even stronger. They are like a rope that has three parts
wrapped together —it is very hard to break.
(Ecclesiastes 4:12, ERV)

THINGS ARE GONNA GET BETTER

Then I saw 'a new heaven and a new earth,' for the first heaven and the first earth had passed away, and there was no longer any sea. I saw the Holy City, the new Jerusalem, coming down out of heaven from God, prepared as a bride beautifully dressed for her husband. And I heard a loud voice from the throne saying, "Look! God's dwelling place is now among the people, and he will dwell with them. They will be his people, and God himself will be with them and be their God. He will wipe every tear from their eyes. There will be no more death or mourning or crying or pain, for the old order of things has passed away." He who was seated on the throne said, "I am making everything new!" Then he said, "Write this down, for these words are trustworthy and true." (Revelation 21:1-5, NIV)

Did you ever play a game of pretend as a child? Usually, little girls were princesses and little boys were cowboys. Then, you grew up, put childish things away, and stopped pretending. However, I surmise that your life would be less stressful if you remembered this childhood game.

Heaven is a prepared place for a prepared people. It isn't an imaginary place that doesn't exist. Of course, we can't know everything that's there, but from the description in Revelation, we know it is far, far better than anything we've ever seen or experienced. It is a real place that you'll see upon death, but in the meantime, you can still play a game of pretend. When things aren't going well, allow yourself to be transported to the place where there are no more tears, or violence, or anger, or destruction, or hatred, or any of the other problems that are of concern to you.

You may be in a challenging place today, but God has promised that things are going to get better. Hang in there until the change comes.

"Let not your heart be troubled. You are trusting God, now trust in me."
(John 14:1, TLB)

JOINED AT THE HIP

"Entreat me not to leave you, or to turn back from following after you; For wherever you go, I will go; and wherever you lodge, I will lodge; Your people shall be my people, and your God, my God. Where you die, I will die, and there will I be buried. The LORD do so to me, and more also, if anything but death parts you and me." (Ruth 1:16-17, NKJV)

There are times we run across people we can't seem to get rid of; every time we look up, they're invading our space. Some are pushier than others; some seem to always be there. They have decided we're to be connected; that's just the way it's going to be, whether we like it or not. Personally, I am leery of those type of people.

One thing I've learned to do is to ask God what purpose everyone I meet will serve in my life. If God put them there as a blessing, okay; however, if the devil put them there as a deterrent, that's not okay! The only way we'll know is to ask God, and then listen and respond to His answer. Sometimes we want to keep people around because they fulfill a need in us; but if God says no, then we must believe God has someone better to satisfy the need. Obedience is the key to less drama.

Naomi and Ruth had a connection that defined their relationship. God orchestrated it from beginning to end. The move to Bethlehem, the marriage of the two sons to Moabite women, the deaths of the sons, the move back to Bethlehem with one daughter-in-law, and the meeting of Ruth and Boaz, followed by their subsequent marriage, were used by God to fulfill His purpose. Throughout the book of Ruth, you see God's hand moving people like pieces on a chessboard to their ultimate destination.

Teach me to do Your will, For You are my God; Your Spirit is good.
Lead me in the land of uprightness. (Psalm 143:10, NKJV)

THIS IS THE DAY TO INTERCEDE

He isn't really being slow about his promised return, even though it sometimes seems that way. But he is waiting, for the good reason that he is not willing that any should perish, and he is giving more time for sinners to repent. (2 Peter 3:9, TLB)

There is a saying, "The road to hell is paved with good intentions," which may be right. I also believe that Hell will be full of good people. Sure, there are plenty of human monsters occupying space there; we live in an evil world. But, more importantly, there will be people there who couldn't or wouldn't accept that God loved them enough to send Jesus Christ to save them. There will also be people there who were never told about the love of God. They had no frame of reference. Those who find themselves spending eternity in Hell are not all bad people.

The job of the Church is to spread the Gospel to everyone we encounter. Unfortunately, we don't always do that well. We criticize the denomination that pesters people by knocking on doors and practically forcing their literature on people, but, at least they're witnessing! Christians have no excuse for not sharing Jesus. After all, we've experienced His faithfulness, trust, love, protection, security, and other attributes, so we have a personal testimony about Almighty God that can't be taken from us.

Today, make it a point to tell at least one person that God loves them enough to want them to spend eternity in Heaven with Him. He is extending a personal invitation through you.

Thank You, Lord, that someone took the time to share the gospel with me. Help me to remember to do the same for someone else.

RESCUE ME

Remember, it is sin to know what you ought to do and then not do it. (James 4:17, NLT)

Do you know that God wants to rescue you from sin? Oh, I can hear your response. "What do you mean? I've been saved for 55 years. I'm not a sinner! Who do you think you are?"

Well, I'm a child of God who makes mistakes, just like you. Sin isn't only murder, fornication, lying, stealing, or cheating. It's also not paying your bills on time, refusing to tithe, mistreating others, gossiping, and pride, to name a few.

Today's Scripture is clear: If you know there is something God requires, and you're not doing it, God calls that sin.

If we claim we have no sin, we are only fooling ourselves and not living in the truth. But if we confess our sins to Him, He is faithful and just to forgive us our sins and to cleanse us from all wickedness. If we claim we have not sinned, we are calling God a liar and showing that His word has no place in our hearts.
(1 John 1:8-10, NLT)

PAY IT FORWARD

GOD wasn't attracted to you and didn't choose you because you were big and important—the fact is, there was almost nothing to you. He did it out of sheer love, keeping the promise he made to your ancestors. . . Know this: GOD, your God, is God indeed, a God you can depend upon. He keeps his covenant of loyal love with those who love him and observe his commandments for a thousand generations. (Deuteronomy 7:7-9, MSG)

There are some people fortunate enough to trace their lineage back to multiple great-grandparents. Some are blessed to spend time with second, third, and fourth generation relatives to hear firsthand the experiences they've endured.

Even more fortunate are those whose relatives have or had a relationship with the Lord and could tell how He blessed and kept them through dangers seen and unseen. Their prayers made it possible for us to live in the 21st century and to experience cultural, scientific, medical, and technological events they could never imagine.

We, too, must ensure that future generations are blessed. How? By paying forward the blessings of God. Every prayer, every tear, every plea before God's throne for our family is the payment. We may not live to see all that God will do in the lives of our loved ones, and that's okay. We can trust that when God hears our prayers, He'll make sure everything happens in His timing.

Whether we can trace our lineage or not, we know that someone, somewhere, at some time prayed for us; and God responded. We're in the Kingdom today because someone took the time to pray for their unborn relatives. So, what's your excuse?

Just make sure you stay alert. Keep close watch over yourselves. Don't forget anything of what you've seen.
Don't let your heart wander off. Stay vigilant as long as you live. Teach what you've seen and heard to your children and grandchildren.
(Deuteronomy 4:9, MSG)

DID YOU JUST DIS ME?

The LORD said to Samuel, "How long will you mourn for Saul, since I have rejected him as king over Israel? Fill your horn with oil and be on your way; I am sending you to Jesse of Bethlehem. I have chosen one of his sons to be king." (1 Samuel 16:1, NIV)

I like watching both the summer and winter Olympics, although the summer ones are my favorite. The Olympians have worked hard, and I enjoy seeing people's dreams come true of making the Olympic teams and possibly winning a medal for their country.

Every year the media picks a few Olympians they think are going to bring home the gold. They do profiles and interviews with them. They fawn over them, build them up, put them on the cover of magazines as a sure bet. . .all before the games even start! Then, when the games begin, sometimes the one nobody paid any attention to walks away with everything. I love the drama of the whole thing.

David can relate. He had no inkling that God would anoint him king or that his father would totally dismiss him from the opportunity when Samuel came to the house. Fortunately, Samuel wasn't willing to assume he had to "settle" for one of the seven sons Jesse presented. Samuel was clear—"The LORD has not chosen these"—and asked the relevant question: "Are these all the sons you have?" (v. 11) Jesse reluctantly had to admit he had another son. He had to have felt 2 feet tall when Samuel made him admit his error, and then even smaller as he watched the one he dismissed as insignificant be anointed king to replace Saul. People may not be aware of you. Thankfully, God is not like people. He sees what others miss.

Then the LORD said, "Rise and anoint him;
this is the one." (1 Samuel 16:12[b], NIV)

ARE YOU SURE YOU WANT TO DO THIS?

David answered, "You come at me with sword and spear and battle-ax. I come at you in the name of GOD-of-the-Angel-Armies, the God of Israel's troops, whom you curse and mock. This very day GOD is handing you over to me. I'm about to kill you, cut off your head, and serve up your body and the bodies of your Philistine buddies to the crows and coyotes. The whole earth will know that there's an extraordinary God in Israel. And everyone gathered here will learn that GOD doesn't save by means of sword or spear. The battle belongs to GOD—he's handing you to us on a platter!" (1 Samuel 17:45-47, MSG)

The story of David and Goliath is a classic example of the underdog being victorious. No one expected David to win the battle. Yet, David was confident that God would show Himself mighty. It's interesting that none of Saul's army was willing to fight a giant, but they allowed a teenager to do what they were reluctant to do. Saul tried to help David out with his armor, but David rejected it. Instead, he used the weapon he was familiar and comfortable with: a slingshot (1 Samuel 17:1-45).

When Goliath moved toward him, "David took off from the front line, running toward the Philistine. David reached into his pocket for a stone, slung it, and hit the Philistine hard in the forehead, embedding the stone deeply. The Philistine crashed, face down in the dirt. That's how David beat the Philistine—with a sling and a stone. He hit him and killed him. No sword for David!" (vv. 48-50).

We may have to face a giant at some point in our life. In that situation we have two choices: we can do like Saul and his army, standing around letting the giant disrespect everything we believe, or we can do like David and run toward the giant, confident that if God is for us, who can be against us!

"But in that coming day no weapon turned against you will succeed. You will silence every voice raised up to accuse you. These benefits are enjoyed by the servants of the LORD; their vindication will come from me. I, the LORD, have spoken!" (Isaiah 54:17, NLT)

SHORT AND TO THE POINT

Friends, when I came and told you the mystery that God had shared with us, I didn't use big words or try to sound wise. In fact, while I was with you, I made up my mind to speak only about Jesus Christ, who had been nailed to a cross. At first, I was weak and trembling with fear. When I talked with you or preached, I didn't try to prove anything by sounding wise. I simply let God's Spirit show his power. That way you would have faith because of God's power and not because of human wisdom. (1 Corinthians 2:1-5, CEV)

Before I accepted Jesus Christ as Lord and Savior, the few times I went to church as an adult I left scratching my head because I had no idea what the preacher was trying to say. They were using words that made absolutely no sense, and for someone who loves words like me, that was very frustrating. However, the reasons I'm saved today are (1) because God deemed the timing was right; (2) I accepted the fact that I was headed to Hell on a Concorde jet and I needed to do something before it was too late; (3) my friend, Deborah Thompson, got saved and I saw a visible difference in her life; and (4) she was able to tell me what her pastor (and now mine) preached and taught. I figured if I could understand it second hand, I'd be able to understand it straight from Bishop Timothy J. Clarke's mouth. And I did, and I do, which is why 30 years later I'm still saved!

Paul was an educated man with an extensive vocabulary. Yet, he didn't try to impress the Corinthians with big words. Paul put it down "where the goats could eat it." When it comes to telling the Gospel story, we need to make sure the people we're witnessing to can understand what we're saying. This isn't the time to try to use every multi-syllable word we know. This is the time to imitate Paul and break the Gospel down in its simplest form—Jesus Christ and Him crucified.

Thank You, Lord, for every opportunity You provide for us to talk about You. Help us to remember to keep You at the center of the conversation.

WEEP NOW, LAUGH LATER

For his anger lasts only a moment, but his favor lasts a lifetime; weeping may stay for the night but rejoicing comes in the morning. (Proverbs 30:5, NIV)

When we experience heartache, we sometimes wonder if we will ever recover from the hurt, loss, disappointment, or betrayal. Logically, we know that we won't feel this way forever; however, in our heart we're not quite sure that's true. The good news is that things do change. A loved one may be gone, but their memories linger. Betrayal and disappointments hurt, especially when it's from someone close.

If we allow it, God will and can restore relationships. If we don't believe that's possible, we only need to look to Jesus for our role model. For the most part, His disciples were nowhere to be found during His trial and subsequent crucifixion. Yet, He chose to reveal Himself after the Resurrection and restore them—especially Peter—back to their rightful place.

It may be challenging now, but rest assured, things are going to get better.

"Blessed are you who weep now, for you will laugh."
(Luke 6:21[b], NIV)

TRUST ME, THIS IS FOR YOUR OWN GOOD

And lest I should be exalted above measure by the abundance of the revelations, a thorn in the flesh was given to me, a messenger of Satan to buffet me, lest I be exalted above measure. Concerning this thing I pleaded with the Lord three times that it might depart from me. And He said to me, "My grace is sufficient for you, for My strength is made perfect in weakness." (2 Corinthians 12:7-9[a], NKJV)

I don't know of anyone who likes being in pain, do you? Most of us want to be as pain-free as possible. In an ideal world, we would be. Unfortunately, that's not where we live. While temporary pain from a toothache or paper cut is irritating, we know it will stop at some point. Then, there's chronic pain defined on www.webmd.com as "pain lasting more than six months." That pain often causes us to ask, "Lord, how much longer will this go on?"

The apostle Paul is someone who can relate to our dilemma. He had been allowed a vision of Paradise, the third Heaven, and after that vision, was given a thorn in the flesh so severe that he asked three times for God to remove it. When God finally responded to Paul's request, the answer wasn't what he expected.

When we receive a response from God that is unfavorable, we can do like Paul, and accept the thorn and move on. Will we resent the thorn, or will we accept God's trust in us to handle the thorn? The thorn's not moving; however, with the right attitude, we can make it work for us.

Therefore, most gladly I will rather boast in my infirmities, that the power of Christ may rest upon me. Therefore, I take pleasure in infirmities, in reproaches, in needs, in persecutions, in distresses, for Christ's sake. For when I am weak, then I am strong.
(2 Corinthians 9[b]-10, NKJV)

BECAUSE YOU SAID I COULD

Some time later, Jesus went up to Jerusalem for one of the Jewish festivals. Now there is in Jerusalem near the Sheep Gate a pool, which in Aramaic is called Bethesda and which is surrounded by five covered colonnades. Here a great number of disabled people used to lie—the blind, the lame, the paralyzed. One who was there had been an invalid for thirty-eight years. When Jesus saw him lying there and learned that he had been in this condition for a long time, he asked him, "Do you want to get well?" "Sir," the invalid replied, "I have no one to help me into the pool when the water is stirred. While I am trying to get in, someone else goes down ahead of me." Then Jesus said to him, "Get up! Pick up your mat and walk." At once the man was cured; he picked up his mat and walked. (John 5:1-9, NKJV)

When someone says—with confidence and authority—that they believe you can do what seems impossible, even if you don't believe it yourself, there's something in you that catches their faith. Sometimes you may think, "Well, I know I can't do this, but I'll just show them." If you fail, you could always say, "Didn't I tell you I couldn't do it?" But, on the other hand, if you succeed, then your only response would have to be "Thank you for making me take a chance!"

The invalid recognized that the request to pick up his mat and walk was unrealistic. Yet, he trusted Jesus enough to at least try. Perhaps no one had ever told him he could help himself. Perhaps his friends and family may have enabled him. Perhaps he was uncertain of what the future held. This man knew how to be an invalid; learning something different would be challenging, so it might be easier to stay with what he knew. It doesn't matter why he hadn't made any progress before the encounter with Jesus. What matters is that he took Jesus at His Word.

Is there something Jesus said you can do that you're reluctant to try? Why not take a page from this invalid's biography? You just may be surprised by the outcome.

God, thank You for believing in us. You said we can,
and that's all we need to hear.

CAN'T YOU SEE WHAT JUST HAPPENED?

One who was there had been an invalid for thirty-eight years. When Jesus saw him lying there and learned that he had been in this condition for a long time, he asked him, "Do you want to get well?". . . Then Jesus said to him, "Get up! Pick up your mat and walk." At once the man was cured; he picked up his mat and walked. The day on which this took place was a Sabbath, and so the Jewish leaders said to the man who had been healed, "It is the Sabbath; the law forbids you to carry your mat." (John 5:5-6,8-10, NKJV)

Unlike some of us who would have immediately gone to hang out with friends and family, the former invalid went to the temple. After 38 years of being unable to walk, he joyfully, expectantly, eagerly went to the temple and ran smack into the naysayers. "It is the Sabbath. The law forbids you to carry your mat." I'll paraphrase what he thought: "What! You can't see that I'm walking *and* carrying a mat? All you notice is that I've broken a law. You can't see the miracle?"

Let's assume that the Jewish leaders who questioned this man knew of his previous disability. Perhaps they knew him personally or even his family. Regardless, they may have noticed him. Unfortunately, they couldn't or wouldn't recognize the important issue: A man who had been in a seriously physical deficit for a long time was standing upright, holding the thing that had been holding him, and walking! They recognized the miracle but wouldn't acknowledge the Miracle Worker and instead majored on a minor, "It is not lawful for you to carry your bed" (v 10).

Let us not have such a narrow focus that we miss the big picture.

LET'S NOT HAVE
THIS CONVERSATION AGAIN

Later Jesus found him . . . and said to him, "See you are well again. Stop sinning or something worse may happen to you." (John 5:14, NKJV)

I like unnamed people in the Bible because I can insert my name into whatever the scenario is, especially if it is something I can relate to. Like the man at the pool, there are issues that have plagued me for years. Praise God, they're getting fewer by the day!

Out of all the people at the pool that day, the Bible only records Jesus singling out this unnamed man. Responding yes to the question of whether you want healing means you no longer will do business as usual. Jesus wants to do something new and different and exciting in your life. But, He can't and won't do it if you're not willing to participate.

Later Jesus found the man at the temple and aren't you glad? Jesus purposely went looking for him because He doesn't leave anything undone. Yes, He had healed him physically, but Jesus needed to solidify this man's spiritual health also. The apostle Paul states something similar in Galatians 5:1 (NIV): "It is for freedom that Christ has set us free. Stand firm, then, and do not let yourselves be burdened again by a yoke of slavery."

Have you experienced the freeing power of Jesus Christ?

NOTHING ORDINARY ABOUT IT

"I am Alpha and Omega, the beginning and the ending, saith the Lord, which is, and which was, and which is to come, the Almighty." (Revelation 1:8, KJV)

Most people while preparing for bed will think about what they need to do the following day. We assume that God will wake us up again, and before we close our eyes that night, we'll get everything accomplished. That's commendable but somewhat unrealistic. None of us knows what will happen between sunrise and sunset; our job is to be available to go with whatever direction God takes us. We often quote, "Order my steps," but what we mean is "Only if it's convenient for me!"

- When Naaman arrived home, he didn't know his wife would tell him about a prophet who could take his secret disease of leprosy away (2 Kings 5).
- When Bathsheba took a bath on the roof of her house, she didn't realize it would be the beginning of an emotional roller-coaster resulting in funerals and remarriage (2 Samuel 11).
- When Mary opened the door for Gabriel, she didn't know her future involved the privilege of giving birth to the Messiah (Luke 1).
- When I went to church on a Sunday morning in 1988, I didn't realize that would be the day I accepted the gift of salvation.

Every day is an adventure. Some are traumatic and dramatic; others are enjoyable and stress-free. But, only God knows everything from the beginning to the end, including what will happen to us within any 24-hour timeframe He created.

It is of the LORD's mercies that we are not consumed because his compassions fail not. They are new every morning: great is thy faithfulness.
(Lamentations 3:22-23, KJV)

SO, WHAT ARE YOU GOING TO DO?

Pay attention, you who say, "Today or tomorrow we will go to such-and-such a town" . . . You don't really know about tomorrow. What is your life? You are a mist that appears for only a short while before it vanishes. (James 4:13[a]-14, CEB)

Every Sunday my newspaper runs photos celebrating significant birthdays of those who are in their 80s, 90s and even 100s! Every birthday you reach is significant because God has allowed you time to accomplish more for Him. Yet, James tells us that our life is but a mist or vapor; here for only a short time and then we're gone. He also tells us to live for today instead of making plans for tomorrow.

My question for you is what are you going to do with the time God gives you? Today is all you have; none of us know how long we will live. There used to be a time when most young people lived to adulthood; that's no longer true. Every day we read or hear about a young person cut down before they've had a chance to live. If today was all you had, how would you spend it? Would you worry about grass not being cut or snow not being shoveled? Would you worry about so and so who doesn't like you or about the so and so who does? Would you plan for the big social event months away or concentrate on the upcoming parent-teacher meeting?

If asked, most people would admit that they want to do something great for God. We need to remember that "great" and "big" are not necessarily the same thing to Him. Great encompasses everything from taking care of your children to building the tallest building; from teaching a Sunday school class faithfully to making an Oscar-winning movie.

Each day we need to ask God how He wants us to spend it; that way we won't waste precious time. Everything points to the fact that time is winding down. I suggest that since today is really all you have, spend it focusing on the Kingdom. The other insignificant concerns will all fade away at judgment. Let's not stand before God on that day and have nothing to show for the life He gave us.

Commit your work to the LORD, and your plans will succeed.
(Psalm 16:3, CEB)

FINISH WHAT YOU START

Having started the ball rolling so enthusiastically, you should carry this project through to completion just as gladly, giving whatever you can out of whatever you have. Let your enthusiastic idea at the start be equaled by your realistic action now. (2 Corinthians 8:11, TLB)

I have a confession. There are times I start a project with enthusiasm only to lose interest the closer I get to completion. Whenever that happens, I ask myself why to ascertain the cause of the problem. I very seldom start a project without God's approval, so when procrastination kicks in, I go to the source: God. Sometimes I only need a little break to get reinvigorated; other times the break may last a while longer. God always reminds me that the assignments He gives me (and you, too) are never for me alone. When we don't complete our tasks, the Kingdom experiences lack because someone is waiting for us to finish what we start.

"When we do the best that we can, we never know what miracle is wrought in our life, or in the life of another."
—Helen Keller

MORE LOVE

And I pray that you and all God's holy people will have the power to understand the greatness of Christ's love—how wide, how long, how high, and how deep that love is. Christ's love is greater than anyone can ever know, but I pray that you will be able to know that love. Then you can be filled with everything God has for you. (Ephesians 3:18-19, ERV)

In some ways, today's Scripture is a contradiction. On the one hand, Paul is telling the Ephesian church that he is praying for them to know the greatness of God's love. On the other hand, he's telling them they can't fully comprehend the greatness of God's love. On the surface, it might appear that Paul can't decide what he wants to pray. But, I believe what he is praying for is comprehension, which comes with maturity. It's inconceivable for me to expect my 3-year-old grandson to do what his 14-year-old brother does. It's the same for Christians. Someone who has walked with the Lord for over 20 years shouldn't be on the same level with a newly saved person (or at least I hope they're not). Comprehension comes with growth.

The fact is we will never fully understand God's love until we reach Heaven. However, the longer we live and walk with the Lord here on Earth, the more we learn about His love. What we've learned so far is mind-boggling. I can't even begin to imagine what Heaven is like!

See how very much our heavenly Father loves us, for he allows us to be called his children—think of it—and we really are!
(1 John 3:1[a], TLB)

DO SOMETHING!

"Once a man had two sons. The younger son said to his father, 'Give me my share of the property.' So the father divided his property between his two sons. Not long after that, the younger son packed up everything he owned and left for a foreign country, where he wasted all his money in wild living. He had spent everything, when a bad famine spread through that whole land. Soon he had nothing to eat. . . Finally, he came to his senses . . ." (Luke 15:11-14, 17, CEV)

There are times when we might find ourselves stuck in a rut of our choosing. Something happened, and we stayed too long in pity-party mode. Something happened, and the pain of moving forward was beyond our capabilities. Something happened, and we enjoyed the attention that resulted from the incident. The danger of being in a rut is that it's not progressive; you're neither moving forward or backward. If you're stuck, you'll stay stuck unless you're willing to do something to change the circumstances.

The Prodigal Son in our Scripture was stuck, although that wasn't his intention when he left home. We're not told how much money his father gave him or exactly how long he was gone. What we are told is that when he hit bottom, he made a conscious decision to change his situation.

If you find yourself in a rut, follow the young man's example. Analyze the situation. Take the first step forward. Go back to people who love and care about you. Seek the forgiveness of those you may have hurt and forgive yourself. Accept their embrace and move forward.

"Forgiveness does not change the past, but it does enlarge the future."—Paul Boese (1923-1976)

CLICKING YOUR HEELS THREE TIMES AND WISHING FOR HOME ONLY WORKS IN THE MOVIES

What good is it, dear brothers and sisters, if you say you have faith but don't show it by your actions? (James 2:14[a], NLT)

When I present publishing workshops, I begin with general information about writing because, after all, there is nothing to publish if nothing has been written. I ask three questions: (1) how many of you have started a manuscript? (2) how many of you have finished a manuscript? (3) how many of you are fixin' to? The last question usually produces a lot of sheepish looks and laughter because most, if not all of us, have something we want to do but haven't started. What we fail to fully realize is that if we don't start, we'll never finish.

Today's Scripture is part of Jesus' brother's discourse on the importance of faith and action. They go hand in hand. When God gives us an assignment, He also enables us to complete it and has given us the blueprint for success. Have faith in Him for giving you the assignment and ask Him for the strength to get started. Once you've taken the initial step, you enjoy a sense of accomplishment. You're far from finish, but since the hardest step is the first one, everything after that is gravy!

Let's agree to stop procrastinating and start (or finish) what God has given us. Regardless of what it is, God wouldn't have trusted us with it if one of His people didn't need it. Take a deep breath, step out on faith, and believe that Father really does know best!

"To love means loving the unlovable. To forgive means pardoning the unpardonable. Faith means believing the unbelievable. Hope means hoping when everything seems hopeless."
—G. K. Chesterton (1874-1936)

I AM A CHRISTIAN!

"If any of you are embarrassed over me and the way I'm leading you when you get around your fickle and unfocused friends, know that you'll be an even greater embarrassment to the Son of Man when he arrives in all the splendor of God, his Father, with an army of the holy angels." (Mark 8:38-39, MSG)

I am tired of so-called celebrities flaunting their lifestyles at the world. Everywhere you turn, we hear about yet another personality coming out of the closet, having a child out of wedlock, living together in sin, being arrested for drugs or alcohol abuse, or any other multitude of things that the news media considers newsworthy. Recently, when yet another celebrity came out of the closet, boldly professing, "I'm gay; always have been," I was heartbroken. Don't misunderstand me. I don't have anything against any individual who has chosen the wrong path—I am able to separate the sin from the sinner and I know how to pray—but I do have something against the enemy, who has convinced the world that making immoral choices will have no repercussions. God is not to be mocked!

When are more Christians going to embrace the world's spirit of boldness? Do people around you even know you're saved? Have they ever seen you reading the Word, praying before a meal, or acting in a Christ-like manner? Or, do you go along to get along because you don't want to rock the boat? What are you afraid of? Those of us who live in America have no excuse for not proclaiming the name of Jesus every chance we get. We are free of religious persecution, unlike our brothers and sisters in other nations. Yet, those in other nations are bolder than we are. Why is that?

Rather than have Jesus ashamed to claim me as His, I've decided to make my own press announcement boldly proclaiming: I AM A CHRISTIAN!

Lord, help me not to be timid about our relationship.
Help me to tell the world that I have what they need,
and then help me lovingly share the Good News.

GOD WILL ANSWER WHEN YOU CALL

Then Moses said to God, "Suppose I go to the People of Israel and I tell them, 'The God of your fathers sent me to you'; and they ask me, 'What is his name?' What do I tell them?" God said to Moses, "I-AM-WHO-I-AM. Tell the People of Israel, 'I-AM sent me to you.'" (Exodus 3:13-14, MSG)

I have five grandchildren whose names all begin with "Que" after their father, my son Quentin. Sometimes I call all five names before getting the one I want. What's funny is that if they're all in the room, all of them will answer!

God always answers us when we call. His "I AM" is everything we need. We can call Him Jehovah, Father, God; joy, peace, love, comfort, and any other name that fills in the blank of where we are at any moment. He wipes tears from our eyes when we're hurt or sad. He smiles when we're having fun interacting with family and friends. He takes pleasure when we pause throughout the day to thank Him for being alive. He wraps His arms around us when we're in need of comfort. He leans in our direction when we praise Him. God's "I AM" can fill any void you have.

Sing praises to the Eternal!
Everyone, everywhere should know that God acts in amazing ways. You
who live in this God-blessed place, this Zion, shout out and sing for
joy! For God is great, and God is here—with us and around us—
the Holy One of Israel.
(Isaiah 12:5-6, VOICE)

GIVE ME THE BAD NEWS FIRST

"Simon, stay on your toes. Satan has tried his best to separate all of you from me, like chaff from wheat. Simon, I've prayed for you in particular that you not give in or give out. When you have come through the time of testing, turn to your companions and give them a fresh start." (Luke 22:31-32, MSG)

You may have noticed when given a choice of receiving bad news or good news, most of us will take the bad news first. I think the reason is that the good news will take the sting out of what we just heard, or so we hope.

Jesus used this tactic with His disciples, especially Peter, right after He had washed their feet. Jesus was preparing the disciples for what He knew was going to happen within the next few days. Peter responded that he would lay down his life for Jesus, to which Jesus said before the cock crowed three times, Peter would deny him (vv. 33-34).

Peter refused to believe himself capable of denying Jesus and had conveniently forgotten what Jesus had said earlier, probably because it was the epitome of bad news. Jesus told Peter that Satan wanted to destroy him, but here's the good news: "I have prayed for you!"

Jesus knew Peter would deny Him and be disappointed in both himself and his actions. However, Jesus also knew Peter would be restored not long after the denial and would be on fire for Him until he took his last breath. That's why Jesus gave him a preview of what he would do with his life: "When you have repented and turned to me again, strengthen your brothers" (Luke 22:32[b], NLT).

Jesus doesn't give us a license to mess up; He does, however, offer us hope for when we do. And that's good news!

Lord, thank You for all the times You've given me another chance.

I'LL SEE YOU AGAIN

Now it happened, the day after, that He went into a city called Nain; and many of His disciples went with Him, and a large crowd. And when He came near the gate of the city, behold, a dead man was being carried out, the only son of his mother; and she was a widow. And a large crowd from the city was with her. When the Lord saw her, He had compassion on her and said to her, "Do not weep." Then He came and touched the open coffin, and those who carried him stood still. And He said, "Young man, I say to you, arise." So he who was dead sat up and began to speak. And He presented him to his mother. (Luke 7:11-15, NKJV)

If you have ever buried a loved one, you know that some of the hardest moments occur on the day of the funeral. You've already experienced the shock and finality of death, and the sadness associated with that event. You've been able to pull yourself together enough to interact with well-meaning friends and family. It's tough to get out of bed on the morning of the funeral because you already know that before the day is over, you will have experienced a wide range of emotions. While Christians don't mourn as those who have no hope (1 Thessalonians 4:13), we still feel pain and heartache.

The woman in today's Scripture was a widow; her husband was gone and now her only son was gone, too. In those days a woman without a man's protection was limited in what she could do. While she focused her strength on putting one foot in front of the other and getting through the upcoming ordeal, the Master took note of her and had compassion upon her. "Do not weep," He said, and presented the young man—alive!—back to his mother. That quickly, her heartache turned to joy.

We may never experience the physical resurrection of a loved one, but we, too, can have our heartache turned to joy. That doesn't mean we won't be sad or feel the loss of the person, but we can trust that God, who is the mender of broken hearts, will carry us through. And, we know that we will be reunited with our loved ones in Heaven.

*"The spirit of the Sovereign Lord is upon me
. . . to comfort the brokenhearted . . ."* (Isaiah 61:1, NLT)

LISTEN UP!

In reply Jesus said to the disciples, "If you only have faith in God—this is the absolute truth—you can say to this Mount of Olives, 'Rise up and fall into the Mediterranean,' and your command will be obeyed. All that's required is that you really believe and have no doubt! Listen to me! You can pray for anything, and if you believe, you have it; it's yours!" (Mark 11:22-24, TLB)

Do you ever listen to the words coming out of your mouth? There are times when we talk about ourselves in such a contrary manner that one would be hard pressed to believe we're a child of God. We say things to ourselves that we would never accept from someone else, like "You're so stupid!" "Where was your brain when you made that decision?" "Are you crazy?"

Words have a profound impact on how we see ourselves and consequently how we pray. Today's Scripture tells us we can have whatever we say, and that we can pray about anything and receive it. But, we need to be consistent. You can't tell yourself, "I'm too dumb," and then ask God for a financial breakthrough to attend college. That's a disconnect. If you believe you're made in the image of God, then there isn't anything you're "too" much of, although there may be issues you've brought upon yourself. Yes, God created you in His image, but did He tell you to eat so much that your physical shape has become distorted? Yes, God made you in His image, but did He tell you to ingest drugs and alcohol until you can no longer think straight?

Listen to what you're saying to yourself, and then ask God to help you "hear" what He is speaking to you. That way, you'll say the right things and pray the right way; then today's Scripture will become a reality in your life.

Your ears shall hear a word behind you, saying, "This is the way, walk in it," whenever you turn to the right hand or whenever you turn to the left.
(Isaiah 30:21, NKJV)

GOD SAID, "STOP PUSHING ME!"

God is jealous over those he loves; that is why he takes vengeance on those who hurt them. He furiously destroys their enemies. He is slow in getting angry, but when aroused, his power is incredible, and he does not easily forgive. He shows his power in the terrors of the cyclone and the raging storms; clouds are billowing dust beneath his feet! At his command the oceans and rivers become dry sand; the lush pastures of Bashan and Carmel fade away; the green forests of Lebanon wilt. In his presence mountains quake and hills melt; the earth crumbles, and its people are destroyed. Who can stand before an angry God? His fury is like fire; the mountains tumble down before his anger. (Nahum 1:2-6, TLB)

If reading the newspaper or watching cable news won't make you pray, I don't know what will. Our world is in trouble. I'm fearful for those who keep pushing the envelope of moral, societal, and humanistic issues. At what point will people realize that their behavior is unacceptable? The day is coming when God will be angry, and it's going to be too late for those who don't know Him. The time is now for us to continue telling a dying world that Jesus saves! Without Him in their lives, people lack the motivation to change their negative behavior.

Jesus saith unto him, "I am the way, the truth, and the life: no man cometh unto the Father, but by me."
(John 14:6, KJV)

Neither is there salvation in any other: for there is none other name under heaven given among men, whereby we must be saved.
(Acts 4:12, KJV)

SHUT MOUTH GRACE

But avoid foolish and ignorant disputes, knowing that they generate strife. And a servant of the Lord must not quarrel but be gentle to all, able to teach, patient, in humility correcting those who are in opposition, if God perhaps will grant them repentance, so that they may know the truth. . . (2 Timothy 2:23-25, NKJV)

I have always been accused of having an answer and an opinion about everything, and I'll confess that the accusation is accurate. However, since salvation I have embraced the concept of "shut mouth grace," which means that when necessary, I keep my answers and opinions to myself. And that's not always easy for someone like me.

There are times when it takes every ounce of Holy Ghost to keep my mouth shut, and whenever I'm tempted to just let someone have it, I remember today's Scripture, which enables me to keep the peace. And, usually, God allows an opportunity for me to say what I felt needed to be said, just in a gentler, calmer manner where the recipient is more amenable to hearing my words. "If it is possible, as much as depends on you, live peaceably with all men" (Romans 12:18, NKJV).

Lord, help me to remember that I represent You at all times.
Help me to represent You well.

A PERSONAL ESCORT

"In My Father's house are many mansions; if it were not so, I would have told you. I go to prepare a place for you. And if I go and prepare a place for you, I will come again and receive you to Myself; that where I am, there you may be also." (John 14:2-3, NKJV)

I love eating out, especially in establishments that have excellent food and good service. I want to enjoy every dining experience. Recently I went to my favorite restaurant. As the hostess turned to take me to a seat, another hostess ran over and said, "Oh, I'll take her. I know exactly where she wants to sit." I felt special because she remembered my preference.

Like deplaning and finding someone holding a sign with your name on it, Jesus is willing to be our guide. He is not going to send a substitute or unnamed escort. Heaven is a prepared place for a prepared people, so who better to take us home? Are you ready to be seated?

Amen! Blessing and glory and wisdom,
Thanksgiving and honor and power and might,
Be to our God forever and ever. Amen.
(Revelation 7:12, NKJV)

I CAN SHOW YOU BETTER
THAN I CAN TELL YOU

For God so loved the world, that he gave his only begotten Son, that whosoever believeth in him should not perish, but have everlasting life. (John 3:16, KJV)

Perhaps you've heard someone use the expression, "I can show you better than I can tell you," which can mean that actions speak louder than words. You hear well-meaning, but empty, expressions all the time such as, "Let me know if you need anything." "I'm just a phone call away." "I'll do anything for you, you know that." And so forth. Even someone saying "I love you" is nice to hear, but better when it's shown. I know people in abusive relationships who are told "I love you" while being beaten, cursed at, or emotionally threatened. Words without actions don't really carry that much weight.

That's why John 3:16 is such a powerful verse. God told us He loved us and then backed His Word up with action . . . the death of our Lord and Savior, Jesus Christ, on the cross. The only question that remains is will you accept the offer of eternal life, which can only be found in a relationship with Jesus? And, if you've already accepted Him as Lord and Savior, are you taking full advantage of this remarkable Gift by building a relationship with Jesus? A gift that's unused isn't fulfilling its purpose.

Jesus came to give us life and that more abundantly (John 10:10[b]). Are you living the abundant life?

> I love you, Lord. And I lift my voice.
> To worship You, O my soul rejoice.
> Take joy my King in what you hear.
> Let it be a sweet, sweet sound in your ear.
> *I Love You Lord.* Laurie Klein. 1978.

SUN STAND STILL

Then Joshua spoke to the LORD in the day when the LORD delivered up the Amorites before the children of Israel, and he said in the sight of Israel: "Sun, stand still over Gibeon; And Moon, in the Valley of Aijalon." So, the sun stood still, And the moon stopped, Till the people had revenge upon their enemies. Is this not written in the Book of Jasher? So, the sun stood still in the midst of heaven, and did not hasten to go down for about a whole day. And there has been no day like that, before it or after it, that the LORD heeded the voice of a man; for the LORD fought for Israel. (Joshua 10:12-14, NKJV)

It takes a person confident in their relationship with the Lord to ask for the unthinkable. But, that's what Joshua did, and God responded by doing as asked. If He did it for Joshua, He will do it for us, too.

God wouldn't allow the sun to stand still even if we begged. The Bible is clear that it happened once and will not be repeated. But, there are days we need extra time, not necessarily because of procrastination but because we want to accomplish something positive. We may need more minutes to finish a project, or to make a hospital visit, or to spend with a loved one. When we say, "God, please give me more time," there are moments when it feels as if time stops. And, that is further testament to the goodness of God and His faithfulness to those who belong to Him.

"Time is nothing to God."—Oswald Chambers.

JUST FOR ME (AND YOU, TOO)

"I pray for them. I do not pray for the world but for those whom You have given Me, for they are Yours. And all Mine are Yours, and Yours are Mine, and I am glorified in them." (John 17:9-10, NKJV)

Growing up as a middle child, I felt invisible. According to experts and those who have experienced this particular placement, we often feel overlooked because of what's going on with our siblings.

As I matured, the invisibility disappeared (no pun intended) and I realized, accepted, and embraced my place in the Universe. One of the things that assisted in this transformation is today's Scripture. It is humbling to realize that when Jesus walked the Earth, He prayed for me before I was conceived and born! He prayed for you, too. He prayed for all of us who would accept Him as Lord and Savior, especially for those who don't know it yet: "People will come from the east and the west, from the north and the south, and sit down at the feast in the Kingdom of God" (Luke 13:29, GNT).

When we know with certainty that Jesus loves us, we'll act like we're someone special—I don't mean in an arrogant or conceited way, but with confidence and boldness that we can do anything but fail.

Christ is the one who gives me the strength
I need to do whatever I must do.
(Philippians 4:13, ERV)

IF IT AIN'T BROKE . . .

It pleased Darius to set over the kingdom one hundred and twenty satraps, to be over the whole kingdom; and over these, three governors, of whom Daniel was one, that the satraps might give account to them, so that the king would suffer no loss. Then this Daniel distinguished himself above the governors and satraps, because an excellent spirit was in him; and the king gave thought to setting him over the whole realm. So the governors and satraps sought to find some charge against Daniel concerning the kingdom; but they could find no charge or fault, because he was faithful; nor was there any error or fault found in him. . . .All the governors of the kingdom, the administrators and satraps, the counselors and advisors, have consulted together to establish a royal statute and to make a firm decree, that "whoever petitions any god or man for thirty days, except you, O king, shall be cast into the den of lions. Now, O king, establish the decree and sign the writing, so that it cannot be changed, according to the law of the Medes and Persians, which does not alter." Therefore, King Darius signed the written decree. Now when Daniel knew that the writing was signed, he went home. And in his upper room, with his windows open toward Jerusalem, he knelt down on his knees three times that day, and prayed and gave thanks before his God, as was his custom since early days. (Daniel 6:1-4, 7-10, NKJV)

I am a creature of habit. I follow the same routine every week day morning—devotional time, shower, dress, eat breakfast, and leave for work. If I deviate from my morning routine, something gets left out or is rushed.

Daniel's prayer routine shows us the importance of priorities. There will always be something or someone who attempts to distract or cause us to deviate from what we know pleases God. Let's make sure that doesn't happen, even when we find ourselves in the lion's den. Like Daniel, God will always protect His people.

Then Daniel said to the king, "O king, live forever! My God sent His angel and shut the lions' mouths, so that they have not hurt me, because I was found innocent before Him." (Daniel 6:21-22, NKJV)

... BUT, IF IT IS BROKE, GET HELP

Now they came to Jericho. As He went out of Jericho with His disciples and a great multitude, blind Bartimaeus, the son of Timaeus, sat by the road begging. And when he heard that it was Jesus of Nazareth, he began to cry out and say, "Jesus, Son of David, have mercy on me!" Then many warned him to be quiet; but he cried out all the more, "Son of David, have mercy on me!" So Jesus stood still and commanded him to be called. Then they called the blind man, saying to him, "Be of good cheer. Rise, He is calling you." And throwing aside his garment, he rose and came to Jesus. So Jesus answered and said to him, "What do you want Me to do for you?" The blind man said to Him, "Rabboni, that I may receive my sight." Then Jesus said to him, "Go your way; your faith has made you well." And immediately he received his sight and followed Jesus on the road. (Mark 10:46-52, NKJV)

We don't know whether Bartimaeus was born blind or lost his sight through accident or disease. Let's assume, he was born blind. He would have no concept of colors or shapes; he had never seen a person, place, or thing. While people could attempt to explain to him what they saw, without a frame of reference, it was virtually impossible to comprehend. Is it any wonder he wanted to see?

When we become desperate for change, we'll leave our comfort zone to obtain help. Bartimaeus had gotten tired of his lifestyle; he believed Jesus could help him. When Jesus asked what he wanted, Bartimaeus was clear: I want to see! Like the begging that had become his means of support, he wasn't too ashamed to beg for help from the only One who could provide it. It was a win-win situation. Bartimaeus received his sight, and Jesus did what He came to do: to help His people.

"The Spirit of the LORD is upon Me. . .To proclaim liberty to the captives and recovery of sight to the blind." (Luke 4:18 NKJV)

I'M STANDING RIGHT IN FRONT OF YOU

Then the Pharisees again questioned the man who had been blind and demanded, "What's your opinion about this man who healed you?" The man replied, "I think he must be a prophet." The Jewish leaders still refused to believe the man had been blind and could now see, so they called in his parents. They asked them, "Is this your son? Was he born blind? If so, how can he now see?" His parents replied, "We know this is our son and that he was born blind, but we don't know how he can see or who healed him. Ask him. He is old enough to speak for himself." (John 9:17-21, NLT)

I was at church talking with a woman when another woman approached us. The woman I was speaking with introduced me to the other woman, who asked, "Why does your name sound familiar?" Before I could respond, the first woman spoke up, "Oh, you probably recognize her name because she writes Christian books." The second woman started asking the first woman questions about what I had written, how to get my books, and the like. I smiled to myself, thinking *"Hmm, I didn't realize I'd hired a publicist!"* when the first woman started responding. About the same time, the second woman realized what she was doing and turned back to me and said, "I guess I should be asking you, huh?" We laughed, and I answered her questions and hopefully gained a new fan.

Jesus healed the man in our Scripture after being born blind. The people were reluctant to believe the miracle and kept asking questions. He patiently answered them, but they didn't like his response (John 9:1-16). Finally, they turned to his parents for clarification, who directed them back to their son for an answer. The man never changed his story about his healing and stuck to the facts. He didn't embellish an already dramatic event, and he didn't hesitate to give God the praise.

Testimonies are more powerful when they come straight from the source. Every child of God has a story to tell about what God has done for them, and nobody can say it like you!

Come and listen, everyone who reveres the True God, and I will tell you what He has done for me. (Psalm 66:16, VOICE)

THE NAME GAME

"Greater love has no one than this, than to lay down one's life for his friends. You are My friends if you do whatever I command you. No longer do I call you servants, for a servant does not know what his master is doing; but I have called you friends, for all things that I heard from My Father I have made known to you." (John 15:13-15, NKJV)

Motivational speaker and author Dale Carnegie taught us, "Remember that a person's name is to that person the sweetest and most important sound in any language."

My son calls me Mom; my parents called me Obieray; my siblings call me Obie; my pastor calls me O-O; a couple of friends call me Ob, and now and then, to get my attention, someone will call me by my entire name, Obieray Rogers. I'll answer to any of the above names. But, there is one name I cherish—Friend. I am so glad Jesus calls me His friend. I'm equally delighted that I allow Him to be a Friend to me. No one does friendship better than the Master.

Lord, thank You for allowing us such a level of closeness
as to be called a friend. Help us not to take it for granted.

GET HOME BEFORE THE
STREET LIGHTS COME ON

And at midnight a cry was heard: "Behold, the bridegroom is coming; go out to meet him!" Then all those virgins arose and trimmed their lamps. And the foolish said to the wise, "Give us some of your oil, for our lamps are going out." But the wise answered, saying, "No, lest there should not be enough for us and you; but go rather to those who sell, and buy for yourselves." And while they went to buy, the bridegroom came, and those who were ready went in with him to the wedding; and the door was shut. Afterward the other virgins came also, saying, "Lord, Lord, open to us!" But he answered and said, "Assuredly, I say to you, I do not know you." (Matthew 25:6-12, NKJV)

Parents of my generation required their children to be in the house, or at least on the porch, before the street lights came on. We had played all day, and it was time to get into the house. We may have fussed about the restriction (under our breath) because we wanted to stay out longer; but, we were obedient to our parents' request. We knew their instructions were non-negotiable and, if disobeyed, we'd be punished.

Our parents gave us the street lights as a guide that it was time to come home; however, none of us know when Jesus is returning. It may be today, tomorrow, next week, or next year. It may be summer, winter, spring, or fall. If we missed our curfew, our parents might have punished us, but that is nothing compared to missing Jesus' return. Enjoy your life, but make sure you're prepared for His arrival. Don't be like the foolish virgins in today's Scripture. Jesus wants you with Him more than you'll ever know.

"But of that day and hour knoweth no man, no, not the angels of heaven, but my Father only." (Matthew 24:36, KJV)

THE NEW MATH

When Jesus' followers heard this, many of them said, "This teaching is hard. Who can accept it?" Jesus already knew that his followers were complaining about this. So he said, "Is this teaching a problem for you? Then what will you think when you see the Son of Man going up to where he came from? It is the Spirit that gives life. The body is of no value for that. But the things I have told you are from the Spirit, so they give life. But some of you don't believe." (Jesus knew the people who did not believe. He knew this from the beginning. And he knew the one who would hand him over to his enemies.) Jesus said, "That is why I said, 'Anyone the Father does not help to come to me cannot come.'" After Jesus said these things, many of his followers left and stopped following him. (John 6:60-66, ERV)

Sometimes when we're beginning a new venture, we invite people to join us. We get those who are willing to help but aren't really of any significant assistance. Or, we get those who offer to help, but really just want to take over the project. Or, we get those who are truly helpful, which are usually in the minority.

When Jesus first began preaching, He had many followers. He was the latest "thing," and everybody wanted to be known for being in the know about Him. However, once He started telling them exactly what was required to be in His group, the people started drifting away.

Those who start out with us don't always finish, usually because they're not willing to follow the rules, to work hard, or to be set apart. In our humanity, we may be disappointed, but we shouldn't be. God often subtracts before He adds. We need to allow people to exit our life, so God can bring the ones in who are supposed to be with us.

"My sheep hear My voice, and I know them,
and they follow Me." (John 10:27, NKJV)

I AIN'T GOT NOBODY BUT YOU

Jesus asked the twelve apostles, "Do you want to leave too?" Simon Peter answered him, "Lord, where would we go? You have the words that give eternal life. We believe in you. We know that you are the Holy One from God." Then Jesus answered, "I chose all twelve of you. But one of you is a devil." He was talking about Judas, the son of Simon Iscariot. Judas was one of the twelve apostles, but later he would hand Jesus over to his enemies. (John 6:67-71, ERV)

Before salvation, I would have been like the others who left Jesus because His teachings were too hard. After salvation, I'm like Peter: "Where would I go?" Once you've seen the difference Christ makes in your life, it's very hard to walk away from the relationship. Even those who do still remember what it was like. There's a part of them that longs to return; yet, for whatever reason, they aren't ready to re-commit to the Lordship of Jesus Christ. They may think they're living and having fun, but they're not. And one day they'll realize it's all been a waste of time and that apart from God they can do nothing. We just need to keep praying that they'll shake themselves and come to their senses before it's too late. God wants them in the Kingdom as much as we do.

Then Jesus said to his followers, "If any of you
want to be my follower, you must stop thinking
about yourself, and what you want. You must be willing to carry the
cross that is given to you for following me." (Matthew 16:24, ERV)

WHY CAN'T I BE ENOUGH?

When Jesus came near the city, He cried as He saw it. He said, "If you had only known on this great day the things that make peace! But now they are hidden from your eyes. The time is coming when those who hate you will dig earth and throw it up around you making a wall. They will shut you in from every side. They will destroy you and your children with you. There will not be one stone on another. It is because you did not know when God visited you." (Luke 19:41-44, NLV)

What do you experience when you've given your best and it's not good enough? Or, you've poured all of yourself into a person and they turn their back on you? It causes you to feel rejection, disappointment, hurt, and anger, doesn't it? You wonder why people can't, won't or don't accept what you offer. You wonder why what you offer isn't enough.

These are the emotions Jesus felt when He saw Jerusalem. It brought tears to His eyes because He knew Jerusalem would be destroyed. He also knew that His efforts had been rejected and He would soon face the agony of the cross. According to Matthew Henry's *Concise Commentary* (Public Domain): "The Son of God did not weep vain and causeless tears, nor for a light matter, nor for himself. He knows the value of souls, the weight of guilt, and how low it will press and sink mankind."

Calvin's *Commentary on the Bible* (Public Domain) further states: "As there was nothing which Christ more ardently desired than to execute the office which the Father had committed to him . . . he wished that his coming might bring salvation to all. . . And when he saw the people, who had been adopted to the hope of eternal life, perish miserably through their ingratitude and wickedness, we need not wonder if he could not refrain from tears."

Jesus' desire was for people to be saved. Please let the salvation He offers be enough for you to turn your life around.

HAVE YOU TOUCHED JESUS TODAY?

Now a certain woman had a flow of blood for twelve years . . . When she heard about Jesus, she came behind Him in the crowd and touched His garment. For she said, "If only I may touch His clothes, I shall be made well." Immediately the fountain of her blood was dried up, and she felt in her body that she was healed of the affliction. And Jesus, immediately knowing in Himself that power had gone out of Him, turned around in the crowd and said, "Who touched My clothes?" But His disciples said to Him, "You see the multitude thronging You, and You say, 'Who touched Me?'" (Mark 5:25, 27-31, NKJV)

The woman in today's Scripture is familiar to most of us, and the fact that she's unnamed allows us all—men and women—to insert our name into this story of faith and persistence.

There was an untold number of people surrounding Jesus the day He met this woman. The Bible calls it a "great multitude." Have you ever experienced a shock after walking on carpet and touching someone? It is a static reaction; although it's not painful, you still notice it. Numerous people had already passed by Jesus, rubbing and brushing against Him. But when He felt the electrical shock of this woman's touch of faith, He stopped what He was doing to respond to her needs.

When we purposely and intentionally come to Jesus in faith, He will always respond to us. Sometimes the response is immediate; sometimes it's not. We can rest on the assurance that our acts of faith will always result in God's reaction.

Reach out and touch the Lord, as He passes by.
You'll find He's not too busy to hear your heart's cry.
He is passing by this moment, your needs to supply.
Reach out and touch the Lord, as He passes by.
Reach Out and Touch the Lord. Bill Harmon and
Paul Wigmore (1958)

STOP IT!

"Therefore, I say to you, do not worry about your life, what you will eat or what you will drink; nor about your body, what you will put on. Is not life more than food and the body more than clothing?" . . ."Therefore, do not worry, saying, 'What shall we eat?' or 'What shall we drink?' or 'What shall we wear?' For after all these things the Gentiles seek. For your heavenly Father knows that you need all these things. . . . Therefore, do not worry about tomorrow, for tomorrow will worry about its own things. Sufficient for the day is its own trouble." (Matthew 6:25, 31-32, 34, NKJV)

Do you know people who don't seem to be happy unless they're worried about something? I do, and it is often irritating to be around them. They live in a constant state of "what if" and always expect the worse.

Today's Scripture asks one question in verse 27: Can you add anything to your stature by worrying? The answer, of course, is no! So, if worrying doesn't change the circumstances, why go through the motion? Now, to be clear, there is a difference between worry and concern. According to www.dictionary.com, *worry* is defined as "to torment oneself with or suffer from disturbing thoughts; fret"; whereas, *concern* is defined as, "to relate to; be connected with; be of interest or importance to; affect." Matthew 6:33 (GWT) gives us the key to a worry-free life: "But first, be concerned about his kingdom and what has his approval. Then all these things will be provided for you." *All these things* are everything that keeps you awake at night. In exchange for staying up, God gives peace, rest, and a good night's sleep. Stop worrying. Turn whatever it is over to God, who can handle things much better than we ever could.

"If you prayed as much as you worry, you'd have nothing to worry about."
—Rick Warren

IF I ONLY KNEW THEN . . .

"I have spoken these words while I am here with you. The Father is sending a great Helper, the Holy Spirit, in My name to teach you everything and to remind you of all I have said to you. My peace is the legacy I leave to you. I don't give gifts like those of this world. Do not let your heart be troubled or fearful. You were listening when I said, 'I will go away, but I will also return to be with you.' If you love Me, celebrate the fact that I am going to be with the Father because He is far greater than I am. I have told you all these things in advance so that your faith will grow as these things come to pass." (John 14:25-29, VOICE)

If we had known how some things would end, we would have handled them differently. Usually, we don't have that much foresight into the future. Wouldn't it be nice if we did?

Jesus gave His disciples a glimpse into the future. He explained that He was leaving to return to His Father. He knew that His departure was going to be sad and painful, and He knew He needed to leave them with an assurance of never being alone. He needed to ensure they would survive future events.

Jesus gives us these same assurances. His return to Heaven allowed the Helper to come to do what the name implies, help us maintain our relationship and life in God. Jesus left us His peace to tap into whenever life's challenges become too much. And, Jesus gave us direction in how to handle the events of our life that are designed to increase our faith.

Lord, thank You for thinking enough of me to give me a heads-up of things to come. Help me to focus on Your promise of help, rather than rely on my senses.

THE WATER BILL

"But anyone who drinks the water I give will never be thirsty again. The water I give people will be like a spring flowing inside them. It will bring them eternal life." (John 4:14, ERV)

I forgot to pay my water bill. I didn't remember until I received a delinquent notice in the mail. I knew I had received the bill, and I usually put all the bills in a specific spot. This time the water bill had slipped under other papers; out of sight, out of mind. Upon seeing the notice, I immediately went online and paid the bill.

Water is necessary for our day to day living, whether we're drinking it, bathing in it, or washing clothes or dishes. It's important to keep the bill paid so that when we turn on the tap, water comes out. Our connection to Jesus is even more important, because of the living water He provides. Once we partner with Jesus and make Him our source, our life will flow out, never to be turned off again.

Jesus stood up and said loudly, "Whoever is thirsty may come to me and drink. If anyone believes in me, rivers of living water will flow out from their heart. That is what the Scriptures say."
(John 7:37-38, ERV)

WAIT FOR IT

And Jesus said to him, "What do you want me to do for you?"
(Mark 10:51, ESV)

Years ago, a friend wanted me to meet her mentor. She had
spoken of the woman often, so I felt as if I already knew her and
looked forward to meeting her. On the day introductions were
made, I was disappointed. My friend excitedly made the
introduction; the woman smiled at me and said, "Hi, how are
you?" and then walked away to speak with someone else before
I could answer. I had heard of the woman, anticipated the
introduction and opportunity to talk with her, only to be
disappointed because, in her humanity, she rushed to someone
else.

I am eternally delighted that Jesus does not act like that
toward us. When He asks a question, He waits for a response,
although He already knows what the answer will be. When Jesus
responded to Bartimaeus' call, He asked the question, waited for
a response, and delivered on everything Bartimaeus had heard
about Him.

Lord, help us not to rush to see what's next
and miss the opportunity in front of us.

ARE YOU WILLING TO DO YOUR PART?

One Sabbath as he was teaching in a synagogue, he saw a seriously handicapped woman who had been bent double for eighteen years and was unable to straighten herself. Calling her over to him Jesus said, "Woman, you are healed of your sickness!" He touched her, and instantly she could stand straight. How she praised and thanked God! (Luke 13:10-13, TLB)

We all know people who want something big or special but who aren't willing to do anything to change their situation. However, unlike lazy people, this unnamed woman did something bold. She had suffered from an ailment for a long time. We're not told what other efforts she had taken to correct her sickness; we *are* told that on this day, she was in the right place (in the temple), at the right time (the Sabbath), doing the right thing (worshiping God), with the right person present— Jesus!

Did you notice that Jesus called the woman to Him; He didn't go to her? Jesus had to know that with her present condition, walking would have been difficult. For Jesus to command her to come to Him seems almost insensitive. But, He needed to know how badly she wanted to be healed. She didn't know what was going to happen; she could have responded (like some of us would) with, "Are you kidding me? Do you know how far I've already walked? Why can't you come to me?" and she would have missed her blessing. Instead, she summoned enough strength to rise and took long and torturous steps toward the Master, who spoke the healing before He touched her. I believe that as she took each step, in obedience and faith, the healing happened. Jesus' spoken Word was for the benefit of the woman and the crowd, and the touch was to solidify the miracle. God knows that we finite humans sometimes need to "hear" and "feel" His move. Are you in need of a touch today? God is waiting for you to make the struggle to Jesus.

Lord God Almighty, we thank You for Your willingness to give us what we desperately need. Help us not to be so lazy that we won't respond to Your call.

DON'T BE SCARED

Now as He drew near, He saw the city and wept over it, saying, "If you had known, even you, especially in this your day, the things that make for your peace! But now they are hidden from your eyes." (Luke 19:41-42, NKJV)

Then, when Mary came where Jesus was, and saw Him, she fell down at His feet, saying to Him, "Lord, if You had been here, my brother would not have died." Therefore, when Jesus saw her weeping, and the Jews who came with her weeping, He groaned in the spirit and was troubled. And He said, "Where have you laid him?" They said to Him, "Lord, come and see." Jesus wept. (John 11:32-35, NKJV)

There is a difference between crying and weeping. Crying is to shed tears nosily; weeping is to express deep sorrow, usually by shedding tears (www.dictionary.com).

I believe people who are reluctant to show their emotions by crying are fearful of what others may think of their behavior. They shouldn't be. Jesus wasn't afraid of His feelings, whether it was anger at moneychangers or hurt at Jerusalem's dismissal of what He came to do or seeing His friends in distress. We, too, should be willing to own our emotions with honesty and integrity. We're human; it's time some of us acted like it.

There is a right time for everything. . .
A time to cry; A time to laugh; A time to grieve;
A time to dance. (Ecclesiastes 3:1, 4, TLB)

NOTHING BUT THE TRUTH

And as He walked by the Sea of Galilee, He saw Simon and Andrew his brother casting a net into the sea; for they were fishermen. Then Jesus said to them, "Follow Me, and I will make you become fishers of men." They immediately left their nets and followed Him. (Mark 1:16-18, NKJV)

Most scholars agree that the book of Mark is a biography of Peter. Mark, who was not one of the Twelve, received firsthand knowledge from his mentor, Peter. (He is also the young man who accompanied Paul and Barnabas on their trips and left them to return to Jerusalem.) It is believed that Mark spent a significant amount of time around Peter listening to his preaching, and he arranged notes from the sermons for first-century Christians and us.

Mark was able to experience Jesus' ministry via Peter's retelling of the amazing events he witnessed. Have you ever heard something so good that you couldn't help but pass it on? That's what happened with Mark; he felt the testimony of Peter needed to be recorded for posterity. Surprisingly, Peter told everything—the good and the bad. He told of the healings Jesus performed, as well as his own failures, including the denial of Jesus in Mark 15:66-72. Peter wasn't afraid for people to know that he was human; he readily owned up to his mistakes.

Who needs to hear your firsthand account of all God, Jesus, and the Holy Spirit have done for you? Your testimony will be more potent if you don't gloss over the parts that don't show you at your best. That doesn't mean tell every detail, but it does say tell enough so that people know you don't possess angel wings yet.

All flesh is as grass, And all the glory of man as the flower of the grass.
The grass withers, and its flower falls away,
But the word of the LORD endures forever. Now this is the word which by
the gospel was preached to you.
(1 Peter 1:24-25, NKJV)

EVIDENCE

"I am the Real Vine and my Father is the Farmer. He cuts off every branch of me that doesn't bear grapes. And every branch that is grape-bearing he prunes back so it will bear even more. You are already pruned back by the message I have spoken. Live in me. Make your home in me just as I do in you. In the same way that a branch can't bear grapes by itself but only by being joined to the vine, you can't bear fruit unless you are joined with me." (John 15:1-4, MSG)

If asked, what evidence could you produce to show your connection to the Vinedresser? What fruit are you bearing? We're called to produce fruit, although not all the same. However, there are some criteria that should be consistent among those who claim the name of Jesus: "But when the Holy Spirit controls our lives he will produce this kind of fruit in us: love, joy, peace, patience, kindness, goodness, faithfulness, gentleness and self-control; and here there is no conflict with Jewish laws" (Galatians 5:22-23, TLB).

God does distribute some specific gifts: "And that same Christ gave these gifts to people: He made some to be apostles, some to be prophets, some to go and tell the Good News, and some to care for and teach God's people" (Ephesians 4:11, ERV).

Except for 2 Corinthians 5:18, KJV—"And all things are of God, who hath reconciled us to himself by Jesus Christ, and hath given to us the ministry of reconciliation"—our assignments are as different as night from day. My assignment is to write; yours may be something else, and that's okay. God is only holding us accountable for what He has called us to do.

"You didn't choose me, remember; I chose you, and put you in the world to bear fruit, fruit that won't spoil. As fruit bearers, whatever you ask the Father in relation to me, he gives you." (John 15:16, MSG)

OKAY

Now it came to pass, when the time had come for Him to be received up, that He steadfastly set His face to go to Jerusalem and sent messengers before His face. And as they went, they entered a village of the Samaritans, to prepare for Him. But they did not receive Him, because His face was set for the journey to Jerusalem. And when His disciples James and John saw this, they said, "Lord, do You want us to command fire to come down from heaven and consume them, just as Elijah did?" But He turned and rebuked them, and said, "You do not know what manner of spirit you are of. For the Son of Man did not come to destroy men's lives but to save them." And they went to another village. (Luke 9:51-56, NKJV)

There are times when you try to help people, and they don't or won't accept your help. When that happens, there isn't much you can do except allow them to be content with whatever is going on in their life that made you extend the offer in the first place.

Jesus came down to Earth because His people needed help. He knew what He was willing and able to do. He also knew that we were created with free will to either accept or reject Him. Jesus is our model in all things, especially when it comes to dealing with confused and stubborn people. When the disciples reported back that the Samaritans wouldn't allow Him to enter their village, He didn't point out that He was the Son of God but left to go where He would be accepted.

Let's follow His example the next time we encounter resistance. We don't need to have the last word. We don't need to try to convince anyone to see things our way. And, we don't need people's approval to fulfill our destiny.

Help me to do Your will, for You are my God. Lead me in good paths, for Your Spirit is good. (Psalm 143:10, TLB)

IF YOU LIVE RIGHT . . .

His Lord said to him, "Well done, good and faithful servant. . ."
(Matthew 25:21, NKJV)

Living the Christian life isn't easy. If we're honest, we'll admit there are times we don't want to turn the other cheek; we want to retaliate against rude and ignorant people. There are times we don't want to love our neighbor; matter of fact, we don't want to know who our neighbor is. There are times it's challenging not to overlook the least of God's people and keep walking forward.

Jesus never said it would be easy; He only commands that we follow Him. Following Him means striving to be more like Him. Although it may be hard, it's not impossible if we keep Jesus first.

More about Jesus let me learn,
More of His holy will discern;
Spirit of God, my teacher be,
Showing the things of Christ to me.
More About Jesus. Eliza E. Hewitt. 1887.
Public Domain.

CHECK
(GOOD FRIDAY)

The soldiers nailed Jesus to a cross. Then they threw dice to divide his clothes between them. The soldiers stayed there to guard him. They put a sign above his head with the charge against him written on it: "THIS IS JESUS, THE KING OF THE JEWS." . . . Again Jesus cried out loudly and then died. . . . That day was the day called Preparation day. The next day, the leading priests and the Pharisees went to Pilate. They said, "Sir, we remember that while that liar was still alive he said, 'I will rise from death in three days.' So give the order for the tomb to be guarded well for three days. His followers might come and try to steal the body. Then they could tell everyone that he has risen from death. That lie will be even worse than what they said about him before." Pilate said, "Take some soldiers and go guard the tomb the best way you know." So they all went to the tomb and made it safe from thieves. They did this by sealing the stone in the entrance and putting soldiers there to guard it. (Matthew 27:35-37, 50, 62-66, ERV)

In chess, "check" is a move that attacks the opposing king. On the day we call *Good Friday*, our enemy used Pilate and others to orchestrate the downfall of Jesus. Preachers often talk of how the devil salivated at the thought of Jesus' death, thinking that he would now be in authority. He counted his chickens before they were hatched—never a good idea.

There are moments when things do appear to be over despite how hard we prayed. Our loved one dies, we lose our job, the house is in foreclosure. In those times, we must *trust* that God always knows what He is doing in every situation. We must *learn* to look at things through our spiritual eyes and not the natural ones. We must *remember* that nothing happens without God's approval, even the things we don't understand. The devil is not in control!

The LORD says, "My thoughts are not like yours. Your ways are not like mine. Just as the heavens are higher than the earth, so my ways are higher than your ways, and my thoughts are higher than your thoughts."
(Isaiah 55:8-9, ERV)

THE DAY AFTER YESTERDAY

God is not a man, that he should lie; neither the son of man, that he should repent: hath he said, and shall he not do it? or hath he spoken, and shall he not make it good? (Numbers 23:19, KJV)

I believe the healing process begins the day after a funeral. The shock of the loss has started to fade, the out-of-town guests are usually gone, and the family is finally able to breathe a little. Oh, you're still in pain from the loss; it will take time for that to disappear. But, you realize that your life is now altered, and an adjustment is required.

On the day after Jesus' death, I would imagine His family, friends, and disciples were sad and at a loss as to what to do next. I think on some level they remembered Jesus telling them He would rise again, and they wanted to believe it. What they didn't count on was the cruelty of the crucifixion and the finality of seeing Jesus give up His spirit. I'd like to believe there was a spark of hope among the group, especially from those who witnessed Lazarus' resurrection. If Jesus did it for Lazarus, is it possible He would do it for Himself? I think that some of the people were on pins and needles, counting down the hours to see what would happen next.

"Be still and know that I am God:
I will be exalted among the heathen, I will be exalted in the earth."
(Psalm 46:10, KJV)

CHECKMATE
(RESURRECTION SUNDAY)

At the crack of dawn on Sunday, the women came to the tomb carrying the burial spices they had prepared. They found the entrance stone rolled back from the tomb, so they walked in. But once inside, they couldn't find the body of the Master Jesus. They were puzzled, wondering what to make of this. Then, out of nowhere it seemed, two men, light cascading over them, stood there. The women were awestruck and bowed down in worship. The men said, "Why are you looking for the Living One in a cemetery? He is not here but raised up. Remember how he told you when you were still back in Galilee that he had to be handed over to sinners, be killed on a cross, and in three days rise up?" Then they remembered Jesus' words. (Luke 24:1-8, MSG)

Merriam-Webster's online dictionary defines the word "checkmate" as a move that attacks the opposing king, where the opponent cannot get free. See, if the devil were as smart as he thought, he would have known better than to mess with Jesus in the first place. Appearances can be deceiving; he thought it was over once Jesus was crucified and placed in the tomb. He may have even rubbed his hands in glee when Pilate had the guards put a large rock at the mouth of the tomb and ordered them to watch over it. What he didn't remember was that God always takes care of His people!

No matter what is happening in your life, God hasn't forgotten about you. He knows all about the situation. So, stand firm in your faith and trust God to make everything turn out all right, even if it's not the way you would have expected.

I remain confident of this: I will see the goodness of the LORD in the land of the living. Wait for the LORD; be strong and take heart and wait for the LORD. (Psalm 27:13-14, NIV)

THE GOOD SON

Jesus' mother stood near his cross. Her sister was also standing there with Mary the wife of Clopas, and Mary Magdalene. Jesus saw his mother. He also saw the follower he loved very much standing there. He said to his mother, "Dear woman, here is your son." Then he said to the follower, "Here is your mother." So, after that, this follower took Jesus' mother to live in his home. (John 19:25-27, ERV)

I had a conversation with a woman who believed that our children should do more for us once they're grown. I disagreed with her statement that, "After all, I took care of them. It's their turn to take care of me!" She and I finally agreed to disagree. My point to her was that our children don't owe us anything because they didn't ask to be here. Yes, we take care of them because it's our responsibility. Yes, we'd like to think they would take care of us if something happened. And, yes, we know honoring our parents has rewards. Still, if our children choose to neglect us, there isn't a lot we can do about it. A parent's role is to raise productive citizens, who may or may not be responsible once they reach adulthood.

Jesus shows us how to be a responsible adult. He was so responsible that He paused death to make sure His mother's future would be assured. Jesus entrusted her to someone He knew would do the right thing. It's interesting that He would pick John since He had brothers, although, at the time of His crucifixion, they didn't believe in Him. He knew His mother would want to remember Him with someone who would know what she was talking about without making lengthy explanations. The Bible isn't clear on Jesus' reasoning for choosing John, but I'm glad the Scripture lets us in on what happened.

You must respect your father and mother. This is the first command that has a promise with it. And this is the promise: Then all will go well with you, and you will have a long life on the earth.
(Ephesians 6:2-3, ERV)

BUT WAIT . . . THERE'S MORE

Mary stood outside the grave crying. As she cried, she got down and looked inside the grave. She saw two angels dressed in white clothes. They were sitting where the body of Jesus had lain. One angel was where His head had lain, and one angel was where His feet had lain. They said to her, "Woman, why are you crying?" She said to them, "Because they have taken away my Lord. I do not know where they have put Him." After saying this, she turned around and saw Jesus standing there. But she did not know that it was Jesus. (John 20:11-14, NLV)

Have you ever been to a concert, movie, or even church and noticed the rush of people leaving before the end? They assume they've heard all the good stuff and nothing more will happen. Usually, that's a wrong assumption.

Peter and John heard that Jesus' body was missing. They hurried to the tomb and confirmed it was empty. Then, thinking that nothing more was to be said or done, they left. But Mary stayed and looked in the tomb again—either in grief or astonishment—and had a conversation with two angels. Then, amazingly, she encountered the One she came to see. "He said to her, 'Woman, why are you crying? Who are you looking for?'. . . She said to Him, 'Sir, if you have taken Jesus from here, tell me where you have put Him. I will take Him away'" (John 20:15, NLV).

Jesus was moved by Mary's statement and revealed Himself to her. In Mary's excitement, she wanted to touch Him but was denied the opportunity. Instead, she received the amazing privilege of being the first recorded human to see Jesus after the Resurrection with a message: "Go to My brothers. Tell them that I will go up to My Father and your Father, and to My God and your God!" (John 20:17, NLV).

Sometimes God saves the best for last—an impromptu encore, deleted scenes from a movie, or a surprise ending to what we thought was finished. Let's not be in such a rush to leave that we miss a movement of God.

The end of a thing is better than its beginning. (Ecclesiastes 7:8, NKJV)

I DON'T HAVE TIME FOR THIS

Now after John was put in prison, Jesus came to Galilee, preaching the gospel of the kingdom of God, and saying, "The time is fulfilled, and the kingdom of God is at hand. Repent, and believe in the gospel." (Mark 1:14-15, NKJV)

I have an acquaintance who, when relaying a story, feels she needs to include *every* minute detail. Shortly after she starts, I'm already ready to say, "Are you kidding me? Get to the point!" Of course, I don't say that; instead I try to keep from falling asleep while praying she'll hurry up.

The book of Mark doesn't have the problem of extraneous details. Mark skips over a lot of inessential information to get to the heart of Jesus' ministry. Jesus came for two reasons: (1) to demonstrate God's love for us, and (2) to confront us to leave sin behind and bring us back into right standing with God. When we understand these two concepts, the rest of the Bible is icing on the cake. It's all good, and it's all relevant.

Jesus answered, "My kingdom is not of this world. If My kingdom were of this world, My servants would fight, so that I should not be delivered to the Jews; but now My kingdom is not from here."
Pilate therefore said to Him, "Are You a king then?"
Jesus answered, "You say rightly that I am a king. For this cause I was born, and for this cause I have come into the world that I should bear witness to the truth. Everyone who is of the truth hears My voice." (John 18:36-37, NKJV)

CHILDLIKE, NOT CHILDISH

Jesus called a little child to come to him. He stood the child in front of the followers. Then he said, "The truth is, you must change your thinking and become like little children. If you don't do this, you will never enter God's kingdom. The greatest person in God's kingdom is the one who makes himself humble like this child." (Matthew 18:2-4, ERV)

Do you know adults who exhibit childish behavior? You know, they throw temper tantrums when they don't get their way. When someone does something they don't like or agree with, they take their toys and go home. If you upset them, they give you the silent treatment instead of verbally communicating their feelings. This is *not* what Jesus is teaching in today's Scripture.

Jesus is encouraging us to retain the faith we had as a child. The faith that caused us to take risks without worrying about details. The faith that believed God is in control of everything and everybody. The faith that allowed us to trust our dreams would come true.

> *When I was a child, my speech, feelings, and*
> *thinking were all those of a child; now that*
> *I am an adult, I have no more use*
> *for childish ways.*
> (1 Corinthians 13:11, GNT)

SPREAD A LITTLE SONSHINE

"You are the light of the world. A city that is set on a hill cannot be hidden. Nor do they light a lamp and put it under a basket, but on a lampstand, and it gives light to all who are in the house. Let your light so shine before men, that they may see your good works and glorify your Father in heaven." (Matthew 5:14-16, NKJV)

I often reflect on people who are no longer part of my life—not only those who are deceased but those who are no longer actively involved due to distance. The distance may be five miles or a few thousand miles; the point is, we're not as connected. During my time of reflection, I ask God to bless and keep them because I hope that's what people pray when I cross their mind. I also wonder if they feel their life was better because I passed through. With every encounter—whether friend or stranger—I strive to make their time spent with me enjoyable. Like all humans, I am more successful some days than others, but my heart is in the right place.

One of our jobs as a Christian is to help everyone see Jesus in us. My daily prayer is, "God, fill me with Your spirit and cover me with Your blood. Let my light so shine that people need sunglasses!" Feel free to make this your prayer, too.

"I have come as a light into the world, that whoever
believes in Me should not abide in darkness."
(John 12:46, NKJV)

HAD ENOUGH YET?

"Are you tired? Worn out? Burned out on religion? Come to me. Get away with me and you'll recover your life. I'll show you how to take a real rest. Walk with me and work with me—watch how I do it. Learn the unforced rhythms of grace. I won't lay anything heavy or ill-fitting on you. Keep company with me and you'll learn to live freely and lightly." (Matthew 11:28-30, MSG)

Life brings so many things at us, and sometimes from so many directions at the same time. Usually, we can handle it, but some days we can't. We feel like the ball in a fast-paced tennis match. You know, the kind where the ball is forcefully whacked from one side of the net to the other for many minutes before a foul? Matches like this are exciting to watch but difficult to live out.

There are times when the pressure becomes too much, and we find ourselves mentally, physically, emotionally, and spiritually tired. We need to take a break before we break! It is in those moments that we must remember today's Scripture.

God is waiting for us to allow Him the privilege and pleasure of helping us. When He watches us butting our head against the wall, I believe He shakes His head in amazement that we haven't figured out the solution to our problem. All we need to do is cast our cares on Him. Instead, some of us don't want to "bother" God with our problems, so we take on more than our share. Yes, there are some things God expects us to do on our own; but, God never told us we couldn't ask for help. God never intended for us to carry the weight of the world. That's His job.

Let him have all your worries and cares, for he is always thinking about
you and watching everything that concerns you.
(1 Peter 5:7, TLB)

AND YOU DIDN'T EVEN HAVE TO ASK

Jesus said, "Father, forgive them, for they don't know what they are doing." (Luke 23:34, NLT)

There are some things we get because we ask for them. There are other things we get because of our connection.

When Jesus hung on the cross and spoke, "Father, forgive them, for they don't know what they are doing," He wasn't only referring to the people standing around watching or to those instrumental in the crucifixion. No, He looked down through eternity and saw everybody who has ever lived—from that time through today—and included them in the prayer. He knew that in the future people would be on a rapid path of destruction—more than ever—and wanted to ensure that a way of escape was available.

A lot of times when we do something wrong, it's easier to ask someone to forgive us than it is to forgive ourselves. Jesus wants to be clear: Forgiveness has already been extended! That's incredible news. Now, we must be cautious not to abuse the forgiveness. It is not a free pass to do anything and everything we think we're grown enough to do. When God looks in our direction, let's make sure He's pleased with what He sees.

For you, O Lord, are good and forgiving,
abounding in steadfast love to all who call upon you.
(Psalm 86:5, ESV)

He does not punish us for all our sins; he does not deal harshly with us, as
we deserve. For his unfailing love toward those who fear him is as great as
the height of the heavens above the earth. He has removed our sins as far
from us as the east is from the west. The LORD is like a father to his
children, tender and compassionate to those who fear him. For he knows
how weak we are; he remembers we are only dust.
(Psalm 103:10-14, NLT)

DON'T MISS THIS

Peter turned around and saw behind them the disciple Jesus loved—the one who had leaned over to Jesus during supper and asked, "Lord, who will betray you?" Peter asked Jesus, "What about him, Lord?" Jesus replied, "If I want him to remain alive until I return, what is that to you? As for you, follow me." (John 21:20-22, NLT)

Have you ever dismissed what *was* happening because you were more concerned about what *would* happen? It probably happens more often than we want to admit. For example, you're eating a delicious dinner, and wondering about dessert. Or, you're spending time with someone you're fond of, and curious about who just dinged your phone indicating a text message or voicemail. Or, you're enjoying a beautiful sun-lit, blue sky, fall day and pondering how much snow your area will receive during the winter. We miss so much wondering about things that we have no control over.

That's where Peter was in today's Scripture. If you're familiar with John 21, you know that Jesus gave Peter the assignment to feed God's people (John 21:15-19). Not only was he given an assignment, but Jesus had also made Peter privy to how he would die. And, yet, despite such earth-shattering news, Peter was more concerned about what John was going to do instead of accepting the role he would play in the Kingdom.

Concern about other people is commendable, and it's okay to be curious about others. Our challenge is to not become so focused on them that we miss what God is saying to us. We need to stay in the moment, so that we not only hear what God is speaking clearly, but we can appreciate the fact that He's saying it to us!

*"For I know the plans I have **for you** . . ."*
(Jeremiah 29:11, KJV, emphasis mine)

WHO'S THERE?

"Simon, Simon, Satan has asked to sift each of you like wheat. But I have pleaded in prayer for you, Simon, that your faith should not fail. So when you have repented and turned to me again, strengthen your brothers." Peter said, "Lord, I am ready to go to prison with you, and even to die with you." But Jesus said, "Peter, let me tell you something. Before the rooster crows tomorrow morning, you will deny three times that you even know me." (Luke 22:31-34, NLT)

When my son was little, he and his babysitter tried to outdo each other telling knock-knock jokes. I knew when I arrived to pick him up, I'd have to endure the latest one. Some of them were pretty good; most needed a lot of work.

Simon Bar-Jonah and Peter was one man with two personas. Simon was the old man; Peter was the new. Peter could no more deny the Simon personality than we can deny our dual characteristics. I'm not saying we're schizophrenic; I'm saying there are two sides to our nature, and we're the only one who controls which is in charge with the help of the Holy Spirit.

Most everything in life is a choice. We can decide whether to go with our Before Christ or After Christ persona. If we allow the Holy Spirit to lead, our new identity will be in charge.

"Flesh and blood give birth to flesh and blood,
but the Spirit gives birth to things that are spiritual."
(John 3:6, GWT)

ME, MY, I

But He was wounded for our transgressions, He was bruised for our iniquities; The chastisement for our peace was upon Him, And by His stripes we are healed. (Isaiah 53:5, NKJV)

Reading and studying the Scriptures is an invaluable tool in the maturity of God's people. One way to enhance the impact is to make the Scriptures personal. Today's Scripture is well-known and often quoted by preachers and laypeople. No doubt, it *is* powerful. However, I suggest that to make it more impactful, we remove the collective tone and make it personal. I'm not saying to rewrite the Scripture, but to re-read it to allow a more intimate knowledge of what is said.

> But He was wounded for *my* transgressions. He was bruised for *my* iniquities. The chastisement for *my* peace was upon Him, and by His stripes *I* am healed!

Isaiah 53:5 is a Messianic prophecy of what Jesus would endure for *you*. If you interpret it that way, it allows for a better sense of connectivity to our Lord and Savior and provides a sense of ownership. Since verse five is so personal, why not pass the message on so that others can have a personal Scripture, too?

Like a meal that takes hours to prepare and we only need to show up and eat, Jesus has already done the hard part for us by taking our place on the cross. Let's invite everyone we encounter to accept the gift of salvation.

THE STORYTELLER

"I'm no longer calling you servants because servants don't understand what their master is thinking and planning. No, I've named you friends because I've let you in on everything I've heard from the Father." (John 15:15, MSG)

I love just about all types of music, with or without lyrics. There are some songs that I know by heart and will sing along whenever I hear them. I'm partial to them because they tell a complete story, such as the rags to riches ode by Paul Henning: "Come and listen to my story 'bout a man named Jed; a poor mountaineer, barely kept his family fed. And then one day he was shootin' at some food, and up through the ground came a bubblin' crude. Oil that is, black gold, Texas tea." (The theme song from the *Beverly Hillbillies*.)

Or, how about the one that offers the best secular advice I've ever heard: "You've got to know when to hold 'em, know when to fold 'em. Know when to walk away; know when to run"? (*The Gambler* by Don Schlitz.)

And then there's one of the best hymns ever written: *What a friend we have in Jesus!* The first verse alone tells you everything you need to know. Jesus wants to be your friend and that's a privilege. Jesus wants to bear your burdens. Jesus is waiting for you to give Him your cares and offers you the opportunity to bring *everything* to Him. In exchange, He'll give you His peace.

There are people who will offer to help you during a crisis. They mean well and have good intentions. However, there's only one Jesus. If you haven't experienced His friendship, you're missing out on a valuable relationship.

What a friend we have in Jesus, all our sins and griefs to bear!
What a privilege to carry everything to God in prayer!
Oh, what peace we often forfeit, Oh, what needless pain we bear,
all because we do not carry everything to God in prayer!
What a Friend We Have in Jesus. Joseph Scriven. 1855. Public Domain.

DON'T LEAVE EMPTY-HANDED

And the LORD said: "I have surely seen the oppression of My people who are in Egypt, and have heard their cry because of their taskmasters, for I know their sorrows. So I have come down to deliver them out of the hand of the Egyptians, and to bring them up from that land to a good and large land, to a land flowing with milk and honey." (Exodus 3:7-8, NKJV)

Then (Pharaoh) called for Moses and Aaron by night, and said, "Rise, go out from among my people, both you and the children of Israel. And go, serve the LORD as you have said. Also take your flocks and your herds, as you have said, and be gone; and bless me also." And the Egyptians urged the people, that they might send them out of the land in haste. For they said, "We shall all be dead." So the people took their dough before it was leavened, having their kneading bowls bound up in their clothes on their shoulders. Now the children of Israel had done according to the word of Moses, and they had asked from the Egyptians articles of silver, articles of gold, and clothing. And the LORD had given the people favor in the sight of the Egyptians, so that they granted them what they requested. Thus, they plundered the Egyptians. (Exodus 12:31-36, NKJV)

There are times we've been caught in adverse situations that may not be of our choosing. And, because of God's mercy, we're able to walk away. However, sometimes we leave things behind that rightfully belong to us.

Today's Scripture reminds us that God does have something better for us—our own land of milk and honey. It may not literally be land; it may be a job, relationship, or ministry. It is whatever God knows we need to survive and finish our assignment. Bad things do happen to good people, and every negative experience takes something out of us. I've decided that when God extracts me from these situations, I'm leaving with everything that belongs to me. I may leave battered or bruised, but I refuse to give the enemy my joy, peace, love, and self-respect. It's mine, and I only need to ask God for it.

We are sure that if we ask anything that He wants us to have, He will hear us.
(1 John 5:14, NLV)

I'VE GOT A BOO-BOO, LORD

GOD made my life complete when I placed all the pieces before him. When I got my act together, he gave me a fresh start. Now I'm alert to GOD's ways; I don't take God for granted. Every day I review the ways he works; I try not to miss a trick. I feel put back together, and I'm watching my step. GOD rewrote the text of my life when I opened the book of my heart to his eyes. (Psalm 18:20-24, MSG)

When my younger grandsons visit, at some point they will come to me for treatment of their various scrapes and scratches. The treatment may require soap and water to wash away debris, a bandage to cover a little blood, or a kiss to make it feel better.

The children's rhyme about Humpty Dumpty tells of a fictitious character that fell off a wall and couldn't be put back together. That is not the case with Christians. Those of us who claim Jesus as Lord and Savior have Someone who is in the putting-back-together business. Hallelujah!

Today's Scripture reminds us that once we realize we can't do things on our own—that we don't know what we're doing and are incapable of handling things; that if we don't allow God to take care of our situations, things will continue to be a mess and will never get better—is when God gives us a fresh start.

Do you need a fresh start today? Take the broken pieces of your life to God and say, "I've got a boo-boo, Lord. I'm broken and hurt, and I need You to put me back together again." And you know what? When you get out of the way to let God work, the words of this Psalm become true.

Thank You, Lord, that we don't have to stay the way we are. We can begin again, brand new, with our broken pieces made whole. Help us to not be ashamed to run to You with our hurts, knowing that You're both willing and able to put us back together again.

WHO'S THE BOSS?

Set a guard, O LORD, over my mouth; Keep watch over the door of my lips. (Psalm 141:3, NKJV)

Have you ever thought of how stress-free your life would be if you allowed God to control everything you said? It seems impossible, doesn't it? We encounter so many challenges throughout the day that present the ideal opportunity to give someone a piece of our mind, or to correct faulty thinking, or to get the upper hand in a conversation. Regardless, God wants us to allow Him to not only order our steps but to order our conversation. We may need to take baby steps to gain victory over our mouths, and that's okay. God wants us to move in the direction of perfection. He knows the more we yield to Him, the more natural things will become.

If God is the Lord of our life,
then He is the Lord of every area of our life,
including our mouths.

IT'S PERSONAL

O Lord, you have given me these wonderful promises just because you want to be kind to me, because of your own great heart. O Lord, there is no one like you—there is no other God. In fact, we have never even heard of another god like you! (1 Chronicles 17:19-20, TLB)

It has been said that when God gives us a promise, we can take it to the bank. In other words, it's good. It could also be said that when God gives us a promise, we need to keep it to ourselves.

Often, we're excited and want to share with people we know. There's nothing wrong with that except that we need to be sure it's the people God chooses. Everybody can't celebrate you (remember Joseph and his brothers?) and will make every effort to distract, distort, or detour your destiny. God doesn't bless everyone in the same way or at the same time. Bishop T. D. Jakes told us years ago that "favor ain't fair," and that hasn't changed.

A promise from God is personal.
Treat it with the proper respect.

AS IS

That's why the Spirit said, "If you hear God's voice today, don't be stubborn as in the past when you turned against God." (Hebrews 3:15, ERV)

We often see things listed for sale "as is," which means that what you're purchasing comes without any guarantees. It may be a blessing or a burden. So, you ask yourself, "Is this going to be worth the risk?"

Aren't you glad God doesn't question whether we're worth the risk? He implores us to come to Him "as is" with our burdens, issues, concerns. Unlike humans, He doesn't wait for us to get it together; He's willing to work with whatever we bring to Him. It is a simple concept: God invites us to come to Him, and all we need to do is say yes!

Just as I am, thou wilt receive,
wilt welcome, pardon, cleanse, relieve;
because thy promise I believe,
O Lamb of God, I come, I come.
Just as I Am.
Charlotte Elliot (1789-1871) and
William B. Bradbury (1816-1868).
Public Domain.

DON'T ASK ME AGAIN

God is not a man; he will not lie. God is not a human being; his decisions will not change. If he says he will do something, then he will do it. If he makes a promise, then he will do what he promised. (Numbers 23:19, ERV)

My grandkids will ask the same question a few minutes apart as if I'm going to forget what my previous answer was. Go figure! They're little people so I expect for them to play that childish game. However, what about when adults do it with God? He'll tell us to do something, we may or may not start on it, and then we'll ask Him if He's sure this is what He wants us to do. God doesn't mumble when He speaks and He's not going to change His answer, regardless of how often we ask the same question.

As we come to the eighth day of a new month, let me ask you something. Is there an unfinished assignment that you carried over into this year? Have you at least started working on it? If you answered yes, God would have me to tell you that He really would like for you to finish what you started. If you answered no, God wants you to step out on faith and do what He's asked. He gave you an assignment for a reason. He doesn't doubt for a moment that you're able to fulfill it. You just need to keep in mind that someone is depending on you. So, get the lead out and get to work!

"Someday is not a day of the week."
—Author Unknown

IN THE MORNING

Weeping may last for the night, but there is a song of joy in the morning. (Psalm 30:5[b], GWT)

Sadness, anxiety, distress, worry will all contribute to a long night, causing it to seem endless. Technically, night encompasses only 12 of a 24-hour period; we all know there are times when the night lasts for a season, not hours. The bad news is that before we leave this Earth, we'll all share an experience of checking the clock to see if the hands have moved. The good news is that we have Someone who will share the time with us. Someone who will rock us in His arms, dry our tears, and tell us—honestly, truthfully, succinctly—that everything *is* going to work out. So, when the journey into the night begins, we can rest assured God has already planned our exit.

Ain't no need to worrying, what the night is gonna bring.
It will be all over in the morning.
Ain't No Need to Worry. Marvin L. Winans. 1987.

MISPLACED LOYALTY

Even after Jesus had performed so many signs in their presence, they still would not believe in him. . . Yet at the same time many even among the leaders believed in him. But because of the Pharisees they would not openly acknowledge their faith for fear they would be put out of the synagogue; for they loved human praise more than praise from God. (John 12:37, 42-43, NIV)

There are times when you must choose sides. To determine which side to choose, it's important to have as much available information as possible so you'll make the right choice. It's too bad the men in today's Scripture didn't heed this suggestion. Of course, we can't come down too hard on these unnamed men because some of us do the same thing. Our friends get a divorce, and in our quest to keep a friendship or relationship intact, we choose sides. It may not be right, but I believe it is human nature. Unfortunately, sometimes we choose the wrong side based on erroneous information.

The men in today's Scripture don't have that excuse. They were around to see Jesus perform miracle after miracle. They knew enough about Him to become one His followers; however, they were interested in "human praise more than praise from God." That's a dangerous choice to make. Let's make sure we don't allow anyone or anything to dictate our relationship with our Lord and Savior.

Lord, at those times when we need to make a choice,
help us to clearly hear your voice saying, "This is the way, walk in it."
(Isaiah 30:21)

SOMETHING TO HOLD ONTO

"If you look for me wholeheartedly, you will find me." (Jeremiah 29:13, ERV)

Isn't it interesting how some people make you jump through hoops for the *possibility* that they may be able to help you? You have no guarantee they will keep their word when you do what they request.

In the movie *The Wizard of Oz,* Dorothy and company need the Wizard's help. He sends them to obtain the broomstick of the Wicked Witch of the West, knowing that to get it meant the witch would die. When Dorothy returns with the broomstick, the Wizard is revealed to be a fraud who can't help them!

Most Christians can easily quote Jeremiah 29:11: "For I know the plans I have for you," says the LORD. "They are plans for good and not for disaster, to give you a future and a hope" (NLT). However, I'm partial to verse 13 because of the promise. The only criteria to obtain the promise is to seek God with your whole heart. He assures you that when you do, you will find Him.

Unlike people who may mean well but are still unable always to keep their word, God assures us that we can trust everything He says.

"My covenant will I not break,
nor alter the thing that is gone out of my lips."
(Psalm 89:34, KJV)

YOU BELONG TO ME!

But the Lord says, "Can a woman forget her baby? Can she forget the child who came from her body? Even if she can forget her children, I cannot forget you. I drew a picture of you on my hand. You are always before my eyes." (Isaiah 49:15-16, ERV)

I was blessed to have a great mother. She was gentle, kind, patient, and very loving, and I wish I were more like her. She instilled in my siblings and me a sense of right and wrong and showed, by example, how to handle difficult people with sweetness. Unfortunately, my mother passed away a few weeks after my 18th birthday and a few months before my high school graduation. It was, and still is, a profound loss.

Anyone who has experienced loss knows that at the most unexpected times a memory may surface. Sometimes it will make you smile or laugh; other times, it may cause a sense of sadness at what used to be. Sometimes you may even experience a sense of abandonment. When those moments come, remember what God said in today's Scripture: "I cannot forget you."

Without mother, father or either set of grandparents still living, I have moments when I feel adrift, separated from those who have not experienced the same level of loss. But, then I remember this Scripture and I can't help but smile because it reminds me that while I may occasionally get lonely, I am never alone.

I thank God for the 18 years I had with my mother. She may no longer physically be on Earth, but her spirit yet remains. I've tried to pass on her knowledge to my son and grandchildren. But, more importantly, I've tried to pass on the knowledge that we all belong to God. Why else would He have our picture on His hand?

God, thank You for fond memories of those who are no longer with us.
Thank You for the time You allowed us to be together.

THE THINGS WE DO FOR LOVE: HANNAH

There was a man named Elkanah from the Zuph family who lived in Ramah in the hill country of Ephraim. Elkanah had two wives. One wife was named Hannah and the other wife was named Peninnah. Peninnah had children, but Hannah did not. (1 Samuel 1:1-2, ERV)

There are times we want things so badly that we negotiate with God in a feeble attempt to make it happen. Once we receive what we've asked Him to do, we often conveniently forget the promise we made. You know, the one that goes like this: "God, I promise if you get me out of this, I'll *never*—said with much emphasis for dramatic effect—do this again. I promise!" So, God, in His faithfulness, extends His mercy and gets us out of the situation. And, surprise, surprise, we don't keep our part of the bargain.

We could take a page from Hannah's book. She was a barren woman during a time when a woman's inability to bear children was considered a curse. Year after year, Hannah suffered the humiliation of not having a child of her own when others, including her husband's other wife, were frequently multiplying. Finally, in desperation, she cried out to God and promised that if He would grant her request, she'd give the child back to Him; God answered her prayer (1 Samuel 1:9-20). However, unlike some of us, Hannah kept her word and turned Samuel over to Eli, the priest, to raise: "When the boy was old enough to eat solid food, Hannah took him to the LORD's house at Shiloh. She also took a bull that was three years old, 20 pounds of flour, and a bottle of wine" (1 Samuel 1:24, ERV).

We don't know how often Hannah got to see Samuel, nor are we told how Elkanah felt about being away from his son. What we do know is that Hannah kept her promise despite the personal pain she endured.

Lord, sometimes we must make hard decisions that may be misunderstood by others. When we're confronted with those situations, please give us the strength to be obedient to You.

THE THINGS WE DO FOR LOVE:
ELIZABETH

There was in the days of Herod, the king of Judea, a certain priest named Zacharias, of the division of Abijah. His wife was of the daughters of Aaron, and her name was Elizabeth. . .But they had no child, because Elizabeth was barren, and they were both well advanced in years. (Luke 1:5, 7, NKJV)

Every parent thinks their child is unique. There are times when a child really is special and is meant to be a blessing to the nation. Then, there are the extraordinary ones whose life will alter the events of the Universe.

John the Baptist was unique from conception. His parents, Elizabeth and Zacharias, were old and may have given up hope of ever holding a child in their arms conceived by their love. . . But God!

John's parents took God at His Word and raised him in accordance to God's specifications (see Luke 1:12-17). They not only had parental pride, they also had God's confirmation that John would indeed change the world.

Lord, thank You for allowing us the privilege of molding children into what You would have them become. Whether biologically or spiritually, we can take pride in what You have planned for them.

THE THINGS WE DO FOR LOVE: RIZPAH

But he gave them Saul's two sons Armoni and Mephibosheth, whose mother was Rizpah, the daughter of Aiah. . . The men of Gibeon impaled them in the mountain before the Lord. So, all seven of them died together at the beginning of the barley harvest. (2 Samuel 21:8-9, TLB)

I recently saw something at church that brought a smile to my face. A man and his young son were walking toward where I was sitting. They were holding hands, and the child was happily skipping along, unconcerned and unaware of any potential harm. His father, on the other hand, stopped close to where I was and stooped down to tie his son's shoe. The son wasn't aware (or didn't care) that the strings were flopping along; the father, on the other hand, knew that with the way the boy was skipping he could easily trip and possibly hurt himself. The thing that touched me the most was that the father was looking out for the son's welfare even when the son was unaware of the need. The event reminded me of Rizpah.

Rizpah and her children paid the price for King Saul's inability to keep his word with the Gibeonites, who had made a truce with Joshua. Once Saul died, the Gibeonites sought revenge, requiring seven of Saul's sons to be hung. King David agreed to their request. Two of the sons were Rizpah's, one of Saul's concubines (see 2 Samuel 21:1-9). Once the children were hung, their bodies were left to rot. Rizpah couldn't tolerate that additional humiliation and set out to do something about it. "Then Rizpah, the mother of two of the men, spread sackcloth upon a rock and stayed there through the entire harvest season to prevent the vultures from tearing at their bodies during the day and the wild animals from eating them at night" (2 Samuel 21:10, TLB). This went on for the entire harvest season, approximately six months! That's a long time to keep a vigil, but love will make you do things that other people think are crazy.

God, we don't understand the things people do in the name of love. Some of it makes no sense, like sending Your Son to save us! Even though we don't understand, we are eternally grateful. Thank You!

THE THINGS WE DO FOR LOVE:
A CANAANITE WOMAN

From there Jesus took a trip to Tyre and Sidon. They had hardly arrived when a Canaanite woman came down from the hills and pleaded, "Mercy, Master, Son of David! My daughter is cruelly afflicted by an evil spirit." Jesus ignored her. The disciples came and complained, "Now she's bothering us. Would you please take care of her? She's driving us crazy." Jesus refused, telling them, "I've got my hands full dealing with the lost sheep of Israel." Then the woman came back to Jesus, went to her knees, and begged. "Master help me." He said, "It's not right to take bread out of children's mouths and throw it to dogs." She was quick: "You're right, Master, but beggar dogs do get scraps from the master's table." Jesus gave in. "Oh, woman, your faith is something else. What you want is what you get!" Right then her daughter became well. (Matthew 15:21-28, MSG)

A fly is one of the most annoying creatures on Earth. Whenever one gets in my house, it follows me around. If I flick it away, it comes back in a few seconds. If I try to hit it with a fly swatter, it evades my maneuvers.

The woman in today's Scripture could be compared to a fly. She was on a mission for her daughter's welfare. She was determined that Jesus was going to help her, even when the disciples attempted to dismiss her, and Jesus appeared to insult her. Unlike some of us, who would have given up after the first reproof, she came back. If you read between the lines, you'd know that she was going to keep coming back until she got what she wanted: help for her daughter.

How badly do you want what you're asking God to do? Is it enough to keep praying even when it seems you're being ignored? Persistence always pays off.

"You just can't beat the person who never gives up."
—Babe Ruth

THE THINGS WE DO FOR LOVE:
AN UNNAMED WOMAN

Love puts up with anything and everything that comes along; it trusts, hopes, and endures no matter what. (1 Corinthians 13:7, VOICE)

I'll admit to having mixed emotions about social media. On the one hand, it's a quick way to get information, whereas before you had to rely on the news at regularly scheduled times. On the other hand, it is somewhat a violation of privacy and it appears that nothing is sacred anymore. Sometimes things aren't as they seem.

A few years ago, there was a photo of a woman hitting a hoodie-wearing teenager. Without an explanation, it would appear the young man was being abused. The reality was a mother protecting her son whom she had seen on television in the middle of a riot. She could have said, "I told that boy not to go down there. Just wait until he comes home. I'm going to have something waiting for him." But, no, this mother did what any mother would. She went to get her child out of harm's way. I don't necessarily agree with everything she did or said, but I am in full agreement with the concept of protection.

I don't know of any parent who would willingly let their child be in danger and not do something about it. Isn't that what God does for us every day? He gives us parameters in which to live, not to keep anything from us but for protection. Yet, like this young man, we don't always do what's right. And, like the mother, God then steps in and intervenes. Sometimes when He does, it becomes common knowledge (like the video that went viral) and it's embarrassing ("I saw your momma hit you on television!"), but it's always for our good ("I didn't want my child to end up dead!"). God always has our best interest in mind.

Lord, thank You for keeping us from hurt, harm, and danger, even when we don't have sense enough to do it ourselves. There is no extent You will not go to for us. We give You praise, honor, and glory.

THE THINGS WE DO FOR LOVE: MARY

Now there stood by the cross of Jesus His mother . . . (John 19:25[a], NKJV)

It has correctly been said that nothing can beat a mother's love. Every woman who carries the title of mother—whether blood related or not—will confirm that there's a bond between a mother and child that isn't easily broken. Oh, it may occasionally get bruised and perhaps a little battered, but the connection is very seldom broken. A mother's love will compel you to hold on tight to a hand taking the first step, to keep vigil at the bedside of a sick child, to look through a glass partition in prison, or to watch your son die for the cause of another.

When Mary was told she was to carry the Messiah, she most likely didn't envision the pain and suffering associated with the blessing. She had been told that Jesus would do great things (see Luke 1:30-33). Mary wasn't prepared to watch her child ridiculed and treated unfairly just because of who He was or to endure the comments of skeptics . . . some of whom were in her own house! She would have gone into protection mode, as most mothers would. I wish the Bible had provided more insight into Mary and Jesus' conversations. (I know the ones I've had with my son, so I can only imagine the ones they had.) Jesus didn't lie, so I know that Mary didn't want to hear some of the things He shared with her, but she would have believed Him.

Love sometimes requires us to allow unpleasant events to happen, even when everything inside us is screaming for release.

"Motherhood: All love begins and ends there."
—Robert Browning (1812-1889)

LIKE WHITE ON RICE

And I am convinced that nothing can ever separate us from God's love. Neither death nor life, neither angels nor demons, neither our fears for today nor our worries about tomorrow—not even the powers of hell can separate us from God's love. No power in the sky above or in the earth below—indeed, nothing in all creation will ever be able to separate us from the love of God that is revealed in Christ Jesus our Lord. (Romans 8:38-39, NLT)

Do you realize how powerful today's Scripture is? There is nothing anyone can say or do that will make God change His mind about loving us! Some people tell us they love us and mean it when they say it. But, sometimes we discover their love is conditional, based on whether we jump through the hoops they've designated to prove our love or our worth to be loved in return.

I am so very grateful that God doesn't play games. He loves us. He wants us to love Him in return. And, even if we don't or won't, He doesn't change His mind. He patiently waits for us to realize our need for His love and welcomes us with open arms. We're connected to Him, and there's nothing we can do to change that fact. Why not embrace God and let Him show you what real love looks like and how it feels?

I pray that Christ will live in your hearts because of your faith. I pray that your life will be strong in love and be built on love. And I pray that you and all God's holy people will have the power to understand the greatness of Christ's love—how wide, how long, how high, and how deep that love is. Christ's love is greater than anyone can ever know, but I pray that you will be able to know that love. Then you can be filled with everything God has for you.
(Ephesians 3:17-19, ERV)

THERE'S NOBODY LIKE JESUS

Now after six days Jesus took Peter, James, and John his brother, led them up on a high mountain by themselves; and He was transfigured before them. His face shone like the sun, and His clothes became as white as the light. And behold, Moses and Elijah appeared to them, talking with Him. Then Peter answered and said to Jesus, "Lord, it is good for us to be here; if You wish, let us make here three tabernacles: one for You, one for Moses, and one for Elijah." (Matthew 17:1-4, NKJV)

The apostle Peter was one of the first Bible characters I fell in love with because he reminds me so much of myself. We mean well, but sometimes in our excitement we end up with our foot in our mouth.

Peter, understandably, had never seen anything like the transfiguration. I imagine I might have had a similar response. When something amazing happens, you want to do something to commemorate the occasion. But, this was not one of those occasions and God made sure Peter, James, and John knew that. "While he was still speaking, behold, a bright cloud overshadowed them; and suddenly a voice came out of the cloud, saying, 'This is My beloved Son, in whom I am well pleased. Hear Him!' And when the disciples heard it, they fell on their faces and were greatly afraid" (vv. 5-6).

God wanted Peter, James, John, and us to know that Jesus has no equal: "When they had lifted up their eyes, *they saw no one but Jesus only"* (v. 8), emphasis mine.

We're in the presence of royalty, It's our sovereign God and King.
Here before Your throne, Bow at Your feet,
worship You holy King.
Royalty. Byron Cage, Darien Mickens, and
Demond Mickens. 2007.

ARE YOU READY?

"At that time the kingdom of heaven will be like ten virgins who took their lamps and went out to meet the bridegroom. Five of them were foolish and five were wise. The foolish ones took their lamps but did not take any oil with them. The wise ones, however, took oil in jars along with their lamps. The bridegroom was a long time in coming, and they all became drowsy and fell asleep. At midnight the cry rang out: 'Here's the bridegroom! Come out to meet him!' Then all the virgins woke up and trimmed their lamps. The foolish ones said to the wise, 'Give us some of your oil; our lamps are going out.' 'No,' they replied, 'there may not be enough for both us and you. Instead, go to those who sell oil and buy some for yourselves.' But while they were on their way to buy the oil, the bridegroom arrived. The virgins who were ready went in with him to the wedding banquet. And the door was shut. Later the others also came. 'Lord, Lord,' they said, 'open the door for us!' But he replied, 'Truly I tell you, I don't know you.' Therefore, keep watch, because you do not know the day or the hour." (Matthew 25:1-13, NIV)

The virgins in this parable were given information that the bridegroom was coming, although they weren't given a specific time. They knew something exciting was going to happen; they just didn't know when. The wise virgins knew to be ready at a moment's notice, which is why they had oil for their lamps. The foolish virgins thought the bridegroom's arrival wasn't going to happen any time soon. They "assumed" they'd have time to get more oil if theirs ran out or would just borrow some from the other women. They were surprised that the women wouldn't share their oil and then disappointed when the bridegroom turned them away.

The bridegroom in this parable is Jesus, and He *is* coming back! Let's just make sure we're prepared for His arrival.

"Prior preparation prevents poor performance."
—James Baker

PUT YOUR WAR CLOTHES ON

Everything in the world is about to be wrapped up, so take nothing for granted. Stay wide-awake in prayer. (1 Peter 4:7, MSG)

Some people purposely do things to get you to react a certain way. They want you to entertain them. I like doing the opposite of what people expect. It throws them off their game and they don't know what to do. The reaction they're looking for in me is usually the reaction they demonstrate themselves.

The enemy would love for us to react to what is happening in the world by wringing our hands and shaking our heads, while he continues to wreak havoc. If ever there was a time when Christians need to step to the plate, it's certainly now. This is not the time to give up or give in. This is the time to make sure our armor is on and we're ready for battle.

"For the Son of man shall come in the glory of his Father with his angels; and then he shall reward every man according to his works."
(Matthew 16:27, KJV)

LORD, SEND ME MICHAEL

Then he said to me, "Do not be afraid, Daniel. Since the first day that you set your mind on understanding and getting rid of your pride before your God, your words were heard. And I have come because of your words. But the ruler of Persia stood against me for twenty-one days. Then Michael, one of the leading princes of honor, came to help me, because I had been left there with the king of Persia." (Daniel 10:12-13, NLV)

Angels are created beings that do nothing except God's will. Although frequently mentioned throughout the Bible, there are only two angels specifically named: Gabriel, the messenger who delivered the good news of the coming of Jesus Christ to Mary, as well as the announcement of John the Baptist's birth to Zacharias in the temple; and Michael, the only angel classified as an archangel, whose specialty appears to be battle (read Revelation 12:7-8, NIV).

The Greek word for archangel is *"archaggelos,"* a combination of *archo,* meaning first in political rank or power; and *aggelos,* meaning messenger. By definition, then, an archangel is the first or highest angel and a leader of angels; however, despite the power and rank Michael possesses, he is still subservient to the Lordship of Jesus Christ: "Yet Michael the archangel, in contending with the devil, when he disputed about the body of Moses, dared not bring against him a reviling accusation, but said, 'The Lord rebuke you!'" (Jude 9, NKJV).

Yesterday we looked at the importance of being fully dressed when doing battle with the enemy. However, there are some battles that require a little extra help. In those times you don't need a messenger; you need someone who knows how to strategize, fight, and win!

God will command his angels to protect you
wherever you go. (Psalm 91:11, CEV)

WHERE'S YOUR FAITH?

And it is impossible to please God without faith. Anyone who wants to come to him must believe that God exists and that he rewards those who sincerely seek him. (Hebrews 11:6, NLT)

We like to think we have faith in God, but when something happens, He is often the last resort. Why is that? Why put faith in something that cannot help you in a crisis? We put our faith in a job until we get laid off or fired. We put our faith in our home until repairs become cost prohibitive. We put our faith in our vehicle until someone runs into us, and the car is totaled.

God is the only substance in this world that never changes. He is consistently consistent! There is no *person* and no *thing* that can make the same claim. Set your eyes above and focus on God, the One worthy of not only our faith and trust but our praise and worship.

Some trust in their war chariots and others in their horses,
but we trust in the power of the LORD our God.
(Psalm 20:7, GNT)

RESTORATION

Everyone who hurt you will be hurt; your enemies will end up as slaves. Your plunderers will be plundered; your looters will become loot. As for you, I'll come with healing, curing the incurable, because they all gave up on you and dismissed you as hopeless—that good-for-nothing Zion. (Jeremiah 30:16-17, MSG)

I am not a vindictive person; however, today's Scripture is one of my favorites. It shows that God is willing and capable of fighting my battles a lot better than I ever could. So, I stand on His Word. When He assures me the battle is His, not mine, I sit back and watch God work. I don't have to give someone a piece of my mind, or plot to get back at them, or take any other negative action. I only need to let God handle the situation.

Dear friends, never avenge yourselves.
Leave that to God, for He has said that He will repay those who deserve
it. Don't take the law into your own hands.
(Romans 12:19, TLB)

GIVE 'EM UP!

"So don't be afraid: I'm with you. I'll round up all your scattered children; pull them in from east and west. I'll send orders north and south: 'Send them back. Return my sons from distant lands, my daughters from faraway places. I want them back, every last one who bears my name, every man, woman, and child whom I created for my glory, yes, personally formed and made each one.'" (Isaiah 43:5-7, MSG)

Hopefully, Christians are daily praying for their family's salvation. I'm not only speaking of the immediate family but every single member, even the unborn. It is a challenge to wait for something that may not manifest quickly. There are times when we pray, and nothing changes. There are times when we pray, and the situation immediately changes for the better. And, there are times when we pray, and things rapidly deteriorate to the point you might question whether God is listening, hearing, and seeing what's going on.

The enemy would have you think that the day you prayed God was on a coffee break, or you weren't entirely clear in conveying the sense of urgency, or that God doesn't care. Allow me to assure you that none of those scenarios are true despite what may be going on. To prove it, God uttered today's Scripture. He said, *"I will . . ."* and that's all you need to know, trust, and believe. God has everything under control, and at the appointed time, He *will* change the situation.

God, we appreciate the access we have to You to bring our concerns and cares. Help us to stand firm and patiently wait for Your timing. And, while we're waiting, help us to continue to praise and honor You, for You alone are worthy.

THE UNFINISHED STORY

You, LORD God, have done many wonderful things, and you have planned marvelous things for us. No one is like you! I would never be able to tell all you have done. (Psalm 40:5, CEV)

As a publishing consultant, part of my job is to calm the nerves of first-time authors. They're anxious and excited about what the end product will be, will they sell any copies of their book, will people like it, and so forth. If the writer is at the beginning stage of the product (as in not having started yet), they often ask how many words should the manuscript contain? My answer is always the same: "Just tell the story. When the story is finished, you're finished."

Psalm 40 was written by David, and as with most of his writings, he spent a lot of time praising God just for being who He is. David was a man who desired God's *presence* more than His *presents*. David was a man who was aware that his help came from God. David was a man who understood the importance of telling the story. Some of his psalms are brief like Psalm 13 with 111 words, while others are quite lengthy like Psalm 119 with 2,561 words. Regardless of the word count, David allows us to visualize what he felt, which is why thousands of years later we're still blessed by his writing.

We, too, are writing a story that will live far beyond our years. Some of our stories will be longer than others; yet, even when we no longer walk the earth, our unfinished story will live on. It may not make the world's best seller list but be assured that it will be on God's.

"Where I was born and where and how I have lived is unimportant. It is what I have done with where I have been that should be of interest."
—D.L. Moody

A SUPERNATURAL EXCHANGE

For the LORD does not see as man sees; for man looks at the outward appearance, but the LORD looks at the heart. (1 Samuel 16:7, NKJV)

As of August 16, 2018, according to the U. S. Department of Health & Human Services, Organ Procurement and Transplantation Network, 21,042 organ transplants had been performed year to date. A transplant occurs when part of one person's body is inserted into another person's body. Some exchanges take place with both parties still alive; unfortunately, most heart transplants do not fall into this category.

According to www.optn.transplant.hrsa.gov, there have been a few transplants in the U.S. involving a living heart donor. This may occur if one patient receives a heart-lung combination transplant, but their heart is in good condition. This patient's heart may then be subsequently transplanted into another recipient. This procedure is known as a "domino" heart transplant.

Do you need a spiritual heart transplant? God said, "I will give you a new heart and put a new spirit within you; I will take the heart of stone out of your flesh and give you a heart of flesh" (Ezekiel 36:26, NKJV). Jesus came to give us life and that more abundantly (John 10:10). Have you taken advantage of God's gift to you? Jesus took our place on the cross on Good Friday and showed Himself alive on Resurrection Sunday! The exchange has already taken place; all you need do is accept the gift. No surgery. No transfusions. No long recovery period. It's already done; just say yes!

"The greatest love you can have for your friends is to give your life for them." . . . (John 15:13, GNT)

ON ASSIGNMENT

"But what do you think? A man had two sons, and he came to the first and said, 'Son, go, work today in my vineyard.' He answered and said, 'I will not,' but afterward he regretted it and went. Then he came to the second and said likewise. And he answered and said, 'I go, sir,' but he did not go. Which of the two did the will of his father?" They said to Him, "The first." Jesus said to them, "Assuredly, I say to you that tax collectors and harlots enter the kingdom of God before you. For John came to you in the way of righteousness, and you did not believe him; but tax collectors and harlots believed him; and when you saw it, you did not afterward relent and believe him." (Matthew 21:28-32, NKJV)

We first hear of John the Baptist when his father, Zacharias, is visited by an angel and told that God has heard his prayer. He and his wife, Elizabeth, would have a son, call him John, and he would be filled with the Holy Spirit from his mother's womb. He would be set apart for God's use (Luke 1:5-17).

When we meet John as an adult, he is already working: "There was a man sent from God, whose name was John" (John 1:6, KJV). John and Jesus were approximately the same age, give or take a few months, and were cousins. We can assume that they may have played together as children. But, none of that was as important to John as his role of precursor for the Lord, Jesus Christ, even though his message was mostly rejected as today's Scripture indicates. John wasn't deterred by their unbelief. He understood that his responsibility was to complete his assignment. God would take care of the results.

It's human nature to want people to support what we do. However, when that doesn't happen, we can either go forward or remain in a dead-end situation. When God tells us to do something, He's already moved ahead. We then can either get left behind or catch up to where God is headed. Stuck is not a good place to be.

So, as the Holy Spirit says: "Today, if you hear his voice, do not harden your hearts . . ." (Hebrews 3:7-8[a], NIV)

HERE, LET ME HELP YOU

Now Amalek came and fought with Israel in Rephidim. And Moses said to Joshua, "Choose us some men and go out, fight with Amalek. Tomorrow I will stand on the top of the hill with the rod of God in my hand." So Joshua did as Moses said to him, and fought with Amalek. And Moses, Aaron, and Hur went up to the top of the hill. And so it was, when Moses held up his hand, that Israel prevailed; and when he let down his hand, Amalek prevailed. But Moses' hands became heavy; so they took a stone and put it under him, and he sat on it. And Aaron and Hur supported his hands, one on one side, and the other on the other side; and his hands were steady until the going down of the sun. So Joshua defeated Amalek and his people with the edge of the sword. (Exodus 7:8-13, NKJV)

Today's Scripture is well-known to most Bible readers and should act as an inspiration to us all. There are times when we see people in need of our help, and we give our assistance. It doesn't necessarily have to be something big like winning a battle; matter of fact, it's often the little things. Some examples are listening as someone shares a burden, seeing a friend walking to the bus stop and giving them a ride, or offering to take the children of a single parent out to the park to provide them and the parent a break. The point is that when we see a need, we should be willing to do our part of fulfilling it. We may never get our name in print. We may never get any type of monetary reward. We may never even get thanked for our effort. But, that shouldn't stop us from doing the right thing. God knows and sees and rewards our efforts in His time, and that's all that matters.

Lord God, help us to be sensitive
to the needs around us. Help us to slow
down enough to see, hear, and feel what others may be going through, and
then help us step in to do our part. Help us to never forget that we
have been and will be in need ourselves one day.

THE BENEFITS OF DEPARTURE

"Now I am going back to the one who sent me. And none of you asks me, 'Where are you going?' But you are filled with sadness because I have told you all this. Let me assure you, it is better for you that I go away. I say this because when I go away I will send the Helper to you. But if I did not go, the Helper would not come. When the Helper comes, he will show the people of the world how wrong they are about sin, about being right with God, and about judgment. He will prove that they are guilty of sin, because they don't believe in me. He will show them how wrong they are about how to be right with God. The Helper will do this, because I am going to the Father. You will not see me then. And he will show them how wrong their judgment is, because their leader has already been condemned." (John 16:5-11, ERV)

Years ago, I watched my son's plane take off with mixed emotions: happy, sad, anxious, and excited. He was going to college over three thousand miles away on a basketball scholarship. On the one hand I was thrilled because it was a wonderful opportunity for him; on the other hand, it would be the first time he would be gone that far away for an extended period.

I believe the disciples shared these same emotions as they listened to what Jesus said. They had spent three years together and understandably were saddened at the thought of not seeing and daily interacting with the Savior. Yet, they had to also be excited about the Helper Jesus promised to send.

We are often selfish when it comes to letting people we love go, whether through death or other circumstances. Sometimes, we need to step back to see the bigger picture. If we try hard enough, we just might be able to see the benefits of their leaving.

"After a short time, you won't see me. Then after another short time you will see me again. The truth is, you will cry and be sad. . . but then your sadness will change to happiness." (John 16:19[b]-20, ERV)

TURN THE PAGE

Why am I so sad? Why am I so troubled? I will put my hope in God, and once again I will praise him, my savior and my God. (Psalm 42:5, GNT)

When something devastating happens, we take the high road when people inquire as to how we're doing. You know, they'll ask, "How are you?" and your automatic response is, "Fine." When life throws a hiccup in your path—whether it's the loss of a loved one, job, or possession—it takes time to adjust to whatever your new normal has become.

I understand not wanting to burden people with our emotions, but God doesn't have a problem with us being honest with Him. We can truthfully say, "God, this hurt! I wasn't expecting this, and I certainly don't deserve this!" When we come clean with God, then we have placed ourselves in a position to be helped by God. When we release the hurt, anger, bitterness, confusion, or any other emotion that has us temporarily immobile, we're then able to receive God's comfort and peace. He knows when we hurt, and He understands our frustration.

The lesson for us is to release the pain and embrace the healing. Once we recognize that whatever happened is only the end of a chapter in our life, we're ready to turn the page to what God has next.

LORD, I have given up my pride and turned away from my arrogance. I am not concerned with great matters or with subjects too difficult for me. Instead, I am content and at peace. As a child lies quietly in its mother's arms, so my heart is quiet within me.
(Psalm 131:1-2, GNT)

DREAM AGAIN

Joseph was a young man, 17 years old. . . . One time Joseph had a special dream. Later, he told his brothers about this dream, and after that his brothers hated him even more. Joseph said, "I had a dream. We were all working in the field, tying stacks of wheat together. Then my stack got up. It stood there while all of your stacks of wheat made a circle around mine and bowed down to it." His brothers said, "Do you think this means that you will be a king and rule over us?" His brothers hated Joseph more now because of the dreams he had about them. Then Joseph had another dream, and he told his brothers about it. He said, "I had another dream. I saw the sun, the moon, and eleven stars bowing down to me." Joseph also told his father about this dream, but his father criticized him. His father said, "What kind of dream is this? Do you believe that your mother, your brothers, and I will bow down to you?" Joseph's brothers continued to be jealous of him, but his father thought about all these things and wondered what they could mean. (Genesis 37: 1, 5-11, ERV)

Joseph is one of the few Bible characters we're allowed to follow from birth to death. He was the product of the union between Jacob and Rebecca, the love of his life. Jacob made no secret about the fact that Joseph was his favorite child. His brothers didn't like him because of Jacob's behavior.

When God gave Joseph the dreams about the future, he was excited. He did what most of us would have done; he shared them with others. Unfortunately, his brothers and father weren't the right audience. His brothers plotted to get rid of him; his father pondered the dreams in his heart.

There may be a significant timespan between promise and fulfillment. We need to remain faithful and remember that if God said it, it's going to happen. When it does, it will be more than we could imagine.

I wait for the LORD, my soul waits, And in His word, I do hope.
(Psalm 130:5, NKJV)

FEET DON'T FAIL ME NOW!

Now Joseph was handsome in form and appearance. And it came to pass after these things that his master's wife cast longing eyes on Joseph, and she said, "Lie with me." But he refused and said to his master's wife, "Look, my master does not know what is with me in the house, and he has committed all that he has to my hand. There is no one greater in this house than I, nor has he kept back anything from me but you, because you are his wife. How then can I do this great wickedness, and sin against God?" So, it was, as she spoke to Joseph day by day, that he did not heed her, to lie with her or to be with her. But it happened about this time, when Joseph went into the house to do his work, and none of the men of the house was inside, that she caught him by his garment, saying, "Lie with me." But he left his garment in her hand and fled and ran outside. (Genesis 39:6[b]-12, NKJV)

You wouldn't willingly touch an open flame, or step in front of a moving car, or jump off the roof of a house, would you? Sometimes the danger is a thing; but frequently, it's a person.

A friend told me of a co-worker who inquired why she gave another co-worker the cold shoulder. My friend clarified that she wasn't giving the man the cold shoulder since she talked with him when needed. My friend further explained that the co-worker was her "type," but since he was married, she kept him at a distance. My friend is a single Christian woman determined to live holy for the Lord. Having the male co-worker at arm's-length was necessary. She believed God would allow her to marry one day and knew flirting or beginning a relationship with a married man would not be pleasing to God. There is no shame in having enough sense to stay away from danger!

No temptation has overtaken you except such as is common to man, but God is faithful, who will not allow you to be tempted beyond what you are able, but with the temptation will also make the way of escape, that you may be able to bear it. (1 Corinthians 10:13, NKJV)

OOPS! MY BAD

It came to pass after these things that the butler and the baker of the king of Egypt offended their lord, the king of Egypt. . .So he put them in custody in the house of the captain of the guard, in the prison, the place where Joseph was confined. And the captain of the guard charged Joseph with them, and he served them; so they were in custody for a while. Then the butler and the baker of the king of Egypt, who were confined in the prison, had a dream... "Do not interpretations belong to God? Tell them to me please"...Now it came to pass on the third day, which was Pharaoh's birthday, that he made a feast for all his servants; and he lifted up the head of the chief butler and of the chief baker among his servants. Then he restored the chief butler to his butlership again, and he placed the cup in Pharaoh's hand...Yet the chief butler did not remember Joseph, but forgot him. (Genesis 40:1, 3-5, 8[b], 20-21, 23, NKJV)

Isn't it irritating when you're counting on someone to do something and they don't? They conveniently aren't available when you reach out to them and then start avoiding you because of guilt. I would prefer someone tell me no and then change their mind, rather than say yes and not come through on the promise.

The butler was ecstatic with Joseph's interpretation. Joseph's request—"Remember me when it is well with you, and please show kindness to me, make mention of me to Pharaoh, and get me out of this house" (v. 14)—was forgotten by the butler once he was restored to his position. You would think that every time he serviced Pharaoh he'd remember, but that didn't happen. Fortunately, the king had a nightmare, which finally triggered the butler's memory.

God, help us to be mature enough to honor our word. Help us to remember that someone is depending on us to do what we promise.

DON'T COUNT ME OUT YET

And it came to pass in the morning that his spirit was troubled; and he sent and called for all the magicians of Egypt, and all the wise men thereof: and Pharaoh told them his dream; but there was none that could interpret them unto Pharaoh. Then spake the chief butler unto Pharaoh, saying, "I do remember my faults this day: Pharaoh was wroth with his servants, and put me in ward in the captain of the guard's house, both me and the chief baker: And we dreamed a dream in one night, I and he; we dreamed each man according to the interpretation of his dream. And there was there with us a young man, a Hebrew, servant to the captain of the guard; and we told him, and he interpreted to us our dreams; to each man according to his dream he did interpret. And it came to pass, as he interpreted to us, so it was; me he restored unto mine office, and him he hanged." Then Pharaoh sent and called Joseph, and they brought him hastily out of the dungeon: and he shaved himself, and changed his raiment, and came in unto Pharaoh. (Genesis 41:8-14, KJV)

Sometimes, it's easy to believe that when people are in a negative place, they don't have anything to contribute. If Pharaoh had thought like this, his dream would never have been interpreted, Joseph wouldn't have been summoned, and the country wouldn't have been prepared for the upcoming famine. Everybody in prison isn't guilty. And, even the ones who are can still have skills that may be useful. Let's not be so quick to judge and dismiss what could be a blessing in disguise.

Lord God, thank You that despite our behavior at times,
You still use the gifts You've given us to bless Your people.

YOU CAN'T TAKE CREDIT FOR THIS

Now Israel loved Joseph more than all his children, because he was the son of his old age: and he made him a coat of many colours. . .When Joseph reached his brothers, they ripped off the fancy coat he was wearing, grabbed him, and threw him into a cistern. . . (Genesis 37:3, 23, 31-32, MSG)

Joseph's brothers hated him for more than being Israel's favorite son. In my book *On the Other Side of Yes: Understanding the Power of Agreement*, I take a thorough look at the factors that led up to today's Scripture. Being dropped in an empty well was just the beginning of Joseph's trials. He would endure a lot before the dreams God gave him as a teenager came to pass. God permitted him to confront his brothers, who were afraid that he would treat them the way they had treated him.

Although Joseph didn't seem to desire it, I think it would have been nice if at least one of his brothers had apologized! Yet, throughout Joseph's entire ordeal we never read of a verbal complaint or even a negative thought toward God or his brothers. That's something all of us should be striving to imitate.

Let no corrupt word proceed out of your mouth, but what is good for
necessary edification, that it may impart grace
to the hearers. (Ephesians 4:29, NKJV)

CREAM ALWAYS RISES

When Joseph's brothers saw that their father was dead, they said, "Perhaps Joseph will hate us and will certainly pay us back for all the wrong we did to him." So they sent a message to Joseph, saying, "Your father gave this command before he died: 'Say to Joseph, "I beg you, forgive the transgressions of your brothers and their sin. For they did evil to you." Now, please forgive the transgressions of the servants of the God of your father.'" And Joseph wept when they spoke to him. Then his brothers also went and fell down before his face and said, "We are your servants." Joseph said to them, "Do not be afraid, for am I in the place of God? But as for you, you intended to harm me, but God intended it for good, in order to bring it about as it is this day, to save many lives. So now, do not fear. I will provide for you and your little ones." So he comforted them and spoke kindly to them. (Genesis 50:15-21, MEV)

The story of Joseph and his brothers has many dynamics: sibling rivalry, favoritism, naïve dreams, hatred, and love. Joseph's brothers hated him; but he never stopped loving them. Joseph was in prime position to destroy his brothers; instead, he forgave them and promised to take care of them and their families.

None of us are going to get away from this life without someone saying or doing things to hurt us. I've tried to embrace Joseph's attitude whenever I encounter such situations. A plot was hatched and launched to distract or destroy me; it didn't succeed. Rather than gloating (as I once would have done), I now pray for the individuals, so they will learn the lesson and decline the temptation to set up someone else. Ditch-digging needs to be left to the professionals.

Love is patient, caring. Love is Kind. Love is felt most when it's
genuine, but I've had my share of love, abuse, manipulated
and its strength misused, and I can't help but give you glory
when I think about my story, and I know you favored me because my
enemies did try but couldn't triumph over me.
Yes, they did try but couldn't triumph over me.
God Favored Me. Jules Bartholomew. 2008.

A PROMISE KEPT

Joseph stayed in Egypt, along with all his father's family. He lived a hundred and ten years and saw the third generation of Ephraim's children. . . Then Joseph said to his brothers, "I am about to die. But God will surely come to your aid and take you up out of this land to the land he promised on oath to Abraham, Isaac and Jacob." And Joseph made the Israelites swear an oath and said, "God will surely come to your aid, and then you must carry my bones up from this place." So Joseph died at the age of a hundred and ten. And after they embalmed him, he was placed in a coffin in Egypt. (Genesis 50:22, 23[a], 24-26, NIV)

Moses took the bones of Joseph with him because Joseph had made the Israelites swear an oath. (Exodus 13:19[a], NIV)

I remember when your word was your bond and some deals were sealed with nothing more than a handshake. Those times are obviously long past. Today, some people have no problem telling you what they think you want to hear, knowing they have no intention of keeping their word. It doesn't mean anything to them and subsequently ends up not meaning anything to you either, once they are proven unreliable.

Joseph was instrumental in having his family move to Egypt. After all that his brothers had done to him, the one thing he asked was that when God delivered them, they would take his bones with them to the Promised Land. Despite all the things the brothers did wrong throughout Joseph's life, in his death they did something right and kept their word.

As Christians we need to attain and then maintain a reputation for being trustworthy.

MAKES ME WANT TO HOLLER AND THROW UP BOTH MY HANDS!

Then I saw a new heaven and a new earth, for the old heaven and the old earth had disappeared. And the sea was also gone. . . I heard a loud shout from the throne, saying, "Look, God's home is now among his people! He will live with them, and they will be his people. God himself will be with them. He will wipe every tear from their eyes, and there will be no more death or sorrow or crying or pain. All these things are gone forever." (Revelation 21:1, 3-4, NLT)

Recently, I was playing with my youngest grandson, who repeatedly wanted me to lift him up. Once in my arms, he'd give me a quick hug and then scramble off my lap. It wasn't until he went home that all of that lifting and hugging came back to haunt me. I hurt in places I didn't even realize could hurt! But, it was worth it, feeling those little arms wrapped around my neck

Recently, we had an event at church that required me to do a lot of walking and standing. While that may be a simple task for some, it isn't for me. By mid-afternoon, that excursion caused muscle spasms that almost brought me to tears. But, it was worth it, being involved in the event to its fullest extent.

Recently, I received numerous calls and voicemails from friends and family regarding deaths, illnesses, and life situations. At one point it was happening so frequently I was reluctant to answer the phone, thinking what now? But, it was worth it, to be able to add my prayers to theirs and to know they trusted me with their concerns.

My point of sharing these scenarios is that sometimes we are tempted to get stuck in the moment; however, a day is coming when these types of situations will no longer matter. Everything will be new, and we will be changed. When that happens, aches, pains, tears, heartache, and concerns will all be gone! We won't remember the bad things because we'll be too busy being in the presence of God. I am looking forward to that time, aren't you?

These troubles and sufferings of ours are, after all,
quite small and won't last very long.
(2 Corinthians 4:17[a], TLB)

TEMPLE OF THE LIVING GOD

Don't you know that you yourselves are God's temple and that God's Spirit dwells in your midst? If anyone destroys God's temple, God will destroy that person; for God's temple is sacred, and you together are that temple. (1 Corinthians 3:16-17, NIV)

Do you not know that your bodies are temples of the Holy Spirit, who is in you, whom you have received from God? You are not your own. (1 Corinthians 6:19, NIV)

I tend to forget to charge my laptop between uses. Consequently, it seems that every time I turn it on, the battery has lost juice. The other day I was in the middle of using it when a pop-up read "Battery is very low. Plug it in now!"

It's the same with us. We are God's temple, but sometimes our power drains like my laptop and we need to re-charge. And, sometimes our battery gets so low that we receive an urgent pop-up message. We recharge by reading the Word, listening to a sermon, inspirational music, or sitting quietly in God's presence. He doesn't mind our busyness (unless it becomes detrimental to our health), but He does have a problem with our neglecting the temple He's temporarily loaned us. Need I say more?

My life is not my own.
To you I belong.
I give myself, I give myself away.
I Give Myself Away. William McDowell. 2009.

YOU AIN'T NEVER LIED!

One day a man arrived from Baal Shalishah. He brought the man of God twenty loaves of fresh-baked bread from the early harvest, along with a few apples from the orchard. Elisha said, "Pass it around to the people to eat." His servant said, "For a hundred men? There's not nearly enough!" Elisha said, "Just go ahead and do it. GOD says there's plenty." And sure enough, there was. He passed around what he had—they not only ate but had leftovers. (2 Kings 4:42-44, MSG)

I have a former co-worker who had an over-the-top personality. Everything about her was dramatic—her hair, her clothes, her speech. Not surprisingly, her character fit her. I can think of no one else who could have pulled it off as well. One of the things she enjoyed saying was, "You ain't never lied!" which was her way of saying she agreed with whatever was said.

I thought of this woman when I read this Scripture. This is but one example of God being faithful to His Word, and a reminder that whatever God has said will happen is going to happen. Elisha knew what God could do. He also knew the man with the bread, his servant, and the one hundred men who ate and burped—and were satisfied—needed to see firsthand that God could be trusted. Even when it doesn't make sense or seems impossible, if God said it, we can act upon it. After all, God ain't never lied!

Thank You, Lord, that in this time of fake news
and not knowing who to believe or trust, we
need only turn to You and the Word
to keep our bearings.

THE POWER OF A BUT

In the past you were spiritually dead because of your sins and the things you did against God. Yes, in the past your lives were full of those sins. You lived the way the world lives, following the ruler of the evil powers that are above the earth. That same spirit is now working in those who refuse to obey God. In the past all of us lived like that, trying to please our sinful selves. We did all the things our bodies and minds wanted. Like everyone else in the world, we deserved to suffer God's anger just because of the way we were. But God is rich in mercy, and he loved us very much. (Ephesians 2:1-4, ERV)

I loved the *Schoolhouse Rocks* television program from the 1970s. Although it was geared toward children, they were interesting, short, animated shows with catchy tunes. It was a fun way for kids of all ages to learn. There was a spin-off called *Grammar Rocks*, which looked at all parts of speech (nouns, verbs, etc.). My favorite episode was *Conjunction Junction,* which focused on the words *and, or, but* and showed how they were used as connectors between words.

   We often hear that if a person uses the word "but" you can usually disregard everything that comes before it. I'm not sure where that teaching came from; however, I am aware of the power of the word. It all comes down to how you use it. The phrase "but God" is used too many times throughout the Bible to get an accurate count; I'm just glad it's in there, aren't you? If verses 1-3 of today's Scripture were the only ones recorded, we'd be in a world of hurt. Thankfully, verse 4 gives us cause for celebration—God's mercy and love! In this case, I'm happy to disregard everything that came before "but God."

He loves me. Even when I fall beneath His will.
He loves me. When my broken heart just won't keep still.
He loves me. Even though He knew sometimes I'd fall.
Yet and still my name He called. He loves me.
Jesus, I'm so grateful for Your love.
He Loves Me. Kirk Franklin. 1998.

LIKE WATER OFF A DUCK'S BACK

Jephthah, a brave soldier from Gilead, was the son of a prostitute. His father Gilead had other sons by his wife, and when they grew up, they forced Jephthah to leave home. They told him, "You will not inherit anything from our father; you are the son of another woman." Jephthah fled from his brothers and lived in the land of Tob. There he attracted a group of worthless men, and they went around with him. (Judges 11:1-3, GNT)

It's true: we can choose our friends, but we can't choose our family. The first thing we learn of Jephthah is that he was a brave soldier *and* the son of a prostitute.

Jephthah's brothers resented his presence and made sure he wouldn't inherit anything from their father. They appointed themselves judge and executioner over what would happen. Jephthah fled rather than argue and lived in another land with a group of men. As is typically the case, when something happens we can't handle, we look for help from any available source. When the Ammonites came against Gilead, the elders sought Jephthah to help them fight. He offered his help if they made him their ruler, and they agreed (vv. 4-11).

Jephthah sent word to the king of Ammon to attempt to negotiate without fighting, but the king ignored him (vv. 12-28). Once Jephthah realized battle was necessary, he made a vow to the Lord. Tomorrow we'll discover the result of the vow.

As a child, we often said, "Sticks and stone may break my bones, but words will never hurt me."
We thought we were correct until we grew up and discovered that words can and do hurt.

IT'S OUT OF MY HANDS

Jephthah promised the LORD: "If you will give me victory over the Ammonites, I will burn as an offering the first person that comes out of my house to meet me, when I come back from the victory. I will offer that person to you as a sacrifice." . . . When Jephthah went back home to Mizpah, there was his daughter coming out to meet him, dancing and playing the tambourine. She was his only child. When he saw her, he tore his clothes in sorrow and said, "Oh, my daughter! You are breaking my heart! Why must it be you that causes me pain? I have made a solemn promise to the LORD, and I cannot take it back!" (Judges 11:30-31, 34-35, GNT)

Have you ever heard this statement: "Don't let your mouth write a check you can't cash!" In other words, don't let what you say land you in trouble.

Only Jephthah knows why he made such an extreme vow. Theologians have debated for years what he meant. Some believe he expected an animal to come out of the door first, and not his only child. Theologians further debate what Jephthah did in response. Some think he offered his daughter as a burnt offering; others believe he consecrated her into service for the Lord. I tend to lean toward the second interpretation.

As a parent, I cannot imagine sacrificing my only child to be burned alive. More importantly, I don't believe God is unstable in that He says something is wrong and then accepts it as okay. Deuteronomy 18:10[a] quotes God: "Don't sacrifice your children in the fires on your altars."

Jephthah's daughter had nothing to do with her father making the vow; nor did she realize that as she ran out of the house in excitement to greet her father, her life would be changed forever. She and her father would have to deal with the consequences of the vow made to God.

If you want to stay out of trouble, be careful what you say.
(Proverbs 21:23, GNT)

THE END OF THE STORY

So, she said to him, "My father, if you have given your word to the LORD, do to me according to what has gone out of your mouth, because the LORD has avenged you of your enemies, the people of Ammon." Then she said to her father, "Let this thing be done for me: let me alone for two months, that I may go and wander on the mountains and bewail my virginity, my friends and I." So, he said, "Go." And he sent her away for two months; and she went with her friends and bewailed her virginity on the mountains. And it was so at the end of two months that she returned to her father, and he carried out his vow with her which he had vowed. She knew no man. (Judges 11:36-39, NKJV)

I mentioned yesterday that I believe Jephthah consecrated his daughter for service unto the Lord as opposed to making her a burnt offering. Today's Scripture further confirms my belief.

We're not told the daughter's age, but we know she's unmarried. Most girls, especially in Old Testament times, looked forward to marriage and children. Being obedient, she resigned herself to fulfilling her father's vow; but she needed to put it in perspective. For her, that meant giving up the childhood dreams of a spouse and family. It wasn't going to happen. Here again is evidence that she wasn't to be burned. She took two months to bewail her virginity, not her death.

The moral of the story of Jephthah and his daughter is to be careful with our words. Let's not be so quick to open our mouth and say something we can't take back. Be sensitive to the spirit of God.

"He who has ears to hear, let him hear!"
(Matthew 11:15, NKJV)

TWO MEN NAMED JOSEPH

This is how the birth of Jesus the Messiah came about: His mother Mary was pledged to be married to Joseph, but before they came together, she was found to be pregnant through the Holy Spirit. . . an angel of the Lord appeared to him in a dream and said, "Joseph son of David, do not be afraid to take Mary home as your wife, because what is conceived in her is from the Holy Spirit". . .When Joseph woke up, he did what the angel of the Lord had commanded him and took Mary home as his wife. But he did not consummate their marriage until she gave birth to a son. And he gave him the name Jesus. (Matthew 1:18, 20, 24-25, NIV)

Now there was a man named Joseph, a member of the Council, a good and upright man, who had not consented to their decision and action. He came from the Judean town of Arimathea, and he himself was waiting for the kingdom of God. Going to Pilate, he asked for Jesus' body. Then he took it down, wrapped it in linen cloth and placed it in a tomb cut in the rock, one in which no one had yet been laid. It was Preparation Day, and the Sabbath was about to begin. (Luke 23:50-54, NIV)

I find it interesting that at the beginning and end of Jesus' earthly life, He was taken care of by a man named Joseph, whose name means to add, increase, or repeat. The addition part is obvious in that both men significantly added to Jesus' life as opposed to those who only wanted something from Him. Both men also had several traits in common: integrity, courage, strength, and great faith. Regardless of the first name, all of us can appreciate having men like these two Josephs in our lives.

"Integrity is keeping a commitment
even after circumstances have changed."
—David Jeremiah

REPRESENT WELL

My dear friend, don't follow what is bad; follow what is good. Whoever does what is good is from God. But whoever does evil has never known God. (3 John 11, ERV)

While I was growing up, my parents—like most parents—told their children to remember they represented the family wherever they went. In other words, we weren't to go anywhere acting crazy. We were to act like we had some home training. I'm not sure parents are instilling that mindset into their children today, and that's unfortunate.

As Christians, we represent God, Jesus, and the Holy Spirit everywhere we go. If you review the last 24 hours, is there any evidence of this relationship? If not, ask for forgiveness, a fresh infilling, and vow to get it right from now on.

We are the only visible evidence of Jesus in the world today.
If we're not reflecting Him accurately,
who's going to help His people?

DON'T FORGET

I will exalt you, LORD, for you rescued me. You refused to let my enemies triumph over me. O LORD my God, I cried to you for help, and you restored my health. You brought me up from the grave, O LORD. You kept me from falling into the pit of death. (Psalm 30:1-3, NLT)

I've been walking with the Lord for 30 years, and I'm pleased to announce that I've matured tremendously from where I started the journey. I'll now confess what is true for all of us who have had a similar experience: We're not where we're going to be tomorrow. Every day is a new adventure, and every day brings new challenges. One of those challenges is being able to remember all that God has done for me—*immediately*. What I mean is that there are moments—a nanosecond of a nanosecond—when something negative happens, and I want to ask, "Why me?" Then, after that miniscule second, I snap out of it and think, "Huh! This is only a test, and I've been tested before."

The opening verses of Psalm 30 remind us that *nothing* can hurt us—not our enemies, sickness, or even death. These things and others are irrelevant and not worthy of our concern. We have Almighty God as our Father, who will respond the way our human fathers may not; and that's okay. The Lord God Jehovah is the only Father who can help us. Just call on Him, and He'll be there.

When challenges come,
don't forget who has your back!

WHY? BECAUSE HE LOVES YOU!

If you make the LORD your refuge; if you make the Most High your shelter, no evil will conquer you; no plague will come near your home. For he will order his angels to protect you wherever you go. They will hold you up with their hands so you won't even hurt your foot on a stone. You will trample upon lions and cobras; you will crush fierce lions and serpents under your feet! The LORD says, "I will rescue those who love me. I will protect those who trust in my name. When they call on me, I will answer; I will be with them in trouble; I will rescue and honor them. I will reward them with a long life and give them my salvation." (Psalm 91:9-16, NLT)

I grew up watching the original Mickey Mouse Club, a fun and engaging show that ran on TV from 1955-1958. I especially liked the song the Mouseketeers sang at the end: "M I C (see you real soon) K E Y (Why? Because we like you!) M O U S E!" For kids like me, this was a welcome escape from our *challenging* job of being a child! Throughout the years, people have fallen in love with Mickey Mouse and what he represents, as indicated by the billions of people who have visited any of the houses that Mickey built.

I thought about the Mickey Mouse Club when I read today's Scripture. God does many things for us just because He loves us! He is so much God that He even blesses those who don't or won't serve Him. However, for those of us who have chosen to make God the head of our lives, He has promised us much more than waking us up each morning or allowing the sun to shine on the just and the unjust. God wants a relationship with us! He loves us and only wants us to love Him back! How hard is that?

Thank You, Lord, for the simplicity of Your message that
You love us just the way we are!
Help us to accept and return the love
You've shown without hesitation.

REJOICE WITH ME

This is the day the Eternal God has made; let us celebrate and be happy today. (Psalm 118:24, VOICE)

The clock of life restarts every day when you open your eyes. You then have a choice as to how you'll spend the next 24 hours. Some choices are out of your hands if you work or go to school. However, there's a lot that is totally in your control.

You are the only one who can determine how productive you'll be. You are the only one who can determine whether at the end of the day you'll be satisfied with what you accomplished. You are the only one who can determine whether you followed the psalmist's instructions in today's Scripture. Choose wisely.

It's been a good day. I thank God for it.
I've got my health and strength.
And I know that I'm His child.
A Good Day. James Cleveland. 1991.

CAN YOU SAY THE SAME?

... because God has said, "Never will I leave you; never will I forsake you." (Hebrews 13:5, NIV)

We often marvel at the above Scripture. Imagine having a promise like that from the God of the Universe, knowing it's personally directed to us. Now, imagine it from God's point of view. He's made the promise to us and is wondering if we can say the same to Him.

Have you forsaken God? You ask how you could do that. Well, it's easy when you allow other things to become more important than your relationship with Him. Remember how excited you were when you first met the Lord? You were on fire for God and the things of God. Has your excitement eased? Have you become comfortable and familiar with the relationship? If so, you only need to make the commitment not to forsake God.

My pastor recently said, "When you get serious about God, God gets serious about you," and I believe that to be true. God's not going to hold it against you that your intensity for Him waned a little; God is much more patient and forgiving than we could ever be. But, as our Heavenly Father, He wants what's best for us, and that's a powerful, intimate relationship with Him.

Lord, please help us never to become so comfortable around
You that we forget who You are and
what You've done for us. You are the king of Kings
and the lord of Lords and should be treated appropriately.
Forgive us for the times we've neglected You and taken You for granted.
From this day forward, we vow to make our relationship with You
our highest priority.

YES, YOU CAN DO THIS!

Keep me from paying attention to what is worthless; be good to me, as you have promised. (Psalm 119:37, GNT)

Today's Scripture is one I remind myself of on a regular basis: Don't waste time on insignificant things that don't or won't increase my spiritual walk with God. Once a day is over, it's done. It will not be repeated.

One of my major weaknesses is television. I love it! Philo Farnsworth (1906-1971) is credited with inventing the first electrical television by showcasing 60 horizontal lines in 1927. Although this occurred a long time before I was born, I am eternally grateful for Mr. Farnsworth's initiatives that showed what could be done. Several other inventors and scientists took his concept far beyond their imagination, resulting in what we have today.

I'll admit that even with technology, everything on television isn't worth viewing. That's where we must learn to edit ourselves and tap into the Holy Spirit's guidance. Just as someone rubbernecks to see an accident, and then turns away in horror when they observe too much, we do the same with television. Let's face it, there's a lot of junk on TV from reality shows to infomercials to scripted dramas and comedies that aren't funny. There are also a lot of good, inspirational, uplifting, family-oriented shows. We have a choice as to how we spend our time.

The question to ask yourself is this: Since we only have a set number of days on this Earth, is what we're watching going to enhance our days? Would God consider it "worthless" or "worthwhile"?

Lord, we depend on You for food, clothing, shelter.
Help us to depend on You to guide the use of our time.

CELEBRATE YOU!

You saw me before I was born. Every day of my life was recorded in your book. Every moment was laid out before a single day had passed. (Psalm 139:16, NLT)

I realize there are some people who for whatever reasons don't celebrate the day they were born. I confess I don't understand why that is. The fact that God allowed you to live is cause for celebration.

Think about what life would be like without you and everything you would have missed. Numerous movies have been made about people seeing what life would have been like without them. One of the reasons most of these movies have been successful is because I believe there is something inside all of us that wonders what would things be like if we weren't around? That is not being conceited; in my opinion, it's realistic.

If I hadn't been born, then I wouldn't have met my son's father and my son wouldn't have been born. Without my son's birth, he wouldn't have met his wife and created their children. Without my grandchildren's births, I wouldn't have anyone to love the way only a grandparent can.

There's only one you, and no one can do what you can. As the saying goes, "do you!" For your next birthday, make plans to celebrate you! You're worth it!

Life is a song worth singing.
Why don't you sing it?
Life is a Song Worth Singing. Thomas Randolph Bell and
Linda Diane Creed. 1979.

SEALED WITH A KISS

Now unto him that is able to do exceeding abundantly above all that we ask or think, according to the power that worketh in us; Unto him be glory in the church by Christ Jesus throughout all ages, world without end. Amen. (Ephesians 3:20-21, KJV)

Once upon a time before cell phones, Instagram, Facebook, Twitter, and all the modern methods of communicating, there was something called a letter. You hand wrote or typed your message on whatever paper you had, put it in an envelope, addressed it, stamped it, and put it in an odd-shaped red and blue contraption called a mailbox. People like me, who enjoyed writing letters, enjoyed receiving a response even more. When I was in high school, I had pen pals from around the country, some even in the military. I looked forward to reading their news and then sharing what was going on in my life.

Some of my friends would apply lipstick and place a kiss on the back of the envelope when they were writing to their boyfriends. It might sound corny to those of you who are younger, but back in the day, this was a big deal. Seeing an envelope with a kiss indicated it was something extraordinary. Although they may not admit it, I'm sure the men savored these letters. They probably waited until they were alone to read them because they were from someone they cared about. And, they most likely didn't throw them away when finished.

God is in the letter writing business and seals each of them with a kiss. Unfortunately, we often take His letters for granted. Oh, we read the Bible—sometimes daily—but do we *truly* realize how special we are to God? Every book of the Bible, every chapter, every promise is a love letter sent directly from God specifically for us! That's incredible!

Thank You, Lord, for thinking enough of us to send us mail that's full of love! Help us to read and re-read Your letters every day.

GOD KNOWS YOU'RE TIRED

Now the gates of Jericho were tightly shut because the people were afraid of the Israelites. No one was allowed to go out or in. But the LORD said to Joshua, "I have given you Jericho, its king, and all its strong warriors. You and your fighting men should march around the town once a day for six days. Seven priests will walk ahead of the Ark, each carrying a ram's horn. On the seventh day you are to march around the town seven times, with the priests blowing the horns. When you hear the priests give one long blast on the rams' horns, have all the people shout as loud as they can. Then the walls of the town will collapse, and the people can charge straight into the town." (Joshua 6:1-5, NLT)

I often wonder what the children of Israel thought about as they walked around the city God promised them. After all, there were enough of them to be noticeable; I'm sure the people of Jericho poked fun at them because of their odd behavior. Then, add in the sound of the trumpets, and there's no way people weren't aware that something was happening.

When God gives us a promise that doesn't manifest quickly, we might tend to think He's forgotten about us or even changed His mind, especially if He requires us to do something unusual or out of our comfort zone. "They that wait upon the Lord shall renew their strength" (Isaiah 40:31[a]) indicates God's awareness of our physical and mental challenges with waiting. We must encourage ourselves with the knowledge that God knows everything, including our impatient nature. Because of that encouragement, we can pray a little longer, hang in there a little more, and wait another day before we throw in the towel and say, "That's enough! I'm done!" After all, God's timing isn't ours. Wouldn't it be a shame if we gave up too soon?

God, please help us tap into Your strength when we grow weary. Help us to keep on keeping on until everything You've promised has come true.

ARE YOU PROPERLY DRESSED?

So, chosen by God for this new life of love, dress in the wardrobe God picked out for you: compassion, kindness, humility, quiet strength, discipline. Be even-tempered, content with second place, quick to forgive an offense. Forgive as quickly and completely as the Master forgave you. And regardless of what else you put on, wear love. It's your basic, all-purpose garment. Never be without it. (Colossians 3:12-14, MSG)

Fashion designers are in business because they recognize that everyone has a specific idea of how they want to look and what they want to wear. If you look around where you are right now, you'll probably see a variety of outfits, some more appropriate than others.

God has a wardrobe preference for us, regardless of our race, creed, color, or gender. It is a one-size-fits-all called love.

"I say to you, I have also decided to stick with love,
for I know that love is ultimately
the only answer to mankind's problems."
—Dr. Martin Luther King, Jr.
"Where do we go from here?" speech. August 16, 1967.

ONE WAY OR ANOTHER

Christ was truly God. But he did not try to remain equal with God. Instead he gave up everything and became a slave, when he became like one of us. Christ was humble. He obeyed God and even died on a cross. Then God gave Christ the highest place and honored his name above all others. So at the name of Jesus everyone will bow down, those in heaven, on earth, and under the earth. And to the glory of God the Father everyone will openly agree, "Jesus Christ is Lord!" (Philippians 2:6-11, CEV)

Whether you accept Jesus as Lord and Savior or not, there is no denying this: There has never been nor will there ever be anyone like Him again. There are a lot of people considered famous, and some of their names are familiar. But, whether they go by one name or two, their name does not have the power to save, heal, and deliver. Their name will also never garner adoration like the name of Jesus Christ! You can bow now or later, but you *will* bow.

There is none like You,
No one else can touch my heart like You do,
I can search for all eternity Lord
And find, there is none like You.
There Is None Like You. Lenny LeBlanc. 1991.

STOP THE OUCH!

"This is my covenant with you and your descendants after you, the covenant you are to keep: Every male among you shall be circumcised. You are to undergo circumcision, and it will be the sign of the covenant between me and you. For the generations to come every male among you who is eight days old must be circumcised, including those born in your household or bought with money from a foreigner—those who are not your offspring. Whether born in your household or bought with your money, they must be circumcised. My covenant in your flesh is to be an everlasting covenant. Any uncircumcised male, who has not been circumcised in the flesh, will be cut off from his people; he has broken my covenant." (Genesis 17:10-14, NIV)

I've had enough surgeries to know that anytime you're cut, it's going to hurt. Circumcision—the cutting away of foreskin on the penis—is a painful procedure. My son had it done as an infant; however, the husband of a friend required the procedure as an adult. I felt sorry for him because he was in excruciating pain for weeks.

The Church must ensure that we don't cause pain to members with a lot of man-made rules. Yes, there is a need for order in the house of God; yes, there are protocols to be kept. That is not what I'm referring to; I'm referencing those requirements that are personal preferences found nowhere in the Bible.

Since there is only one God—and it's not us—
let's be careful not to make
others jump through unnecessary hoops.

WHO ARE YOU?

That is, the LORD passed in front of Moses and said, "YAHWEH, the LORD, is a kind and merciful God. He is slow to become angry. He is full of great love. He can be trusted. He shows his faithful love to thousands of people. He forgives people for the wrong things they do, but he does not forget to punish guilty people. Not only will he punish the guilty people, but their children, their grandchildren, and their great-grandchildren will also suffer for the bad things these people do." (Exodus 34:6-7, ERV)

If asked to describe themselves, most people would only mention their good qualities. That makes sense, because who wants to admit that some days they get up on the wrong side of the bed and stay there? We want people to see us at our best.

Today's Scripture takes us to Mount Sinai for the second meeting between God and Moses regarding the Ten Commandments. God had already given them to Moses on two stone tablets, which Moses broke when he came down from the mountain and found the children of Israel having a party (Exodus 31:18-32:19). God was gracious enough to allow a do-over with the tablets and called Moses back to Mount Sinai (Exodus 34:1-4). God determined that Moses and the children of Israel needed a clear understanding of who He is and provided a self-description. Unlike some of us, God's description was all-inclusive and very clear. He *is* a God of mercy and love. He *is* a God of faithfulness and truth. He *is* a God of understanding and compassion. But, He *is* also a God of order; the guilty will be punished!

God is our heavenly Father—the ultimate parent—and we don't get to pick and choose which of His attributes we'll love, honor, and obey.

But the LORD has always loved his followers, and he will continue to love them forever and ever. He will be good to all their descendants, to those who are faithful to his agreement and who remember to obey his commands.
(Psalm 103:17-18, ERV)

SIMPLE REQUEST, HUGE RESULTS

And when the servant of the man of God arose early and went out, there was an army, surrounding the city with horses and chariots. And his servant said to him, "Alas, my master! What shall we do?" So he answered, "Do not fear, for those who are with us are more than those who are with them." And Elisha prayed, and said, "LORD, I pray, open his eyes that he may see." Then the LORD opened the eyes of the young man, and he saw. And behold, the mountain was full of horses and chariots of fire all around Elisha. (2 Kings 6:15-17, NKJV)

The kings of Syria and Israel were at war. The king of Syria wanted to meet Elisha because he couldn't figure out how the king of Israel knew every move he was making. He sent a "great army" to bring Elisha to him, and this is where our Scripture picks up. Elisha's servant looked out, saw "the city surrounded by a great army, horses and chariots," and was getting ready to go into full-fledge panic mode. He wouldn't have been any good to anybody, especially Elisha, so Elisha did what he always did—he sought the Lord. He made a simple request, "Open his eyes that he may see."

A lot of times we are walking into walls with our eyes wide open. It's during these times that we need to pray the prayer of Elisha: Lord, open *my* eyes that I may see. God has things for us to do, but at times we're not focused on what we're called to do. We allow distractions to keep us from completing our tasks and then complain of being tired because we're too busy!

Lord, please keep my eyes open so I may clearly see what is going on around me.

ACKNOWLEDGE THE HURT AND MOVE ON

In the church at Antioch there were some prophets and teachers. They were Barnabas, Simeon (also called Niger), Lucius (from the city of Cyrene), Manaen (who had grown up with King Herod), and Saul. These men were all serving the Lord and fasting when the Holy Spirit said to them, "Appoint Barnabas and Saul to do a special work for me. They are the ones I have chosen to do it." So the church fasted and prayed. They laid their hands on Barnabas and Saul and sent them out. Barnabas and Saul were sent out by the Holy Spirit. They went to the city of Seleucia. Then they sailed from there to the island of Cyprus. When Barnabas and Saul came to the city of Salamis, they told the message of God in the Jewish synagogues. John Mark was with them to help. (Acts 13:1-5, NLT)

A few months ago, a friend told me how painful it was to end a non-romantic relationship she had for seven years. She had tried everything she could to make the relationship work and finally concluded that it had run its course, which doesn't mean the relationship was bad. She was sad and even a little hurt but understood that to everything there is a season. Sometimes it's easier on all parties to recognize that before the relationship deteriorates.

Paul and Barnabas started out as partners in the Gospel. A disagreement about Barnabas's cousin, Mark, caused a conflict and ultimately a separation (Acts 15:36-39). Paul and Barnabas were sad at their parting, but both realized it was best for the Gospel to continue going forth. Paul would become the better known of the two, although Barnabas also continued doing God's work. At one point, God allowed them to reconnect, along with Mark, to further bring the Kingdom to God's people (Colossians 4:10; 2 Timothy 4:11).

William Shakespeare told us that, "Parting is such sweet sorrow." I want to add, "But, it's often necessary to move to the next level." When God says, "Time's up," we can trust that He knows what's best for us.

PRAYER AND INTERCESSION: A DYNAMIC DUO

Make this your common practice: Confess your sins to each other and pray for each other so that you can live together whole and healed. The prayer of a person living right with God is something powerful to be reckoned with. Elijah, for instance, human just like us, prayed hard that it wouldn't rain, and it didn't—not a drop for three and a half years. Then he prayed that it would rain, and it did. The showers came, and everything started growing again. (James 5:16-18, MSG)

My friend had given me a new notebook to keep sermon notes in because my other one was full. I always staple a copy of my prayer list to the front of my notebooks to keep it readily at hand. As I was retyping and updating the list, I thanked God for the items that could be crossed off: a sick child who was healed, a relationship that was restored, a new job, new members added to the Kingdom, and so forth.

    The list reminded me that Christians have two of the most powerful tools ever invented—prayer and intercession! Yet, they are often two of the least used. Prayer and intercession are such wonderful things that take so little effort. You can do it anywhere at any time. You can speak out loud or whisper in your spirit. You can do it with your eyes open or shut. You can do it sitting, standing, or kneeling. You can do it without knowing all the details. You can do a quick "God bless" or a more prolonged session. You don't even have to be eloquent or use correct grammar! It's so simple, yet so powerful.

"And whatever things you ask in prayer,
believing, you will receive."
(Matthew 21:22, NKJV)

SEEK AND FIND

Now God gives us many kinds of special abilities, but it is the same Holy Spirit who is the source of them all. There are different kinds of service to God, but it is the same Lord we are serving. There are many ways in which God works in our lives, but it is the same God who does the work in and through all of us who are his. The Holy Spirit displays God's power through each of us as a means of helping the entire church. (1 Corinthians 12:4-7, TLB)

For years, we've heard about finding our purpose, which is undoubtedly beneficial to the Kingdom. The challenge comes when the purpose isn't clear, and people become frustrated. My suggestion would be to do something on the way to finding your purpose.

I thought my passion for cooking was tied to my purpose, but it isn't. It's just something I enjoy. While I was pursuing culinary school and enhancing my cooking skills, I discovered my real purpose and passion—explaining the Word of God in an easy to understand way via teaching and writing. When I was newly saved, I used the *Living Bible* as my study guide. The result was that I learned to paraphrase the Bible. I didn't know at the time that God would use that specific learning method to help His people. Words are my purpose. Writing and helping other Christians with their work are my passion. Once I discovered my mission, I focused my attention on that area.

The other thing I discovered is a passion for everyone coming into the Kingdom. Of course, we're instructed to spread the Good News, and some do it better than others. There are so many ways to spread the Word; I do it primarily through writing. My point is not to use an unclear purpose as an excuse to do nothing. While waiting, why not increase your prayer life, witness more, and focus attention on spreading the Gospel to a lost world?

Lord, thank You, we're not all called to do the same thing. Help us to find our place and pursue the purpose You've designed for us.

SAVED . . . AGAIN!

But me he caught—reached all the way from sky to sea; he pulled me out of that ocean of hate, that enemy chaos the void in which I was drowning. They hit me when I was down, but GOD stuck by me. He stood me up on a wide-open field. I stood there saved—surprised to be loved! (2 Samuel 22:17-20, MSG)

We don't realize how many times God saves us. Oh, sure, those who claim the name of Jesus know that we're saved from sin when we accept Jesus Christ as Lord and Savior. But, I'm thinking specifically of those times when God steps in, and we didn't even realize we were in danger! Or, the times we jump ahead of God and end up in a precarious situation that we can't get out of on our own. Or, the times we get impatient, not knowing that God is rearranging events that would have devastating results.

Think a moment of the situations that had a reversed outcome only because God stepped in to save us. Perhaps you should be in jail or a hospital or a grave. Maybe your child should have been suspended or expelled because of interacting with peers who didn't have their best interest at heart. Conceivably, you could be married to a spouse who enjoys physically, mentally, or emotionally abusing you. These are just a few examples of what *could* have happened if God hadn't stepped in to save us because He loves us. Why not take a moment to give God praise for what didn't happen?

With all my heart I praise the LORD, and with all that I am
I praise his holy name!
With all my heart, I praise the LORD!
I will never forget how kind he has been.
(Psalm 103:1-2, CEV)

ONLY GOD KNOWS

Then as he lay and slept under a broom tree, suddenly an angel touched him, and said to him, "Arise and eat." Then he looked, and there by his head was a cake baked on coals, and a jar of water. So he ate and drank, and lay down again. And the angel of the LORD came back the second time, and touched him, and said, "Arise and eat, because the journey is too great for you." So he arose, and ate and drank; and he went in the strength of that food forty days and forty nights as far as Horeb, the mountain of God. (1 Kings 19:5-8, NKJV)

God had just shown Himself in a miraculous way by destroying all the prophets of Baal by fire. When Ahab's wife, Jezebel, heard of it, she vowed to do the same to Elijah. He left Mount Carmel and ended up in the wilderness. He sat under a tree, prayed that he might die, and fell asleep (1 Kings 18:20-40; 19:1-4).

God calls us to rest for a reason. In Elijah's case, he had expended so much energy dealing with the prophets that he became depressed when Jezebel issued her threat. God knew he was tired, so He allowed him to sleep, eat, and sleep again. There are benefits to getting the proper amount of rest. It allows us to recharge, renew, and re-energize ourselves for what's ahead. Elijah ran on in the strength of rest and food for 40 days!

Only God knows what the next 40 days hold for you. It may be a project at work that gets accelerated. It may be a diagnosis from a loved one that may require your time and energy. It may be the beginning of a new relationship that absorbs your attention. God calls us to rest because He alone knows what's coming. Stop resisting and follow God's lead.

"When your soul is resting, your emotions are okay, your mind is okay, and your will is at peace with God, not resisting what He's doing."
—Joyce Meyer

IT'S NEVER-ENDING

LORD, help me learn your ways. Show me how you want me to live. Guide me and teach me your truths. You are my God, my Savior. You are the one I have been waiting for. (Psalm 25:4-5, ERV)

When I returned to college at the age of 40, a very young person made what he considered an astute observation: "You're too old for school!" His mother shushed him, but I assured her I wasn't offended. The child's statement provided an opportunity for me to explain to him that one is never too old to learn and that as the saying goes, we should "learn something new every day." I obtained a promise from him that he would never forget that learning is fun. Some lessons are more fun than others, but we can gain something from every experience.

You don't have to go to college to gain an understanding of God. Regardless of your age, if you allow God to become your professor, your level of education will far surpass the achievements of those with the most initials behind their name.

Do you realize that if you live to be 1,000 years old, you won't even touch the surface of God's knowledge? That's incredible!

Lord, thank You for being willing to allow us to
tap into Your knowledge. When we allow You
to guide and teach, we become more like the
image of Your Son, Jesus Christ.

FATHER KNOWS BEST

Trust GOD from the bottom of your heart; don't try to figure out everything on your own. Listen for GOD's voice in everything you do, everywhere you go; he's the one who will keep you on track. Don't assume that you know it all. (Proverbs 3:5-7[a], MSG)

I think if you were to look back over your life, you would agree that there have been moments when you clearly didn't know what you were doing and did it anyway. We don't often like delays, denials, or disappointments, but they are usually for our good.

This year why not commit to following Solomon's advice and save yourself a headache or two. When we surrender our lives to Jesus, we're giving Him permission to control our lives. . . to tell us where to go and when; what to do and how to do it. Is it possible to have two people in control? Yes, but only if you want to drive yourself and everybody else crazy! It's not easy for humans to surrender our will; if it were, then everyone would do it. It takes love and discipline; discipline and love. But, when you experience the euphoric response of being in God's will, you'll always want to be there.

> The safest place in the whole wide world,
> is in the will of God.
> Trials may come, great and small,
> just stay in the will of God.
> Come what may, from day to day.
> Keep the faith and be still.
> It remains to be seen what God will do,
> for the one who submits to His will.
> *It Remains to be Seen,* David Curry. 1993.

RELAX, TAKE A BREAK

Cast your burden on the LORD, And He shall sustain you; He shall never permit the righteous to be moved. (Psalm 55:22, NKJV)

Most adults have a lot of responsibility and sometimes you just get tired of having to deal with it all. I know I do. There are times when I get fed up and want to throw up my hands and walk away from everything. I know that's not realistic, but it's nice to imagine being unencumbered for a few moments. In those times—which don't happen often—I give myself a break and have an impromptu one-on-one with God. I immediately feel better and am then ready to get back in the race.

Trust in Him at all times, you people;
Pour out your heart before Him;
God is a refuge for us. Selah.
(Psalm 62:8, NKJV)

IT'S ALL A MATTER OF PERSPECTIVE

The LORD delights in those who fear him, who put their hope in his unfailing love. (Psalm 147:11, NIV)

One of my friends pointed out that whenever she asks about my son, I start smiling. I didn't realize I did that, but it makes sense. My son is one of my all-time favorite people in the world, so why wouldn't I smile? When he was growing up, there were moments I wasn't pleased with his actions; however, that didn't negate the fact that he is my son and I love him. See, it's all a matter of how you want to look at things.

I thought about this in connection to our relationship with God. When someone asks about God, do you start smiling, thinking of His goodness, or frowning, thinking of all the things you believe He hasn't done for you? All of us have unanswered prayers. We can choose to stay stuck on what God hasn't done, or we can focus on God's unfailing love, mercy, faithfulness, and goodness. When we do that, we then realize that if God hasn't moved yet, it must be because He knows more than we do about the situation.

Lord God, help us to reign in our impatience.
Help us to focus on what we have
instead of what we don't.

AIN'T TOO PROUD TO BEG

And Christ did die for all of us. He died so we would no longer live for ourselves, but for the one who died and was raised to life for us. We are careful not to judge people by what they seem to be, though we once judged Christ in that way. Anyone who belongs to Christ is a new person. The past is forgotten, and everything is new. God has done it all! He sent Christ to make peace between himself and us, and he has given us the work of making peace between himself and others. What we mean is that God was in Christ, offering peace and forgiveness to the people of this world. And he has given us the work of sharing his message about peace. We were sent to speak for Christ, and God is begging you to listen to our message. We speak for Christ and sincerely ask you to make peace with God. (2 Corinthians 5:15-20, CEV)

Have you ever wanted something for someone so badly that you were willing to do whatever was necessary? Have you ever loved someone enough to put your pride aside and beg on their behalf? Have you ever wanted something for someone enough to make a nuisance of yourself with whoever had what they needed? Have you ever loved someone so much that you didn't want them lost forever?

If you answered "Yes" to any of the above questions, you're well-qualified for the position of Minister of Reconciliation. You won't get a robe, collar, position, or salary. What you will get is the satisfaction of being in God's will. You may not be able to physically reach everyone in need, but you have the power of prayer to intercede—beg—on their behalf and to stand in the gap for them. The people you are trying to reach are the seekers (as one of the ministers of my church calls them). They are the lost and the uncovered; they don't know what they're seeking, but we do. We alone have the answers to their questions, and it's our responsibility to share.

Lord, help me not to neglect my assignment as a
minister of reconciliation. Help me to share the
Good News with those who need to hear it. When I can't physically touch
someone, remind me to lift them before You in prayer.

I THANK GOD FOR YOU

Every time you cross my mind, I break out in exclamations of thanks to God. Each exclamation is a trigger to prayer. I find myself praying for you with a glad heart. I am so pleased that you have continued on in this with us, believing and proclaiming God's Message, from the day you heard it right up to the present. There has never been the slightest doubt in my mind that the God who started this great work in you would keep at it and bring it to a flourishing finish on the very day Christ Jesus appears. (Philippians 1:3-6, MSG)

God has already ordained everything that will happen to us, including the people who will touch our lives. Do you ever thank God for the people He places in your life?

Where would you be without some of the people who poured faith, favor, and love into your life? Where would you be without your parents, who instilled values into you as a child that you still maintain, even in adulthood? Where would you be without your pastor, who labors to bring a Word from God week in and week out? What about your family, who puts up with you, encourages you, supports you and, yes, occasionally disagrees with you? And, of course, there are those secondary people who touch us daily: The bus driver who drives us safely from point A to point B; the mechanic who repairs our car; or the person who cuts our grass and shovels our snow.

Everyone who comes into your life is instrumental in making you the person God wants you to be. Don't forget to thank God for them.

Lord, I pause now to say thank You for everyone
You have sent into my life. Some were assigned
to me for only brief moments in time; others
will be with me until the end. Either way,
I bless You for sending them my way.

AN IDEAL MATCH

When David was settled in his palace, he summoned Nathan the prophet. "Look," David said, "I am living in a beautiful cedar palace, but the Ark of the LORD's Covenant is out there under a tent!" Nathan replied to David, "Do whatever you have in mind, for God is with you." But that same night God said to Nathan, "Go and tell my servant David, 'This is what the LORD has declared: You are not the one to build a house for me to live in.'" . . .Then David said, "This will be the location for the Temple of the LORD God and the place of the altar for Israel's burnt offerings!" David said, "My son Solomon is still young and inexperienced. And since the Temple to be built for the LORD must be a magnificent structure, famous and glorious throughout the world, I will begin making preparations for it now." So David collected vast amounts of building materials before his death. (1 Chronicles 17:1-4; 22:5, NLT)

John Stockton, a retired NBA point guard, holds the record for the most assists: 15,806! That's amazing! An assist means that you're responsible for getting the ball into the hands of the person who can make the basket. It requires skill and unselfishness.

Stockton spent 19 seasons with the Utah Jazz where he and Karl "The Mailman" Malone became what www.NBA.com refers to as "The most consistently productive guard-forward combination" during the 18 seasons they played together. To assist effectively requires a willingness to make the other person look good and shine. John Stockton did that very well.

Likewise, David did the same for his son, Solomon. When David's desire to build the temple was denied, he turned his attention to making sure Solomon had everything he would need to complete the project. David may have been hurt that God didn't allow him to do it, but instead of pouting, he got busy. Assisting means we set the stage for someone else's success. Who can you support today?

"No one is useless in this world who lightens the burdens of another."
—Charles Dickens

THE POWER OF COMMITMENT

"Is there no one still alive from the house of Saul to whom I can show God's kindness?" Ziba answered the king, "There is still a son of Jonathan; he is lame in both feet." "Where is he?" the king asked. Ziba answered, "He is at the house of Makir son of Ammiel in Lo Debar." So King David had him brought from Lo Debar. . . Mephibosheth . . . bowed down to pay him honor. David said, "Mephibosheth!" "At your service," he replied. "Don't be afraid," David said to him, "for I will surely show you kindness for the sake of your father Jonathan. I will restore to you all the land that belonged to your grandfather Saul, and you will always eat at my table". . . So Mephibosheth ate at David's table like one of the king's sons. (2 Samuel 9:3-7, 11[a], NIV)

None of us know when the end of a relationship will occur. Sometimes it happens through death or distance. Sometimes it happens because priorities and people change.

David and Jonathan demonstrate what brotherly love and commitment look like. As young men they anticipated having a long friendship; unfortunately, Jonathan and his father, Saul, were killed at Mount Gilboa (1 Samuel 31:1-8). When Jonathan's son's nurse heard of the deaths, she sought to protect the five-year-old Mephibosheth. In her haste, she tripped and as a result Mephibosheth was lame in both feet. The nurse and the boy found refuge in Lo Debar, which is where David found him. David honored his friendship with Jonathan by restoring Mephibosheth to his rightful place, remembering the covenant he and Jonathan had made: "At last," Jonathan said to David, "Go in peace, for we have sworn loyalty to each other in the LORD's name. The LORD is the witness of a bond between us and our children forever" (1 Samuel 20:42, NLT).

Jesus, like David, is ready to restore us to our rightful
place in Him. And, like Mephibosheth,
all we need do is accept the invitation.

OKAY, I'M OFFICIALLY AMAZED

Jesus said, "Would you give me a drink of water?" . . . The Samaritan woman. . . asked, "How come you, a Jew, are asking me, a Samaritan woman, for a drink?". . . Jesus answered, "If you knew the generosity of God and who I am, you would be asking me for a drink, and I would give you fresh, living water." The woman said, "Sir, you don't even have a bucket to draw with, and this well is deep. So how are you going to get this 'living water'? . . .Jesus said, "Everyone who drinks this water will get thirsty again and again. Anyone who drinks the water I give will never thirst—not ever. The water I give will be an artesian spring within, gushing fountains of endless life." The woman said, "Sir, give me this water so I won't ever get thirsty, won't ever have to come back to this well again!" He said, "Go call your husband and then come back." "I have no husband," she said. "That's nicely put: 'I have no husband.' You've had five husbands, and the man you're living with now isn't even your husband. You spoke the truth there, sure enough." (John 4:7, 9-11, 13-18, MSG)

When this unnamed woman went to the well, the last thing she expected was for her life to be transformed. Yet, God knew it was time for her to change. She was ostracized by the women of the community because of her loose living. She didn't need them to tell her she was better than what she had become, but she had gotten stuck in the cycle of going from man to man. She had plenty of internal dialogues with herself about her lifestyle, and her unspoken questions were answered the day she met Jesus.

Jesus and the woman continued their dialogue, and every word was another revelation more astonishing than the previous one. When Jesus told her that whoever worships God must do so in spirit and in truth, she said, "I don't know about that. I do know that the Messiah is coming. When he arrives, we'll get the whole story." "I am he," said Jesus. "You don't have to wait any longer or look any further" (John 4:25-26, MSG).

Lord, I thank You for revealing Yourself to me and allowing me to become part of the Kingdom. That is truly amazing!

SEE, WHAT HAD HAPPENED WAS

"Go and get your husband," Jesus told her. "I don't have a husband," the woman replied. (John 4:16-17, NLT)

I admire the Samaritan woman because she accepted the truth about herself and her situation. Isn't it irritating to talk with someone who has a revisionist view of the circumstances of their life? Sure, some things happen that we have no control over. But, there are a lot of things that occur when we are in full control. Those are the times we can't blame anyone else.

The Samaritan woman liked (loved?) men. That was a weakness. She had been married five times and was presently living with a man who wasn't her husband. She may have been one of those women more comfortable with men than women, so being ostracized by the women of the community may not have been that big of a deal for her. However, she was honest in her assessment of herself; she didn't make excuses. When Jesus met her at the well, and they began talking, she willingly responded to His request for her husband. That alone is significant because most people are reluctant to show themselves in an unfavorable light.

God knows everything about us. Why not be honest with yourself about anything that's hindering you from moving forward? God wants us healthy and whole. We can't do that if we're in denial. Take a page from the Samaritan woman and boldly profess the truth to God. You'll be astonished at His response.

The Lord hates lying lips,
but those who speak the truth are His joy.
(Proverbs 12:22, NLV)

COME, SEE A MAN

Just then his disciples came back. They were shocked. They couldn't believe he was talking with that kind of a woman. No one said what they were all thinking, but their faces showed it. The woman took the hint and left. In her confusion she left her water pot. Back in the village she told the people, "Come see a man who knew all about the things I did, who knows me inside and out. Do you think this could be the Messiah?" And they went out to see for themselves. (John 4:27-30, MSG)

This woman could have taught a class on witnessing. She heard and received the message of salvation. She knew it needed to be shared. And, she knew the women of the village probably wouldn't listen to anything she had to say. However, she also knew something about the male psyche, so that's who she approached. The men listened to her and then followed her (which may further explain why the women didn't like her), so she had to have been convincing in her statements.

"Many of the Samaritans from that village committed themselves to him because of the woman's witness: 'He knew all about the things I did. He knows me inside and out!' They asked him to stay on, so Jesus stayed two days. A lot more people entrusted their lives to him when they heard what he had to say" (John 4:39-41, MSG).

It doesn't matter who you share with or why they decide to at least listen to what you're saying. We need to invite people to experience Jesus for themselves, so they will say, "We're no longer taking this on your say-so. We've heard it for ourselves and know it for sure. He's the Savior of the world!" (John 4:42, MSG).

Lord, help me recognize who is receptive to the
message of salvation, and then give me
boldness to share what I know.

YOU NEVER KNOW WHAT WILL HAPPEN

There was a relative of Naomi's husband, a man of great wealth, of the family of Elimelech. His name was Boaz. So Ruth the Moabitess said to Naomi, "Please let me go to the field, and glean heads of grain after him in whose sight I may find favor." And she said to her, "Go, my daughter." Then she left and went and gleaned in the field after the reapers. And she happened to come to the part of the field belonging to Boaz, who was of the family of Elimelech. (Ruth 2:1-3, NKJV)

I have a maintenance man who has loved my house since the first day he came to do a job. He immediately offered to buy it, although it is not for sale. Because of his fondness for the house he believes will be his if or when I ever sell it, he treats it as though it's already his. He takes pride in the work he does to ensure that the work is done correctly and will hold up as well. He has no way of knowing if I'll ever sell, nor does he know if my son or niece would want the house, but he acts as if he already owns it.

Ruth was a widow who needed income. She went to work in a field that happened to belong to a kinsman redeemer, although she didn't know it at the time. Nor did she know she'd eventually own the field. She worked to the best of her ability and treated the field as if it were her own. She did her job and reaped not only the immediate blessing of having enough to eat but a long-term blessing in being in the lineage of our Lord, Jesus Christ!

My point is to treat everything as if you own it. The job you go to daily may become the first business you own. The house you perform maintenance on may become yours. The car you detail at the shop may be the first of many in a fleet.

In all the work you are given, do the best you can.
Work as though you are working for the Lord, not any earthly master.
(Colossians 3:23, ERV)

TIT FOR TAT

"Give, and it will be given to you: good measure, pressed down, shaken together, and running over will be put into your bosom. For with the same measure that you use, it will be measured back to you." (Luke 6:38, NKJV)

We think of today's Scripture as concerning money only. I believe that is doing a disservice to the text. Giving doesn't just involve money. It includes giving of your time, talent, *and* treasure. We are giving when we take time to talk with someone in need of conversation; or when we use the gifts God has given us to make someone's day brighter; and yes, even when we provide money for a meal for someone who cannot return the favor.

While we shouldn't give to get, the actuality is that none of us will leave this world without needing assistance from someone at some point for something. Keep that in mind the next time your life is interrupted by someone else's need. Instead of getting frustrated or irritated, thank God for putting you in the right place at the right time.

And the King will answer and say to them, "Assuredly, I say to you, inasmuch as you did it to one of the least of these My brethren, you did it to Me." (Matthew 25:40, NKJV)

IT'S ALREADY ALRIGHT!

Then he said to Gehazi his servant, "Call this Shunammite woman." When he had called her, she stood before him. And he said to him, "Say now to her, 'Look, you have been concerned for us with all this care. What can I do for you?'" . . . She answered, "I dwell among my own people." So he said, "What then is to be done for her?" And Gehazi answered, "Actually, she has no son, and her husband is old." So he said, "Call her." When he had called her, she stood in the doorway. Then he said, "About this time next year you shall embrace a son." . . . the woman conceived, and bore a son when the appointed time had come, of which Elisha had told her. And the child grew. Now it happened one day that he went out to his father, to the reapers. And he said to his father, "My head, my head!" So he said to a servant, "Carry him to his mother." When he had taken him and brought him to his mother, he sat on her knees till noon, and then died. And she went up and laid him on the bed of the man of God, shut the door upon him, and went out. Then she called to her husband, and said, "Please send me one of the young men and one of the donkeys, that I may run to the man of God and come back." So he said, "Why are you going to him today? It is neither the New Moon nor the Sabbath." And she said, "It is well." (2 Kings 4:12-23, NKJV)

The only song I remember my mother ever singing or humming was *It Is Well*, which I thought was such a drab, slow song. I didn't understand what the words meant and especially what they meant to my mother.

When I got saved and started attending church, within the first week or so, the congregation sang this song. I hadn't thought of it in a long time, but still considered it to be a dull, drab song. However, as time passed, and I went through some things that only God could have brought me out of, I began to realize there is a lot of truth to the lyrics. I finally understood why my mother hummed or sang it all the time. I only wish she was here; I would tell her I've finally got it.

> When peace, like a river, attendeth my way,
> When sorrows like sea billows roll;
> Whatever my lot, thou has taught me to say,
> It is well, it is well, with my soul.
> *It Is Well*. Horatio P. Spafford. 1873.

NEVER ALONE

"I will not leave you comfortless: I will come to you." (John 14:18, KJV)

God has been good to me, and there's nothing I lack. However, that doesn't mean there aren't situations I wish were different, and I confess there is only one thing I envy other people. Envy is one of the emotions that can be either constructive or destructive; it's destructive when it pushes one to the brink of violence and constructive when it drives us to count our blessings.

According to dictionary.com, *envy* is "a feeling of discontent or covetousness with regard to another's advantages, success, possessions, etc." What I envy is directly related to parents and grandparents, of which I have neither, and it saddens me. Technically, I'm an orphan even though I am of retirement age. Each loss created a void in my heart. Before salvation, the vacuum was filled with a variety of things to ease the pain. I didn't realize at the time that the efforts to seek other avenues only resulted in more pain. However, one of the best revelations I received after salvation was the knowledge that if I allowed, God would fill the void in unimaginable ways.

Despite missing those who may no longer physically be in our lives, we are never alone. Today's Scripture tells us so. It, therefore, can become our new reality when we personalize the Scripture. I know God will wrap His arms around us, dry our tears, and not only fill the void but flood the void with His love. He doesn't erase the memories of long-gone loved ones; He helps us remember them better.

Lord God, we thank You for being willing and able to fill the voids in our lives. Help us to turn to You for comfort and not fall into the trap of self-medicating with things that in the end will cause more harm than good.

THREE DAYS IN THE DARK

Meanwhile, Saul was uttering threats with every breath and was eager to kill the Lord's followers. . . .As he was approaching Damascus on this mission, a light from heaven suddenly shone down around him. He fell to the ground and heard a voice saying to him, "Saul! Saul! Why are you persecuting me?" "Who are you, lord?" Saul asked. And the voice replied, "I am Jesus, the one you are persecuting! Now get up and go into the city, and you will be told what you must do." The men with Saul stood speechless, for they heard the sound of someone's voice but saw no one! Saul picked himself up off the ground, but when he opened his eyes he was blind. So his companions led him by the hand to Damascus. He remained there blind for three days and did not eat or drink. (Acts 9:1, 3-9, NLT)

I believe there are times God gives us spiritual blindness because we're not ready for the next phase of our journey. When He opens our eyes, allowing us to see what was previously hidden, God wants us to apply our new insight to bring about change. Sometimes He teaches us how to respond to an area of lack in our life. Other times, He teaches us the actions necessary to correct an injustice in our community.

When Jesus opened Saul's eyes, he not only had a new name—Paul—but an exciting new assignment that would reach people throughout future generations. I think Paul would agree, the prize was worth the price of being blind for three days.

Saul stayed with the believers in Damascus for a few days. And immediately he began preaching about Jesus in the synagogues, saying, "He is indeed the Son of God!" (Acts 9:20, NLT)

STOP IN THE NAME OF LOVE

And David arose and went with all the people . . . to bring up from there the ark of God, whose name is called by the Name, the LORD of Hosts, who dwells between the cherubim. So they set the ark of God on a new cart, and brought it out of the house of Abinadab, which was on the hill. . . Then David and all the house of Israel played music before the LORD on all kinds of instruments . . . So David went and brought up the ark of God from the house of Obed-Edom to the City of David with gladness. And so it was, when those bearing the ark of the LORD had gone six paces, that he sacrificed oxen and fatted sheep. . . So David and all the house of Israel brought up the ark of the LORD with shouting and with the sound of the trumpet. (2 Samuel 6:2-4[a], 5, 12[b]-13, 15, NKJV)

If you have ever experienced one of God's do-overs, you'll appreciate David's actions. The first time he went to get the ark he did everything wrong. He didn't consult with God (1 Chronicles 13:1-3), which ultimately resulted in the death of Uzzah. He put the ark on a new cart in direct violation of God's specific command that the ark was to be carried by Levites of the family of Kohath (Numbers 4:15). And, he thought that good intentions would cause God to overlook his disobedience. David loved God and God loved him in return, but God is a God of order. David evidently forgot that.

When David went to get the ark the second time, he did everything according to custom. Is it any wonder that after taking six steps, David had to stop to offer a sacrifice and then start dancing?

When you remember what God has done, how He delivered you out of a particularly difficult situation, how He healed your body, restored your finances, saved your family . . . love will make you stop and give God praise.

Love GOD, your GOD, with your whole heart: love him with all that's in you, love him with all you've got! (Deuteronomy 6:5, MSG)

SHUT UP!

The rabble with them began to crave other food, and again the Israelites started wailing and said, "If only we had meat to eat! We remember the fish we ate in Egypt at no cost—also the cucumbers, melons, leeks, onions and garlic. But now we have lost our appetite; we never see anything but this manna!" Moses heard the people of every family wailing at the entrance to their tents. The LORD became exceedingly angry, and Moses was troubled. (Numbers 11:4-6, 10, NIV)

We don't often like to use the term "shut up" because it implies a level of disrespect. We prefer to say something more politically correct like, "please stop talking" or "be quiet." But, there are times when you just need to emphatically get to the point and what better way than to say, "Shut Up!"

The children of Israel were complaining—again—and wanted to go back to what they knew. We sometimes revise history to make things seem better than they were. The fact of the matter is that while they may have had a more varied diet, they were slaves! What about you?

Yes, gas is high, but you used to ride the bus. You had to wait for the bus in inclement weather, suffer too many people (some who hadn't bathed in a while), sit crammed into a seat or stand shoulder-to-shoulder, and deal with a bus driver who may have been having a bad day.

Yes, your house needs repairs, but you used to live in an apartment where nothing got fixed, the walls were too thin, the rent was too high, you couldn't find a parking space, and the neighbors were too loud.

Yes, your co-workers may work every nerve you have, but you used to be unemployed without any benefits. Or, you had to wait until the first of the month for your welfare card to be reloaded.

The next time you're inclined to complain, review your history. And, with all due respect, shut up!

> "What you're supposed to do when you don't like a thing is change it. If you
> can't change it, change the way you think about it. Don't complain."
> Wouldn't Take Nothing for My Journey Now. Maya Angelou. 1993.

THE PROMISE

"Behold, I am with you and will keep you wherever you go and will bring you back to this land; for I will not leave you until I have done what I have spoken to you." (Genesis 28:15, NKJV)

There are times I explicitly remember the dreams I have during sleep. Other times, I only remember bits and pieces. Either way, I write down what I can recall.

Jacob left Beersheba going toward Haran. When the sun set, he laid his head on a rock and went to sleep. He experienced a dream of watching angels ascending and descending a ladder between heaven and earth (vv.10-12). God spoke to Jacob, repeating the promise He had given to his ancestors: "I am the LORD God of Abraham your father and the God of Isaac; the land on which you lie I will give to you and your descendants. Also, your descendants shall be as the dust of the earth; you shall spread abroad to the west and the east, to the north and the south; and in you and in your seed all the families of the earth shall be blessed" (vv.13-14). Jacob awoke, recognizing the awesomeness of God. He placed a memorial stone on the spot and changed the name of the city from Luz to Bethel (vv. 16-19).

It's been said that we can take a promise from God to the bank; meaning, we can trust what He has said. I believe we can do better (after all, banks can fail and then what do you have?). God's Word can stand on its own. The only place we need to take it is into our hearts.

For all the promises of God in Him are Yes, and in Him Amen, to the glory of God through us. (2 Corinthians 1:20, NKJV)

ISN'T THAT SO AND SO?

And they said, "Is not this Jesus, the son of Joseph, whose father and mother we know? How is it then that He says, 'I have come down from heaven?'" (John 6:42, NKJV)

Have you encountered an acquaintance you haven't seen in a while and started catching up? The problem with running into people from our past is that they want us to be the same person they used to know. That's impossible. Like water flowing down a river, we are constantly evolving as we encounter various challenges, obstacles, mountains, and valleys.

After Jesus fed the 5,000 (John 6:1-15), He and His disciples left the area. The crowd followed and then began to play a game of "Twenty Questions." Unfortunately, they didn't like the answers Jesus gave, including telling them, "I am the bread of life. He who comes to me will never go hungry, and he who believes in me will never be thirsty" (John 6:35, NIV) and ". . . I have come down from heaven not to do my will but to do the will of him who sent me" (John 6:38, NIV). The crowd was enraged at His responses and began to grumble, "Ain't that Joseph and Mary's boy? What's He talking about coming down from heaven and being bread of life? He's lost His mind!" (my paraphrase).

Whenever you bump into people who believe that knowing something about your past entitles them to predict your future, just remember how Jesus handled the naysayers. He never argued or debated. Jesus simply walked in the anointing of who He is, and you can, too. You're a child of God. It doesn't matter what you may have done or what you may have been. Once you come to Jesus, you're forgiven; the slate is wiped clean, and you can begin to walk in newness of life.

God, Your eraser is bigger than any human's finite mind to try to dredge up all we used to do or be. When people want to start the "isn't that so and so" conversation, we don't have to be ashamed of what was, because ". . . if anyone is in Christ, he is a new creation; old things have passed away; behold, all things have become new." (2 Corinthians 5:17, NKJV)

REVIVED!

My flesh and my heart may fail, but God is the strength of my heart and my portion forever. (Psalm 73:26, ESV)

On the days when it feels like the world is on top of you instead of the other way around, remember today's Scripture. It will energize you and provide strength to run on a little while longer as you let God's strength become yours.

Seek the LORD and his strength;
seek his presence continually!
(1 Chronicles 16:11, ESV)

WHO KNEW?

One of the two who heard John speak, and followed Him, was Andrew, Simon Peter's brother. He first found his own brother Simon, and said to him, "We have found the Messiah" (which is translated, the Christ). And he brought him to Jesus. (John 1:40-42, NKJV)

Have you ever wondered what becomes of the people you witness to? The Bible tells us that some plant, some water, but God gets the increase (1 Corinthians 3:6). This means we may not all "see" the benefits of our witnessing; yet, we believe by faith that the seed planted will eventually bear fruit.

The apostle Andrew has the distinction of being the first disciple to accept John the Baptist's statement about the Messiah: The next day John saw Jesus coming toward him, and said, "Behold! The Lamb of God who takes away the sin of the world! This is He of whom I said, 'After me comes a Man who is preferred before me, for He was before me.' I did not know Him; but that He should be revealed to Israel, therefore I came baptizing with water" (John 1:29-31, NKJV). Instead of keeping the Good News to himself, Andrew immediately found his brother, Peter, and unknowingly set in motion a strategic event that would turn the world upside down.

Andrew wasn't jealous of his brother being part of Jesus' inner circle. He could have stomped his foot, had a temper tantrum, and reminded Jesus that he was there first. He could have pointed out that his brother was a hot-head with a bad temper. He could have shared the secrets that only siblings know to make Peter look bad. But, no, Andrew chose to share Jesus with his brother and then stepped out of the way.

We may never know how many people have come to know Christ because of our actions, and that's okay. We only need to tell everyone we encounter, "Come meet a man," and then get out of the way, so God can work. You never know what may become of those we introduce to Christ. They may be the next one to turn the world upside down.

God, help me to be mindful that sharing the Good News of
Jesus Christ is never about me.

NAME-DROPPER

Now Peter and John went up together to the temple at the hour of prayer, the ninth hour. And a certain man lame from his mother's womb was carried, whom they laid daily at the gate of the temple which is called Beautiful, to ask alms from those who entered the temple; who, seeing Peter and John about to go into the temple, asked for alms. And fixing his eyes on him, with John, Peter said, "Look at us." So he gave them his attention, expecting to receive something from them. Then Peter said, "Silver and gold I do not have, but what I do have I give you: In the name of Jesus Christ of Nazareth, rise up and walk." And he took him by the right hand and lifted him up, and immediately his feet and ankle bones received strength. (Acts 3:1-7, NKJV)

I am not impressed when people name-drop because most of the time they don't know the person, only their name. Plus, even if they know the person, that doesn't necessarily mean it will be helpful to me. Aren't you glad that God has allowed you to join in a relationship where you can both use the name and know the name of the One who is above all?

When the man at the gate in today's Scripture met Peter and John, he thought he'd get another handout. That was his typical routine—get up, get taken to the gate, beg all day, get taken home, get in bed, go to sleep, get up the next morning, and start the routine all over again. However, God decided that the routine had gone on long enough. That day, the beggar unknowingly approached the right two people and thought he'd get money; what he got was so much more and was precisely what he needed. Instead of receiving a hand-out, he received a hand-up! Peter dropped the Name that could change this man's situation; and to ensure there was no confusion as to whom he was talking about, Peter used the full name—Jesus Christ of Nazareth!

Help us, Lord, to drop Your name everywhere we go.
You're the only One who can turn situations around.

YOU HAVE TO ANSWER FOR SONNY

"If My people who are called by My name put away their pride and pray, and look for My face, and turn from their sinful ways, then I will hear from heaven. I will forgive their sin and will heal their land." (2 Chronicles 7:14, NLV)

In the 1972 mega-hit movie, *The Godfather,* the fictitious Carlo Rizzi sets up Santino "Sonny" Corleone to be killed. He thinks he's gotten away with it until Sonny's brother, Michael, pays him a visit. Carlo is understandably nervous. During his visit with Carlo, Michael tells him that he's known all along that it was he who set Sonny up and it was time to answer for what he did. In other words, it was time to reap what he had sown. Carlo begs for his life; Michael tells him he will be exiled from the family but he's not going to kill him (which is a true statement; someone else does it for him).

America and the world have pushed the envelope so far, I believe, because we think that since God hasn't done anything too drastic in response to our behavior, it's okay to continue acting crazy. There is going to come a time when all of us will have to answer for what we've done, both before and after salvation. However, unlike the crime family portrayed in the movie, which doesn't listen to your excuses or repent of their intentions once a decision has been made, God told us we can change His mind when we sincerely repent as an individual, a nation, and a world.

The LORD is compassionate and merciful, slow to get angry and filled with unfailing love (Psalm 103:8, NLT),
and aren't you glad about that?

A NECESSARY INTERRUPTION

But as the Scriptures say, "No one has ever seen, no one has ever heard, no one has ever imagined what God has prepared for those who love him." (1 Corinthians 2:9, ERV)

I have two confessions: I hate commercials, and I believe the fast forward button on the DVR remote is one of the most phenomenal breakthrough inventions of my lifetime! I very seldom watch anything in real time anymore because of the unnecessary interruptions called commercials. Some last only a few seconds—literally long enough to pause for station identification—while others are over five minutes long! It is irritating because commercials seem to come right when whatever you're watching gets to the good part.

Now, having said that, I'm asking you to pause for a "necessary" interruption. I want you to take a moment and reflect over the last three months of your life. Aren't you amazed at the things you've experienced? If God had told you what was going to happen, you would have missed out on some of the greatest adventures of your life, both good and bad, because you may have attempted to avoid the situation.

When I think back over the past three months, and my life as a whole, today's Scripture is fitting. The things God has allowed me to experience are so far out of the realm of vision, hearing, and imagining that all I can say is Thank You!

God, I will never understand why or how You have chosen to bestow
favor on me. Because of Your unfailing love and mercy and grace,
I will bless Your name forever. I love You!

FRESH START

Rain down, you heavens, from above, And let the skies pour down righteousness; Let the earth open, let them bring forth salvation, And let righteousness spring up together. I, the LORD, have created it. (Isaiah 45:8, NKJV)

When I was a child, we often said, "Rain, rain, go away. Come again another day," because we wanted to be outside playing. Last summer in Columbus, Ohio was one of the rainiest I can remember in a long time. It seemed like it rained five days out of seven, week in and week out. My arthritic knees did not appreciate the wetness, and I found myself thinking of the childhood chant!

One thing I noticed about the rainfall was that once it was over, the air smelled fresh and clean. The grass was greener, the flowers were brighter, and the plants were bigger. So, in the end, the rain was beneficial.

As rain is necessary for the Earth, it is also essential for our spiritual growth. We don't like it when we're saturated with issues and problems; but in the end, we realize it was worth getting wet to move up higher in God.

We know that all things work together for the good of those who love
God—those whom he has called according to his plan.
(Romans 8:28, GWT)

IT'S OKAY TO DO IT AGAIN

"So why do you keep calling me 'Lord, Lord!' when you don't do what I say? I will show you what it's like when someone comes to me, listens to my teaching, and then follows it. It is like a person building a house who digs deep and lays the foundation on solid rock. When the floodwaters rise and break against that house, it stands firm because it is well built. But anyone who hears and doesn't obey is like a person who builds a house right on the ground, without a foundation. When the floods sweep down against that house, it will collapse into a heap of ruins." (Luke 6:46-49, NLT)

If you enjoy HGTV as much as I do, you're accustomed to seeing renovations made on homes that start out barely habitable and end up jaw-dropping fabulous! Sometimes, you'll see where the house is beyond the scope of renovation and must be torn down and rebuilt because the foundation isn't correct.

Just like the houses on HGTV, Christians are also a work in progress. Sometimes we're in the remodeling stage where only a few cosmetic changes are required. Other times we're in the renovation stage where a good makeup job isn't going to cover the damages. Finally, there's the rebuilding stage where we're torn completely down and rebuilt from the ground up. This, I confess, is the most painful stage of our transition; however, it's also the most rewarding. Being rebuilt means you're given another chance to get it right. This is where you stop letting the threat of a storm turn your world upside down. This is where you take a deep breath and allow God to pour a firm foundation so that you'll be able to withstand, survive, and excel through the storms of life. Isn't that what you want? If it is, the Master Carpenter is ready to assist you.

For the Lord your God is a God of loving-pity. He will not leave you or destroy you or forget the agreement He promised to your fathers.
(Deuteronomy 4:31, NLV)

SUSTAINED

Then I heard a loud voice in heaven say, "The victory and the power and the kingdom of our God and the authority of his Messiah have now come. These things have come, because the accuser of our brothers and sisters has been thrown out. He is the one who accused them day and night before our God. (Revelation 12:10, ERV)

I watch mostly dramas on television, especially those that will have courtroom scenes. I enjoy the tension of the shows, realizing that it is a form of fantasy. Most crimes aren't solved in 44 minutes without commercials!

One thing all courtroom scenes have is a time when either the defense attorney or prosecutor asks the witness a question that is inappropriate. The other attorney hollers "Objection!" and the judge decides what happens. He or she will either "overrule" the objection, which means the witness has to answer, or "sustain" the objection, which means the witness *doesn't* have to answer.

Our enemy stands before God day and night accusing us. God knows to ignore him. We, on the other hand, often want to engage in unnecessary conversation with the enemy when he brings something to our remembrance. He's out of order, and we have been authorized to put him in his proper place—the pit from which he came. In other words, when the devil says, "You messed up. God isn't going to forgive you for that one," just say "sustained!" You're not required to respond to anything he says.

"He is the enemy but know that I have given you more power than he has. I have given you power to crush his snakes and scorpions under your feet. Nothing will hurt you." (Luke 10:19, ERV)

OVERRULED!

But keep the Lord Christ holy in your hearts. Always be ready to answer everyone who asks you to explain about the hope you have. But answer them in a gentle way with respect. Keep your conscience clear. Then people will see the good way you live as followers of Christ, and those who say bad things about you will be ashamed of what they said. (1 Peter 3:15-16, ERV)

Yesterday, we looked at why we don't have to respond to the devil's accusations because of the price Christ paid on the cross. We discovered that if during a trial an inappropriate question is asked, the judge will either *sustain*—meaning we don't have to answer—or *overrule*—which means an answer is expected.

When our enemy comes against us, there are times we can ignore him; other times we can't. When in a situation where the judge has overruled the objection, go ahead and answer the question. Tell the devil and his imps and everyone else exactly what God, Jesus Christ, and the Holy Spirit have done for you. Tell how you were snatched from the jaws of Hell; how doors were opened and shut; ways made, bodies healed, and souls saved. Be quick to respond. No one can stop you or take your testimony away.

From my heart to the Heavens,
Jesus be the center.
It's all about You.
Yes, it's all about You.
Jesus at the Center. Israel Houghton, Adam A. Ranney,
and Micah Massey. 2011.

FREE WITH PURCHASE

But he was being punished for what we did. He was crushed because of our guilt. He took the punishment we deserved, and this brought us peace. We were healed because of his pain. (Isaiah 53:5, ERV)

In my Sunday paper there is usually at least one ad promising something "free with purchase," which I personally think is an oxymoron. Anytime there is a price associated, it's not free. Free is free!

I'm not sure who coined the phrase, "The best things in life are free," but the only "thing" I can think of that would successfully fall into this category would be Jesus willingly giving His life for mine. It cost Him everything; it cost me nothing! For that, I am eternally grateful! Thank You, Jesus!

I had a debt I could not pay.
He paid the debt He did not owe.
I needed someone,
To wash my sins away.
And now I sing a brand new song,
"Amazing grace" all day long,
Christ Jesus paid the debt,
That I could never pay.
I Had a Debt I Could Not Pay. Ellis J. Crum. 1982.

WHAT DID GOD SAY?

"That's because I am the LORD, and if I say something will happen, it will happen! I will not wait any longer. Those troubles are coming soon—in your own lifetime. Hear me, you people who always refuse to obey! When I say something, I make it happen." This is what the Lord GOD said. (Ezekiel 12:25, ERV)

Most of us know this story: A child goes to the mother and asks permission to go outside to play. The mom asks, "Have you done your chores?" to which the child gives a half-hearted response. Then the mom says, "Go ask your father." The child goes to the father and asks permission to go outside. The father says, "Did you ask your mother?" The child responds that he did. And, then, the ultimate question: "What did she say?" God is no different.

There are times when God asks us to do something that we're reluctant to do, so we ask other people about it. It doesn't matter what they respond, because God is the one who told you to do it. Just like running from one parent to the other didn't get the child his desired response, our going from person to person won't get us our desire either. When God asks us to do something, He's saying that He trusts our ability to handle the request and be successful at it.

It's humbling to think that the God of the Universe wants to partner with us to get something done! It's a privilege that isn't afforded to everyone. If we look at it in that light, we won't be so quick to try to get out of the assignment.

The one who chose you can be trusted, and
he will do this. (1 Thessalonians 5:24, CEV). *God always finishes what He starts. We need to make sure we can say the same.*

SHAKE IT OFF!

"Whoever does not receive you or does not listen to what you say, as you leave that house or city, shake off the dust from your feet." (Matthew 10:14, NLV)

Jesus was sending out His disciples with clear instructions: "As you go, proclaim this message: 'The kingdom of heaven has come near.' Heal the sick, raise the dead, cleanse those who have leprosy, drive out demons. Freely you have received; freely give" (Matthew 10:7-8, NIV). If they refused, the disciples were to shake the dust off their feet and keep going.

We need to embrace that behavior. There are too many times we hold onto attitudes, thoughts, and people who should have been released a long time ago. It's not healthy or productive. In some ways we're stuck, and because of that we're not growing in the Lord as we should. I know it's easier said than done; sometimes we want to keep what's comfortable even when it makes us miserable. However, keep in mind that anything you're holding onto so tightly prevents God from filling your hands with something new. And, when God gives us something new, it's always something better!

Now I don't know what you think about that or how you feel about it, but as for me, I'll take God's new over my stale any day of the week!

Morning by morning new mercies I see.
All I have needed Thy hand hath provided;
Great is Thy faithfulness, Lord, unto me!
Great Is Thy Faithfulness.
Thomas Chisholm (lyrics)
William M. Runyan (music)
1923. Public Domain.

YOU CAN IF YOU WANT TO

And it happened when He was in a certain city, that behold, a man who was full of leprosy saw Jesus; and he fell on his face and implored Him, saying, "Lord, if You are willing, You can make me clean." Then He put out His hand and touched him, saying, "I am willing; be cleansed." Immediately the leprosy left him. (Luke 5:12-13, NKJV)

The leprous man worded his request in such a way that he put all the pressure on Jesus because he didn't want to be disappointed if Jesus wasn't who he thought Him to be. In that case, he would have his fallback response, "Well, *he* wasn't willing to do it, so that's why *I* wasn't healed." The word "if" denotes uncertainty, as in "I'm not really sure you can do this, but I'm going to ask anyway just in case." But, aren't you glad for Jesus' response: "I am willing!" That is such a wonderful phrase and one Jesus is waiting to give to us when we bring our needs, concerns, and cares to Him.

Hold on, help is on the way.
He said he'd never leave you or forsake you.
Stay strong.
Help is on the way.
He'd said he'd help you.
Just reach out and take his hand.
Help Is on the Way. Michael W. Smith, Christa Black,
Debbie Smith, and Israel Houghton. 2008.

HMM

Your statutes are my heritage forever; they are the joy of my heart. My heart is set on keeping your decrees to the very end. (Psalm 119:111-112, NIV)

I agree with the commentators who believe that David wrote Psalm 119, partly because it sounds too biographical to not have been authored by him. However, Psalm 119:112 brings up an interesting question that I think we should all ponder on a regular basis: If man looks at the outward appearance, but God looks at the heart (1 Samuel 16:7), and the psalmist states his heart is set on keeping God's decrees, then what is your heart set on?

Lord, teach us to rely solely on You so that
You will always be a "lamp for our feet, a light for our path."

A SIMPLE FORM OF COMMUNICATION

This is why I have never stopped praying for you since I heard about you. I ask God that you may know what He wants you to do. I ask God to fill you with the wisdom and understanding the Holy Spirit gives. Then your lives will please the Lord. You will do every kind of good work, and you will know more about God. I pray that God's great power will make you strong, and that you will have joy as you wait and do not give up. I pray that you will be giving thanks to the Father. He has made it so you could share the good things given to those who belong to Christ who are in the light. (Colossians 1:9-12, NLV)

I love to hear people pray. Some prayers are eloquent and paint a masterpiece of what God will do in response. Some are staggered in that the words may not be strung together as eloquently; yet, they're so sincere that you can visualize God stopping to listen. Still, others are put together with so much power and passion; I wish I could pray like that.

In today's Scripture, Paul is praying for the saints at Colossae the same prayer we need *and* must pray for both ourselves and others. His prayer is profound in its simplicity. Verse nine asks that we know what God wants us to do. We could stop right there! Our lives would be less stressful if we only asked God what He wants instead of jumping from thing to thing, project to project, wearing ourselves out. Paul then goes on to pray for God's wisdom, power, and patience to be upon us. He concludes by reminding us to give thanks unto God and not to forget to share God with others.

Prayer doesn't have to be stressful or painful. Prayer is taking advantage of the privilege of speaking directly to the Creator, who is willing to listen, anxious to hear, and eager to respond.

God, in a world filled with people who think they're too important to speak to the "common man," we thank You for allowing us the privilege of communicating with You. While others may pretend to be important, we know who holds the real power! Thank You, Lord!

YOU DON'T HAVE TO BEG

"If your child asks for bread, do you trick him with sawdust? If he asks for fish, do you scare him with a live snake on his plate? As bad as you are, you wouldn't think of such a thing. You're at least decent to your own children. So don't you think the God who conceived you in love will be even better?" (Matthew 7:9-11, MSG)

When you were a child, do you remember begging for something from your parents? Perhaps it was an opportunity to go outside to play after they said no. Or, to get something special to eat after Mom said it would spoil your dinner? Or, to stay up late on a school night because you just "had" to watch something on TV? When our parents said no, they weren't mean; they were responsible. They knew what was best for our well-being even if we didn't like or understand their rationale. And, no matter how dramatic our begging was, their answer didn't change.

God is our parent; He knows what we need and when we need it. And, if it is His desire for us to have something, He'll release it at the appropriate time. The reverse is also true. If what we're asking for isn't in our best interest, God says no. We don't like being denied, but begging won't change God's mind.

We need to learn the difference between "asking" and "begging." God doesn't have a problem with our asking—"Ask, and it shall be given you. . . For everyone that asketh receiveth . . ." (Matthew 7:7-8, KJV). Just as our parents were irritated with our begging, God gets irritated also. Begging implies that we don't trust the original answer or the person who gave it. Let's be careful not to disrespect God by begging for something we aren't ready to handle.

Trust the LORD! Be brave and strong and trust the LORD.
(Psalm 27:14, CEV)

AT THE INTERSECTION OF
MERCY STREET & GRACE BOULEVARD

O LORD, I will honor and praise your name, for you are my God. You do such wonderful things! You planned them long ago, and now you have accomplished them. . . . Therefore, strong nations will declare your glory; ruthless nations will fear you. But you are a tower of refuge to the poor, O LORD, a tower of refuge to the needy in distress. You are a refuge from the storm and a shelter from the heat. For the oppressive acts of ruthless people are like a storm beating against a wall, or like the relentless heat of the desert. But you silence the roar of foreign nations. As the shade of a cloud cools relentless heat, so the boastful songs of ruthless people are stilled. (Isaiah 25:1,3-5, NLT)

"As I look back over my life, and I think things over. I can truly say that I've been blessed. I've got a testimony" are the opening lines to the song, *I've Got a Testimony* written by Anthony Tidwell.

It is good to occasionally take a stroll down Memory Lane to reflect on how far we've come from where we started. God is good! He allows us to experience ups and downs, highs and lows, mountains and valleys, all while holding our hand. We're never alone, despite how it may seem. That's the blessed assurance that lets us sleep at night.

In that day the people will proclaim, "This is our God!
We trusted in him, and he saved us!
This is the LORD, in whom we trusted.
Let us rejoice in the salvation he brings!"
(Isaiah 25:9, NLT)

LEAVE ME ALONE!

Then Jesus, being filled with the Holy Spirit, returned from the Jordan and was led by the Spirit into the wilderness, being tempted for forty days by the devil. And in those days He ate nothing, and afterward, when they had ended, He was hungry. (Luke 4:1-2, NKJV)

But when it pleased God, who separated me from my mother's womb and called me through His grace, to reveal His Son in me, that I might preach Him among the Gentiles, I did not immediately confer with flesh and blood, nor did I go up to Jerusalem to those who were apostles before me; but I went to Arabia, and returned again to Damascus. (Galatians 1:15-17, NKJV)

There are times when God calls us to seasons of aloneness because He knows there are some things that can only be learned alone. Jesus and Paul are two examples of men who knew the power of one-on-one encounters with God. The wilderness, or the desert, is part of the maturing process God uses with His children. We don't like either location, but the trip is necessary to accomplish God's will, because it is there that we:

1. Gain clarity of our purpose or vision.
2. Receive stamina to run the race set before us.
3. Gather strength for the journey.
4. Garner the ability to maneuver around obstacles.
5. Develop tunnel vision to dismiss distractions.
6. Embrace the favor of God.

You will not receive any of the above benefits staying in a crowd. With life issues and obligations, you may not spend 40 days in the wilderness or the desert. As a matter of fact, you may only have 40 minutes, but you must use whatever time you have wisely. Challenging times are coming. You overcome them by spending time with God, being prayed up, and holding on to what God has said. Why not call your heavenly travel agent today and schedule your trip?

Even the unpleasant things we face have benefits.
Lord, help us to see beyond the obvious to what You have for us.

DON'T EVEN TRY IT!

For His loving-kindness for those who fear Him is as great as the heavens are high above the earth. He has taken our sins from us as far as the east is from the west. The Lord has loving-pity on those who fear Him, as a father has loving-pity on his children. (Psalm 103:11-13, NLV)

People who allow the devil to use them to remind me of my past irritate me beyond belief. I *know* that God has forgiven me; these people haven't accepted the message yet. They think it's their job to remind me of what used to be.

    It's bad when other people do it; it's worse when I do it to myself and take a stroll down the wrong street of Memory Lane. That's the street that makes me think I had it better living a life of sin—more fun, more friends, more enjoyment. The truth is that while my experience of sin wasn't bad, it wasn't necessarily as great as the enemy would have me believe. I can't fault him because he's only doing his job. I blame myself when I give in to the temptation to revise history.

    When I finally got sick and tired of being sick and tired of the enemy bringing that particular test to me, I started shaking my head whenever a thought occurred that wasn't of God. I went so far as to verbally state, "Don't even try it!" and rebuked the devil in the name of Jesus because I know that no good thing will come from taking that trip. That may sound too simplistic, but it works. Thoughts are going to come, and I have a choice as to what I'll do with the ones that aren't from God. You do, too.

And now, brothers, as I close this letter, let me say this one more thing: Fix your thoughts on what is true and good and right. Think about things that are pure and lovely, and dwell on the fine, good things in others. Think about all you can praise God for and be glad about. (Philippians 4:8, TLB)

YOU'RE NOT DELUSIONAL!

But it is just as the Scriptures say, "What God has planned for people who love him is more than eyes have seen or ears have heard. It has never even entered our minds!" God's Spirit has shown you everything. His Spirit finds out everything, even what is deep in the mind of God. You are the only one who knows what is in your own mind, and God's Spirit is the only one who knows what is in God's mind. But God has given us his Spirit. That's why we don't think the same way that the people of this world think. That's also why we can recognize the blessings that God has given us. (1 Corinthians 2:9-12, CEV)

Songwriters Barrett Strong and Norman Whitfield penned the lyrics for one of R&B's most celebrated groups, The Temptations, and one of their greatest hits, *Just My Imagination*. The song speaks to a man's desire for a specific woman. He goes so far as to imagine being married and having a life with her. Unfortunately, the man doesn't know the woman, and she certainly doesn't know him. Chances are that if he told his friends about this woman, they would say to him he was crazy for letting his imagination get so out of control. The chances are also that because of their response, the man might agree and put his dreams aside.

I submit that we as Christians need to follow Pastor Joel Osteen's admonition to "dream big and pray bold!" There is no dream we have that is ever going to be bigger than what God can handle. I also submit that we need to free our imagination and allow the sky to be the limit. Even then, we still will not have fulfilled all that God has in store for us. So, go ahead and take the reins off. Don't worry about what your friends will say if you decide to share your dreams with them. The only one you need to be concerned about is God, and if He hasn't said no to the dream, it's yours!

You can't out dream God! You haven't seen it, heard it,
or imagined it, and that's some of the best news
I've ever heard!

DON'T START TRIPPIN'

Uzziah was sixteen years old when he became king and reigned for fifty-two years in Jerusalem. . . He behaved well in the eyes of GOD, following in the footsteps of his father Amaziah. He was a loyal seeker of God. He was well trained by his pastor and teacher Zechariah to live in reverent obedience before God, and for as long as Zechariah lived, Uzziah lived a godly life. And God prospered him. . . But then the strength and success went to his head. Arrogant and proud, he fell. One day, contemptuous of GOD, he walked into The Temple of GOD like he owned it and took over, burning incense on the Incense Altar. The priest Azariah, backed up by eighty brave priests of GOD, tried to prevent him. They confronted Uzziah. . .But Uzziah, censer in hand, was already in the middle of doing it and angrily rebuffed the priests. He lost his temper; angry words were exchanged—and then, even as they quarreled, a skin disease appeared on his forehead. . . Uzziah had his skin disease for the rest of his life and had to live in quarantine; he was not permitted to set foot in The Temple of GOD. (2 Chronicles 26:3-5, 16-18[a], 19, 21[a], MSG)

The story of Uzziah's leprosy is a cautionary tale for all of us. We must guard against thinking that anything we achieve that remotely resembles success is our doing. It is not! We must keep things in their proper perspective, especially when God allows us to do something for *His* glory. It's never about us.

God graciously allowed Uzziah to achieve fame and power (2 Chronicles 26:6-15). But, there's one line that explains why Uzziah started ego-tripping — "As long as he sought the Lord, God gave him success"—2 Chronicles 26:5[b]. When Uzziah stopped seeking God and started believing his own press reports, he was headed for a downfall. Let's make sure we don't follow his example. Yes, it's nice when people admire what we do, but we must be careful that we don't start thinking we don't need to continue seeking God for direction.

Know that the LORD, He is God;
It is He who has made us, and not we ourselves;
We are His people and the sheep of His pasture.
(Psalm 100:3, NKJV)

FAITH TO ASK, FAITH TO BELIEVE

When Jesus had again crossed over by boat to the other side of the lake, a large crowd gathered around him while he was by the lake. Then one of the synagogue leaders, named Jairus, came, and when he saw Jesus he fell at his feet. . ."My little daughter is dying. Please come and put your hands on her so that she will be healed and live." So Jesus went with him. . .While Jesus was still speaking, some people came from the house of Jairus, the synagogue leader. "Your daughter is dead," they said. (Mark 5:21-22, 23[b]-24, 3[a], NIV)

I am a busy woman, and there are times when I can't immediately fulfill a request. But, being a woman of my word, if I agree to do something, I'm going to do it to the best of my ability as soon as I can.

Jesus agreed to go with Jairus to see about his daughter, but along the way He was interrupted by a woman with an issue of blood. While Jesus was dealing with her, someone told Jairus his daughter was dead. The Bible doesn't record any anxiousness on Jairus' behalf upon hearing the news because I believe he rested in two absolutes: (1) his personal belief that since Jesus agreed to go with him, his daughter wouldn't die, and (2) the reminder that Jesus had given him: "Don't be afraid; just believe" (v. 36). Jairus didn't respond when the crowd told him to forget about Jesus coming (v. 35[b]), and he didn't respond when he arrived home and Jesus took him, his wife, Peter, James, and John into the child's room (v. 40). He may have been anxious about the state of his daughter's health, but he held fast to his faith.

When we're faced with situations that seem impossible, we need to remind ourselves of what Jesus told Jairus, "Don't be afraid, just believe." God is going to work things out for our good and His glory despite how things look. We need to hold fast to our faith and watch God do what He does best.

Don't waste God's time asking for something if you're not going to believe He can fulfill your request.

MEMORY WIPE

"So don't remember what happened in earlier times. Don't think about what happened a long time ago, because I am doing something new!" (Isaiah 43:18-19[a], ERV)

There are products on the market that claim to permanently erase hard drive data on your computer. God does the same for us once we're saved: "How far has the LORD taken our sins from us? Farther than the distance from east to west!" (Psalm 103:12, CEV). Unfortunately, we sometimes run into people who knew us when and who think it's their job to remind us of past behavior. They usually start the conversation with, "Remember when you . . ." to which I always respond, "No, I don't remember" because for the most part I don't. I used to be concerned about the things I couldn't remember, but then I realized God has allowed me to disregard things He considers trivial, especially if it's under the Blood. They're not necessarily bad things; remembering them just serves no purpose. Since God has removed them, what would be the point of straining to remember something that, in the words of my late mother, "aren't going to amount to a hill of beans"? There is no point!

We need to let the past stay in the past and focus on the future. If God has something He wants you to remember, then He—not the devil or any of his imps—will bring it to your mind. Until He does, use today's Scripture as a gentle reminder that what's done is done!

I focus on this one thing: Forgetting the past and looking forward to what lies ahead, I press on to reach the end of the race and receive the heavenly prize for which God, through Christ Jesus, is calling us.
(Philippians 3:13[b]-14, NLT)

CAN YOU BELIEVE HOW BIG THEY'VE GROWN?

But to obtain these gifts, you need more than faith; you must also work hard to be good, and even that is not enough. For then you must learn to know God better and discover what he wants you to do. Next, learn to put aside your own desires so that you will become patient and godly, gladly letting God have his way with you. This will make possible the next step, which is for you to enjoy other people and to like them, and finally you will grow to love them deeply. (2 Peter 1:5-7, TLB)

My niece was sharing that she had seen a recent picture of one of her cousins on a social media page. She was astonished that he had gotten so tall since the last time we saw him and said what we often say: I can't believe how big he's getting! Then, we started calculating where my nephew would have obtained his height. On his mother's side (including her parents and grandparents), people weren't taller than 5'7"; however, on his father's side (including his father, his parents, and grandparents) people were well over 6'3". We shouldn't have been surprised at my nephew's height, even at the age of thirteen.

When people interact with us, are they amazed at how much we've grown? They should be. After all, we get our spiritual height from our Father's side, so people shouldn't be surprised at our size. I'm not referencing our physical size but our spiritual capacity to become more like God. Regardless of how long you've been walking with the Lord, there's always room for more growth. Why not stretch your faith to see just how large you can grow?

But the fruit that the Spirit produces in a person's life
is love, joy, peace, patience, kindness, goodness,
faithfulness, gentleness, and self-control.
There is no law against these kinds of things.
(Galatians 5:22-23, ERV)

TWEET THIS

"I am the Gate for the sheep," he said. "All others who came before me were thieves and robbers. But the true sheep did not listen to them. Yes, I am the Gate. Those who come in by way of the Gate will be saved and will go in and out and find green pastures. The thief's purpose is to steal, kill and destroy. My purpose is to give life in all its fullness. I am the Good Shepherd. The Good Shepherd lays down his life for the sheep. A hired man will run when he sees a wolf coming and will leave the sheep, for they aren't his and he isn't their shepherd. And so the wolf leaps on them and scatters the flock. The hired man runs because he is hired and has no real concern for the sheep. I am the Good Shepherd and know my own sheep, and they know me, just as my Father knows me and I know the Father; and I lay down my life for the sheep. I have other sheep, too, in another fold. I must bring them also, and they will heed my voice; and there will be one flock with one Shepherd." (John 10:7-16, TLB)

I freely admit that I don't get the whole tweeting, texting, or social media thing. I also admit I am in the minority and that social networking is going to be around for a while. But, truly, some of the information shared on this technology makes absolutely no sense to me. Jesus has a universal message that is well worth sharing with every human. So, if you need something to tweet, allow me to suggest:

- Jesus is the only way and the only One who can save you (vv. 7-9).
- Be aware of what the thief wants to do in your life (v. 10[a]).
- Jesus wants you to enjoy the good life (v. 10[b]).
- Jesus is willing to die for you; no one else can make that claim (vv. 11-13, 17).
- Jesus knows you and wants you to know Him, too (vv. 14-15).

"The Father loves me because I lay down my life that I may have it back again. No one can kill me without my consent—I lay down my life voluntarily. For I have the right and power to lay it down when I want to and also the right and power to take it again. For the Father has given me this right."
(John 10:17-18, TLB)

TIME'S UP!

And if it seem evil unto you to serve the Lord, choose you this day whom ye will serve; whether the gods which your fathers served that were on the other side of the flood, or the gods of the Amorites, in whose land ye dwell: but as for me and my house, we will serve the Lord. (Joshua 24:15, KJV)

I love the game show *Jeopardy*. It's an excellent way to increase my knowledge and stimulate my mind. I would never make a good contestant, though, because when I play at home, I always blurt out the answers without putting them in the form of a question. If I were on the show, I'd be disqualified. During "Final Jeopardy," the contestants are given an allotted amount of time to respond. Then, I get to hear the music that gets in my head and that I find myself humming at times when I'm waiting for something or someone. When the time is up, the contestants show their question/answer, even if it's incorrect.

In the times we currently live in, anyone willing to play Russian roulette with their salvation is in danger of being disqualified from life. You can't keep straddling the fence when it comes to the decision to spend eternity with God. At some point you must decide whether you will willingly serve God, or you can wait for judgment; the choice is yours. Why not get a jump on the crowd and come on over to the Lord's side while you still have time?

For we shall all stand before the judgment seat of Christ. For it is written: "As I live," says the LORD, "every knee shall bow to Me, And every tongue shall confess to God." So then each of us shall give account of himself to God. (Romans 14:10[b]-12, NKJV)

ARE YOU IN TUNE?

My dear, dear friends, if God loved us like this, we certainly ought to love each other. No one has seen God, ever. But if we love one another, God dwells deeply within us, and his love becomes complete in us—perfect love! (1 John 4:11-12, MSG)

A few years ago, I watched a documentary on one of the major orchestras in our country. I noticed how in tune the conductor was with every single instrument. So much so that during one of their rehearsals, out of the 150 pieces playing, he heard the one instrument that hit the wrong note and stopped rehearsal! I found it interesting that his ear was so finely tuned. Of course, he's trained; whereas to me, it all sounded good.

I realize that God does what the conductor did. He knows what individual sound we make, especially when we're in harmony with Him and each other. That also means He knows the individual sound we make when we're out of step with both Him and each other.

Let's make sure the sound we're producing is pure so that the Maestro doesn't have to call us out.

Sing through me, Lord.
Sing through me.
Your heart. Your simple melody.
Orchestrate Your symphony through me.
I Am Your Song. Jonathan Nelson. 2010.

GOING UNDER THE KNIFE

So ever since we first heard about you we have kept on praying and asking God to help you understand what he wants you to do; asking him to make you wise about spiritual things; and asking that the way you live will always please the Lord and honor him, so that you will always be doing good, kind things for others, while all the time you are learning to know God better and better. (Colossians 1:8-10, TLB)

I pray to God I never see the inside of another hospital operating room! I've had enough surgeries to last a lifetime, even if they were all necessary. Fortunately, I haven't experienced any of the horror stories we hear others relate. I believe one of the reasons is my prayer for the surgical team: (1) that they will have good rest the night before the procedure; (2) that they don't have any personal problems with drugs or alcohol that will prevent them from being at their best; and (3) that they didn't argue with their spouse, boyfriend, girlfriend, or kids before leaving for work. I know the surgical team is educated and trained, but they're also very much human. I need and want the entire team to bring their "A" game to work without distractions.

The only elective surgery I've endured was asking God to do a new work in me. When I knelt at the altar and asked Jesus to come into my life, I knew there were things left there when I got up. Since salvation, God has shown me areas that need work; not necessarily sins but things He doesn't like. When that happens, I can pretend I don't know what He's talking about or I can willingly submit to surgery. Unlike surgical teams, God doesn't have off days, and the above prayers aren't necessary. My only prayer is, "God, please help me learn the lesson the first time, endure the procedure willingly, and quickly recover so I can move on to the next adventure."

Who Himself bore our sins in His own body on the tree, that we, having died to sins, might live for righteousness—
by whose stripes you were healed. (1 Peter 2:24, NKJV)

I'M OUTTA HERE!

Then GOD said, "You've been going around in circles in these hills long enough; go north . . . GOD, your God, has blessed you in everything you have done. He has guarded you in your travels through this immense wilderness. For forty years now, GOD, your God, has been right here with you. You haven't lacked one thing." (Deuteronomy 2:2-3, 7, MSG)

Comfortable, complacent, and contrary. Stale, stagnant, and stuck. This is what happens when you either stay too long at one location or do the same thing for a long time.

They say there is nothing worse than a reformed smoker, which I know from personal experience is true. I first started smoking when I was around 10 or 11. I would sneak my father's unfiltered cigarettes. That habit continued until I was 35 years old, stopping about 6 months after I got saved. Three things happened simultaneously that caused me to quit: (1) Someone saw me light up while driving down the street after church and told the deaconate member who was assigned to me. She called me and *suggested* that I might not want to continue smoking; (2 and 3) I belonged to an organization that had weekly meetings. This was before smoking in public buildings had been banned, so I was sitting in the women's lounge smoking before going back to the meeting. One of the members of my group, who was also a Christian, asked me if I was ready to stop smoking. I thought about it and realized that I really didn't enjoy smoking, but I had done it for so long that it was just automatic. I also realized I wanted to quit. When I said yes, she said, "Good, let's pray," and proceeded to pray right then and there!

God is a habit breaker, but we first must recognize we have a habit, and then accept His mandate: "You have roamed around this mountain country long enough" (Deuteronomy 2:3[a], AMP). Just because you've always done something doesn't mean you have to continue doing the same thing. When God says, "Pack your bags," you need to pack your bags.

God, I appreciate Your clarity of instruction and directions.
Help me not to hesitate to move when I hear You say, "Go!"

ECHOING PRAYERS

Let this record be kept for posterity so that people not yet born may praise the Eternal. (Psalm 102:18, VOICE)

According to an online article on www.bbc.com in January 2014, Professor Trevor Cox set a certified Guinness World Record for the longest echo in a man-made structure, an underground fuel depot constructed before World War II. Professor Cox shot a pistol loaded with blanks inside the Inchindown Tunnels near Invergordon in Scotland. The vibration lasted 112 seconds!

Professor Cox's achievement was indeed remarkable; but, I know something that's even more incredible—the prayers of the saints that have reverberated throughout the generations!

Many of us can attest to a family member praying for us, even when we were actively pursuing something other than godly intentions. That didn't stop their prayers from going forth. It's been said before and bears repeating: We *cannot* stop praying for those outside the arc of safety. We know it is not God's will for anyone to be lost. We owe it to our brothers and sisters to do for them what someone did for us. The praying saints didn't get tired, and neither can we. It is our responsibility to stand in the gap for those who are unable to do it for themselves.

Now to the God who can do so many awe-inspiring things,
immeasurable things, things greater than
we ever could ask or imagine through the power at work in us,
to Him be all glory in the church and
in Jesus the Anointed from this generation
to the next, forever and ever. Amen.
(Ephesians 3:20-21, VOICE)

THINGS COULD HAVE BEEN SO DIFFERENT

"And if that had been too little, I also would have given you much more!" (2 Samuel 12:8[b], NKJV)

We spend an inordinate amount of time unconsciously comparing ourselves to others. Oh, I can already hear you saying, "Well, maybe other people do, but I don't!" Let's see:

Someone at church shares about their healing. You're also facing sickness, but you're focused on God healing you the way He healed the other person. You miss the fact that you're being healed, too.

A friend shares about a financial blessing. You're facing financial need and expect God to move the way He did for the other person. You miss the fact that God has already made a way financially for you, too.

A parent shares his child's success in a specific area. Your child is still struggling to "find" her place. You miss the fact that God has allowed you to raise a God-fearing, law-abiding, productive citizen.

When we hear about what God does for others, we sometimes forget what He does for us. We get excited when we hear the song *What God Has for Me Is for Me* written by Pastor Marc Cooper because of the inherent promise: God has something for me. But, I propose that we need to embrace the phrase "for me!" God has what we need and knows how to give it to us. He knows the when, the where, and the how of blessing us.

Second Samuel 12:8 is God's chastisement of David for sleeping with Bathsheba and killing Uriah (2 Samuel 11). God points out all he had done for David—a significant amount of blessing and favor—and ends by telling David that he could have asked for more. You can, too. Ask God for *your* specific blessings; not your neighbors. Ask God to show you everything He has for you. Don't expect Him to move the way He did for someone else.

What God has planned for people who love him is more than eyes have seen or ears have heard. It has never even entered our minds!
(1 Corinthians 2:9, CEV)

STEADFAST

"I, the LORD, have put a curse on those who turn from me and trust in human strength. They will dry up like a bush in salty desert soil, where nothing can grow. But I will bless those who trust me. They will be like trees growing beside a stream—trees with roots that reach down to the water, and with leaves that are always green. They bear fruit every year and are never worried by a lack of rain." (Jeremiah 17:5-8, CEV)

People are fickle. One day you're the greatest thing since sliced bread; the next, you're treated like a stale, moldy loaf.

The prophet Jeremiah is reminding us there is One who is consistently consistent. When we put our faith and trust in God, we never need to worry about Him turning His back on us.

> My hope is built on nothing less,
> Than Jesus' blood and righteousness;
> I dare not trust the sweetest frame,
> But wholly lean on Jesus' name.
> On Christ, the solid Rock, I stand;
> All other ground is sinking sand.
> *My Hope Is Built on Nothing Less.* Edward Mote.
> (1797-1874).

YOU AREN'T THAT GROWN!

But the Spirit produces love, joy, peace, patience, kindness, goodness, faithfulness, humility, and self-control. There is no law against such things as these. (Galatians 5:22-23, GNT)

I take spiritual inventory to see where I'm at in my walk with the Lord on a regular basis. I would recommend that you do the same. The fruit of the Spirit is a good barometer to use. There are times I think I've got these nine areas under control and then . . . BAM! Out of nowhere, something happens that proves my thinking incorrect. It's not that I haven't made strides; it's that I haven't arrived at perfection yet, and I won't until I reach Heaven. (By the way, neither will you in case you're wondering.)

Life on Earth is rough. Every day the opportunity is presented for us to detour from our spiritual path into the world's definition of how to handle things. Go ahead and tell someone off. Go ahead and hate your neighbor. Go ahead and be disloyal. We have options. Hopefully, the choice we make is to be more like Christ.

The good thing about the fruit of the Spirit is that it's an evolution. You don't go to bed one way and wake up another. How long you've been saved has nothing to do with where you're at in your walk. What you *can* do is strive every day with the goal of obtaining the fruit God has for us. That's a goal we can all reach. Unlike a race where there's only one winner, it doesn't matter who comes in first. God recognizes and honors effort.

Thank You, Lord, that on the days we don't get it quite right, You give us another chance. Help us in our walk with You.
The closer we get to You, the riper our fruit will become.

FOR SUCH A TIME AS THIS

A certain man from Cyrene, Simon, the father of Alexander and Rufus, was passing by on his way in from the country, and they forced him to carry the cross. (Mark 15:21, NIV)

When Simon left Cyrene for Jerusalem to celebrate the Passover, the last thing he expected to encounter upon arrival was a beaten and bloody man struggling with a one-hundred-pound crossbeam! Cyrene (present day Libya) was over 700 miles from Jerusalem. The journey would have been made on foot, on a donkey, on a horse, or a combination of all three. The Scripture states Simon was coming in from the country, which most likely means he hadn't had a chance to rest from his journey. The thought of carrying a crossbeam through the narrow streets of the *Via Dolorosa* (Latin for the Way of Grief) wasn't appealing to a tired man. Yet, perhaps, he was familiar with who Jesus was and didn't consider this a burden at all.

Jews from all over made their way to Jerusalem for the Passover; and out of all those people in town during the feast, God appointed Simon to be instrumental in the crucifixion story. Jesus was physically unable to carry the beam because of the beatings He had already endured. His humanity kicked in and He collapsed. But, even weak and weary, Jesus would have acknowledged Simon's help. Theologians don't know whether Simon embraced Jesus' teaching that day, but I believe he was forever changed. You cannot have an encounter with Jesus and not be! Some theologians and commentators believe that Simon's two sons, Rufus and Alexander, did become Christians perhaps in part because of their father's encounter with Jesus.

Lord, help us to always be ready to assist anyone who needs help. Doing so is not only the right thing but may have far-reaching results. We never know what those watching will interpret from our actions. We may be instrumental in bringing them to You.

FRIENDSHIP 101

So, chosen by God for this new life of love, dress in the wardrobe God picked out for you: compassion, kindness, humility, quiet strength, discipline. Be even-tempered, content with second place, quick to forgive an offense. Forgive as quickly and completely as the Master forgave you. And regardless of what else you put on, wear love. It's your basic, all-purpose garment. Never be without it. Let the peace of Christ keep you in tune with each other, in step with each other. None of this going off and doing your own thing. And cultivate thankfulness. (Colossians 3:12-17, MSG)

Did you know that according to *Strong's Exhaustive Concordance of the Bible,* the word "friend" is used 53 times throughout the Old and New Testaments? That's a lot, which shows how important this relationship is to God.

Friends are those people God brings into your life to make it richer, fuller, and deeper. I am thankful for the people who have enhanced my life in ways I would never have imagined. Today's Scripture offers a blueprint for improving our relationships with those whom we call friend:

1. Don't take your friends for granted.
2. Treat your friends the way you want to be treated.
3. Accept their idiosyncrasies, the way they accept yours.
4. Forgive when necessary. Don't take everything so personally.
5. Remember, love covers a multitude of sins and issues, including your own.
6. Calm down and accept the peace of God.
7. Be grateful for every one of your friends.

Celebrate and enjoy every friend God has given you. Why not contact your friends today and let them know how much you value your relationship?

Lord, help me to be the kind of friend my friends need.

YOU HAVE ANOTHER CHOICE

"Wash yourselves clean. Stop all this evil that I see you doing. Yes, stop doing evil and learn to do right. See that justice is done—help those who are oppressed, give orphans their rights, and defend widows." The LORD says, "Now, let's settle the matter. You are stained red with sin, but I will wash you as clean as snow. Although your stains are deep red, you will be as white as wool. If you will only obey me, you will eat the good things the land produces. But if you defy me, you are doomed to die. I, the LORD, have spoken." (Isaiah 1:16-20, GNT)

Have you ever done something and concluded you might as well keep doing it since you started? For example, you're watching what you eat but crave something sweet, so you have a cookie. Then "something" inside urges you to have another one because, after all, you've already blown your diet. Logically, you know that's not true; one cookie isn't going to affect you one way or another. In those times you have a choice whether to give into the "something" that you *know* isn't from God, or to exhibit discipline and walk away from the cookies.

We make numerous conscious and subconscious choices throughout the day. Let's make sure the choices we make are pleasing to God. He's the only One worthy of judging our actions.

When people live to please the LORD,
even their enemies will be at peace with them.
(Proverbs 16:7, ERV)

SOMEDAY, WE'LL BE TOGETHER. . . I PROMISE

Jesus said to his disciples, "Don't be worried! Have faith in God and have faith in me. There are many rooms in my Father's house. I wouldn't tell you this, unless it was true. I am going there to prepare a place for each of you. After I have done this, I will come back and take you with me. Then we will be together." (John 14:1-3, CEV)

Little kids often cry when their parents leave them because they don't know if their parents are coming back for them.

I think the disciples felt that same way, although as grown men, they may have been reluctant to shed tears. Jesus had told them what was going to happen to Him and that He would be leaving them. He hurriedly told them that He'd be back, and they could stand on that promise.

When the parents return, the child is all smiles again, because the parents kept their promise. It will be the same for us. We'll grin from ear to ear on the day we see Jesus return. It will be a day unlike any other. The trumpet will sound and the dead in Christ will rise, and we will be caught up to meet Him in the air.

I can only imagine what it will be like, when I walk by your side. I can only imagine what my eyes will see, when your face is before me. I can only imagine.
Surrounded by your glory, what will my heart feel?
Will I dance for you Jesus, or in awe of you be still?
Will I stand in your presence, or to my knees will I fall?
Will I sing Hallelujah
Will I be able to speak at all? I can only imagine
I Can Only Imagine. Bart Millard (composer). 2002.

IS THERE ANY MORE?

The hearing ear and the seeing eye were both made by the Lord.
(Proverbs 20:12, NLV)

Money was tight in our household of six kids and two parents. We had the basics without a lot of extras. My father worked to provide shelter, clothing, and food. My mother worked until I was in the third grade. I didn't realize she stopped working due to health reasons; I was just happy to know that when I came home from school, she'd be there. My mother was an excellent cook and knew how to create nutritious and filling meals out of only a handful of items. I don't remember being hungry; I *do* remember there were times we had more food than others and some that I enjoyed more than others. When we had something I liked, I ate slowly and savored every bite. I knew there wasn't enough for seconds, so I didn't bother to ask for more. I also knew my mother had already put up my father's plate and that definitely was off-limits!

When I came to the Lord, I accepted His gift of the basics: forgiveness for my sins, acceptance into the Kingdom, and a place in Heaven. As I matured in faith, I realized there was more available. Once I moved past feeling guilty for not being satisfied, I started asking God for more. Not more stuff such as a bigger house, a newer car, or a better job, but more of Him. More love for His people. More patience with His timing. More understanding of His Word.

God gave us sight and hearing; these are the basics. Using our God-given sight and hearing to fulfill our assignment is the more. I discovered that God doesn't have a problem with our asking for more if we're using the more for the Kingdom. My Bible tells me I can ask with confidence for what I want, so I did. Have you?

"Keep on asking, and you will receive what you ask for. Keep on seeking, and you will find. Keep on knocking, and the door will be opened to you."
(Matthew 7:7, NLT)

SURPRISE! SURPRISE! SURPRISE!

Now there were four lepers sitting outside the city gates. "Why sit here until we die?" they asked each other. "We will starve if we stay here and we will starve if we go back into the city; so we might as well go out and surrender to the Syrian army. If they let us live, so much the better; but if they kill us, we would have died anyway." So that evening they went out to the camp of the Syrians, but there was no one there! (For the Lord had made the whole Syrian army hear the clatter of speeding chariots and a loud galloping of horses and the sounds of a great army approaching. "The king of Israel has hired the Hittites and Egyptians to attack us," they cried out. So they panicked and fled into the night, abandoning their tents, horses, donkeys, and everything else.) (2 Kings 7:3-7, TLB)

On the 1960s television show, *Gomer Pyle,* the title character often showed up at the most inopportune times and then state in his Southern drawl, "Surprise! Surprise! Surprise!"

The lepers had a dilemma and came to what they considered to be the best solution. They concluded they were going to die but decided they had a choice as to how and where it would happen: sitting outside the city gates or at the hands of the enemy. They thought they had it all figured out and probably congratulated themselves on coming to a logical decision.

Today's Christians often do the same thing. We come to what we believe to be a logical conclusion to our problems. However, like the lepers, we don't take God's part into account. Whenever we think we know how God is going to work, we're always going to be wrong! God is so creative that He doesn't ever have to repeat an action unless it's His desire. And, just like He made the lepers' footsteps sound like chariots, horses, and a great army, He can certainly handle whatever situation we find ourselves facing.

"My plans aren't your plans, nor are your ways my ways,"
says the LORD. (Isaiah 55:8, CEB)

HOPEFUL, NOT HOPELESS

But let me reveal to you a wonderful secret. We will not all die, but we will all be transformed! It will happen in a moment, in the blink of an eye, when the last trumpet is blown. For when the trumpet sounds, those who have died will be raised to live forever. And we who are living will also be transformed. (1 Corinthians 15:51-52, NLT)

I am an avid newspaper reader. I don't want to read news online or watch it on the television. I like holding a newspaper in my hand and hearing the crackle of the pages as I turn them. One reason is so I can take my time to thoroughly read the articles, which is something I can't do when listening to the TV. I suppose I could take my time online, too, but I prefer paper. I start with the front section and conclude with the comics because after reading the negativity in today's news, I need to smile (if not laugh) at the antics of my favorite comic characters.

Yesterday after reading about yet more bombings, starvations, deaths, hatred, destruction, and the discord of our government, even the comics couldn't lift my spirit. I closed the paper and started talking to the Lord. Our world is in a mess, and our only help is the Second Coming of Jesus Christ. I'm not necessarily ready to leave this world—I believe I still have more to do—but I'm like the apostle Paul in that I'm torn: "For to me, living means living for Christ, and dying is even better. But if I live, I can do more fruitful work for Christ. So, I really don't know which is better" (Philippians 1:21-22, NLT). I continue to be hopeful that God knows what He's doing. When enough becomes enough, He'll send Jesus back. My only hope is that we will all be ready.

But I really believe that I will see the LORD's goodness before I die.
(Psalm 27:13, ERV)

OPEN THE WINDOW

"Will a man rob God?" (Malachi 3:8, NKJV)

My former job was housed in a warehouse with several large bays (I worked in the office). At Christmastime we often had huge potluck parties with over 100 people. We paid a nominal fee for the meat and poultry and then brought a side dish. While we didn't expect anyone to provide a side dish for 100 people, some went to the opposite end and would bring one individual size bag of potato chips or something similar. Some people didn't want to bring anything and would donate extra money. My point is that everyone contributed something to the event.

The question in Malachi 3:8 refers to robbing God of the tithe—10% of your first fruits. Some of you may have an issue with giving 10% of your gross earnings to God. If that's the case, allow me to remind you of two things: (1) It is not your money! If God withheld the ability to work and earn a living from you, what would you have? and (2) You're not giving the money to an individual person, you're giving it to the Kingdom to help spread the Gospel.

You may have to work your way up to 10%, but don't let that stop you from tithing something. Everything you contribute is appreciated. And, before you know it, 10% will only be the minimum you contribute.

"Bring all the tithes into the storehouse so that there will be food
enough in my Temple; if you do,
I will open up the windows of heaven for
you and pour out a blessing so great
you won't have room enough to take it in!
Try it! Let me prove it to you!"
(Malachi 3:10, TLB)

TAKE IT UP WITH GOD

But David said, "What have I done now? Was it not just a question?" Then David turned away from him to another and asked the same question. And the people gave him the same answer. (1 Samuel 17:29-30, NLV)

It's unfortunate but true: All of us have people who don't like us although we haven't done anything to them. Some are jealous because of God's favor; others are just plain mad at everything and everybody. David shows us how to deal with both groups effectively.

David was sent to check on his brothers, who were in King Saul's army. Upon arrival, he saw how Goliath was taunting the Israelites. He questioned why nothing was being done to stop the giant Philistine. David's brother, Eliab, overheard the conversation and got angry and made several disparaging remarks about David and his sheep. David asked his brother "What have I done now?" and received no response (1 Samuel 17:12-28). With Eliab's lack of response, David gives us a blueprint of how to handle negative people. He didn't argue, debate, or continue a dialogue with his brother, who wouldn't or couldn't get it. He could have said, "Don't get mad at me because God's anointed me. Don't get mad at me because God has blessed me. Don't get mad at me because God has put His hand on my life. Do you have a problem with me? Take it up with God! And perhaps if you weren't so negative, God might bless you, too!" Instead, he turned to another person and asked the same question. That response set in motion Goliath's downfall.

David shows us how to choose our battles carefully and not waste energy or emotions on haters. We can all follow his example.

If I hold my peace and let the Lord fight my battles,
I know that victory shall be mine.
Victory Shall Be Mine. James Cleveland. 1985.

JUST WHEN YOU NEED IT THE MOST

The Lord wants to use you for special purposes, so make yourself clean from all evil. Then you will be holy, and the Master can use you. You will be ready for any good work. (2 Timothy 2:21, ERV)

I love reading mail, so much that I ignore offers to go paperless. I like opening my mailbox and seeing something inside other than bills. I enjoy reading catalogs, brochures, and advertisements, what we refer to as "junk" mail. But, I especially like getting something unexpected. The other day I received a card from a friend for no reason other than she was thinking about me. It was a beautiful card with beautiful words and a beautiful sentiment. The fact that someone thought enough to send a card made me happy. The fact that it came at a time when I needed a hug from God also put a smile on my face.

People often cross our mind, and we make a mental note to contact them. However, with the busyness of life, our good intentions sometimes go by the wayside. Consider that when people cross your mind, God wants you to do something about it—send a card, make a phone call, pray. Mental notes are all well and good, but sometimes God needs us to act. We don't know what the person is going through; God does, and He uses us to extend His message of love.

"When I count my blessings, I count you twice."
—Author Unknown

YOU PICKED THE WRONG ONE TODAY

The LORD says this to you: "Don't be afraid or worry about this large army, because the battle is not your battle. It is God's battle!" (2 Chronicles 20:15, ERV)

As the time was drawing close when I needed to have this project to my editor, Cynthia Donaldson, in time for the scheduled release, a series of events came with the sole purpose of distracting me from the goal.

Three days before the deadline, I experienced an attack unlike any other. I had stayed up late writing and awoke in severe pain; everything hurt. I felt as if I had been run over by a car twice. Have you ever tried to pray in pain? It's challenging because you can't even concentrate. (That's when it's good to know the Holy Spirit interprets our moans and groans.) It took over an hour to get dressed because I had to stop to catch my breath. In addition to the body aches, my stomach was upset. I knew this wasn't because of anything I had eaten or done the night before. Then, a migraine started, and that's when I finally said, "Enough!" I declared war, and I knew my side would be victorious.

See, one thing I know for sure is that God is the author of this book—He only allows me to put my name on the cover. It's written to bless His people—something we know the enemy doesn't want to happen. So, I changed strategies. I released my faith and bound the devil, sending him and his imps back to the pit from where they came. Almost immediately, the pain left. I thanked God for responding to my prayer! And, just to make sure the devil knew who was in charge, God gave me more devotionals to write! To God be the glory!

There is no pain that Jesus can't feel.
There is no hurt, he cannot heal.
All things work according to His perfect will. No matter, what you're going through. Remember God is only using you.
For the battle is not yours. It's the Lord's.
The Battle Is the Lord's. V. Michael McKay. 1993.

NO MORE, FOREVER

"Tell the people of Israel to turn back and camp across from Pi-Hahiroth near Baal-Zephon, between Migdol and the Red Sea. The king will think they were afraid to cross the desert and that they are wandering around, trying to find another way to leave the country. I will make the king stubborn again, and he will try to catch you. Then I will destroy him and his army. People everywhere will praise me for my victory, and the Egyptians will know that I really am the LORD." The Israelites obeyed the LORD and camped where he told them. . .When the Israelites saw the king coming with his army, they were frightened and begged the LORD for help. But Moses answered, "Don't be afraid! Be brave, and you will see the LORD save you today. These Egyptians will never bother you again. The LORD will fight for you, and you won't have to do a thing." (Exodus 14:2-4, 10-14, CEV)

There is a scene in *The Wizard of Oz* where Dorothy, Scare Crow, Tin Man, Toto, and the Cowardly Lion are getting ready to enter the haunted forest on their way to the Emerald City. There's a sign posted on a tree, "I'd Turn Back If I Were You!", giving those who entered fair warning that what was ahead wasn't going to be pleasant. Of course, the Cowardly Lion was all for retreating, but Dorothy and the gang wouldn't allow it.

There are moments when we're facing issues that seem insurmountable. We see no way out, around, or through; retreat seems to be our only option. That's when we need to remember what God did for the Israelites at the Red Sea. The sea was in front of them and the Egyptians were behind them in full pursuit.

God will put your enemies in a position where they can't pursue you, when you trust Him to work things out.

The LORD is my strength and my song; he has given me victory. This is my God, and I will praise him—my father's God, and I will exalt him!
(Exodus 15:2, NLT)

HEY, WAIT FOR ME!

As Pharaoh approached, the Israelites looked up, and there were the Egyptians, marching after them. They were terrified and cried out to the LORD. They said to Moses, "Was it because there were no graves in Egypt that you brought us to the desert to die? What have you done to us by bringing us out of Egypt? Didn't we say to you in Egypt, 'Leave us alone; let us serve the Egyptians'? It would have been better for us to serve the Egyptians than to die in the desert!" Moses answered the people, "Do not be afraid. Stand firm and you will see the deliverance the LORD will bring you today. The Egyptians you see today you will never see again. The LORD will fight for you; you need only to be still." Then the LORD said to Moses, "Why are you crying out to me? Tell the Israelites to move on. Raise your staff and stretch out your hand over the sea to divide the water so that the Israelites can go through the sea on dry ground." (Exodus 14:10-16, NIV)

Can you imagine being the last person crossing the Red Sea? I know I would have been nervous walking on the floor of the sea, with water to the right and left. I'd be tempted to tell the people in front of me to hurry up.

There are times when we feel we're going to be left behind or left out. Others are getting blessed with things we've prayed for, and we wonder when our turn is coming. Like the last person crossing the Red Sea on that memorable day and night, we, too, can be assured that God hasn't forgotten about us.

For the word of the LORD is right and true;
he is faithful in all he does. (Psalm 33:4, NIV)

THE ONLY STUPID QUESTION
IS THE ONE YOU DON'T ASK

"So I say to you, ask, and it will be given to you; seek, and you will find; knock, and it will be opened to you. For everyone who asks receives, and he who seeks finds, and to him who knocks it will be opened." (Luke 11-9-10, NKJV)

Have you ever had someone say, "That's a stupid question!" when you asked for clarification about something? What about those people who would never use the word "stupid" but whose body language and facial expression clearly show what they're thinking? I am a person who often needs clarification because the time frame for processing what I thought I heard and what was said takes a moment. Instead of responding to the wrong question, I'll often ask for more details. I admit some of the looks I've received would be daunting if I didn't know who I was in God.

One thing that brings me great pleasure about my relationship with God is that He doesn't give me the "look" when I ask for more information. He won't give it to you, either. God doesn't make us feel as though there's something wrong because we don't immediately grasp what He is saying or doing.

Gideon questioned what mighty man of valor was the Angel of the Lord talking about (Judges 6:12-16); Nicodemus questioned how a grown man was expected to re-enter his mother's womb (John 3:1-18); and Mary questioned how a virgin was to give birth to the Messiah (Luke 1:26-38). In all these examples, the questions were taken seriously and thoroughly explained to the recipient's understanding. God doesn't mind our asking questions—even if the answers appear to be a no-brainer to someone else—that's the only way you'll learn and grow in knowledge.

The apostle Paul used the phrase, "I would not have you ignorant"
consistently throughout his writings, especially in the book of Romans and
I and II Corinthians. Perhaps he did that for a reason.

THERE'S ONLY ONE WAY

Now the serpent was more cunning than any beast of the field which the LORD God had made. And he said to the woman, "Has God indeed said, 'You shall not eat of every tree of the garden'?" And the woman said to the serpent, "We may eat the fruit of the trees of the garden; but of the fruit of the tree which is in the midst of the garden, God has said, 'You shall not eat it, nor shall you touch it, lest you die.'" Then the serpent said to the woman, "You will not surely die. For God knows that in the day you eat of it your eyes will be opened, and you will be like God, knowing good and evil." So when the woman saw that the tree was good for food, that it was pleasant to the eyes, and a tree desirable to make one wise, she took of its fruit and ate. She also gave to her husband with her, and he ate. Then the eyes of both of them were opened, and they knew that they were naked; and they sewed fig leaves together and made themselves coverings. (Genesis 3:1-7, NKJV)

Some people are wired to always look for the shortcut. They don't want to adhere to the rules (perhaps they don't believe they apply to them, only everyone else), so they have no problem cheating, lying, or conniving to get their way. Shortcuts may work for a while; but in the end, everything in the dark is revealed in the light (Luke 8:17).

Just as there is only one way to heaven—"Nor is there salvation in any other, for there is no other name under heaven given among men by which we must be saved" (Acts 4:12, NKJV)—there are no shortcuts in God. He doesn't mumble when He speaks and has made clear the path for us to take. He even left us a blueprint called the Bible. All we need do is follow His instructions. Don't let anyone steer you in the wrong direction. If you're in doubt, ask, "God, is this You?" You'll know which way to go when He responds, and He will.

Nevertheless, I am continually with You; You hold me by my right hand. You will guide me with Your counsel, and afterward receive me to glory.
(Psalm 73:23-24, NKJV)

ARE YOU STILL ANOINTED?

And she said, "The Philistines are upon you, Samson!" So he awoke from his sleep, and said, "I will go out as before, at other times, and shake myself free!" But he did not know that the LORD had departed from him. (Judges 16:20, NKJV)

The story of Samson and Delilah has so many facets to it: The danger of being involved with someone who isn't what they seem; the danger of telling your secrets to the wrong person; and the danger of assuming that what *was* still *is*. We know that the story of Samson ends with his death. God allowed his hair to grow back after Delilah had someone shave it off. With the renewed anointing, he was able to kill more of the Philistines in death than he did in life.

We often see people doing something for a long time, unaware that God has no longer anointed them for that particular task. It's not that God doesn't want to continue to use them. God is ever-moving, and He may now have something else for them, but they won't let go of what they're doing to find out what it is.

Why not ask God if the area you're working in is the area He still wants you to work in? Let's not be like Samson and "assume" that everything is as it was.

"See, I will do a new thing. It will begin happening now.
Will you not know about it?" (Isaiah 43:19[a], NLV)

YOU'RE TOO GOOD FOR HELL!

"Look at what I've done for you today: I've placed in front of you Life and Good, Death and Evil." (Deuteronomy 30:15, MSG)

I believe people stay in sin because they just don't believe they can live better or change their current lifestyle. The enemy has convinced them that they've done so much wrong, there's no way God would ever forgive them. The devil has done his job well. Christians need to do their job better.

God is faithful and just to forgive those who are truly repentant. "The Lord is . . . patient with you, not wanting anyone to perish, but everyone to come to repentance. . ." (2 Peter 3:9, NIV).

God gave us free will and expects us to use it wisely. Please don't make Him regret that decision. "This commandment that I'm commanding you today isn't too much for you, it's not out of your reach. It's not on a high mountain—you don't have to get mountaineers to climb the peak and bring it down to your level and explain it before you can live it. And it's not across the ocean—you don't have to send sailors out to get it, bring it back, and then explain it before you can live it. No. The word is right here and now—as near as the tongue in your mouth, as near as the heart in your chest. Just do it!" (Deuteronomy 30:11-14, MSG).

People are destined to die once
and then face judgment.
(Hebrews 9:27, CEB)

A MARRIAGE MADE IN HEAVEN

"Return, O backsliding children," says the LORD; "for I am married to you. I will take you, one from a city and two from a family, and I will bring you to Zion." (Jeremiah 3:14, NKJV)

I am declaring today National Claim a Backslider Day. It's not an official holiday, but it should be. All of us know at least one person, and probably more, who used to walk with the Lord. We need to pray for them. If God releases you to share a Word with them, do so. They need to know they don't have to be embarrassed or worried about people knowing what they did. They need to know that God will forgive them as soon as they ask for forgiveness! It really is that simple. People may want them to jump through a lot of hoops, but God doesn't. He faithfully keeps His marriage vows.

We can't stop praying for those who once belonged to the Lord. You would do anything in your power to reclaim what was taken from you; Jesus feels the same way about backsliders. Those of us who claim the name of Christ are obligated to fulfill God's desire that all should come to repentance.

Backsliders are challenging. They remember what walking with the Lord was like. They remember the joy of serving God. They remember the love and fellowship of the saints. They remember the laughter and the fun. When they compare it to what they now experience—backbiting, envy, jealously, false friends—they already know they need to come back to God.

I have a list of those I pray for daily who were once part of the family. My prayer list consists of family, friends, love ones, and acquaintances. Also included on my list are the uncovered—the lost, the forgotten, the yet to be claimed. Somebody prayed for me; I'm happy to return the favor.

Thank You, God, for Your faithfulness to all of us. Extend Your mercies to those who are still outside the family.
Help us to bring them home.

A TRIBUTE TO MY FRIEND

The next day John was back at his post with two disciples, who were watching. He looked up, saw Jesus walking nearby, and said, "Here he is, God's Passover Lamb." The two disciples heard him and went after Jesus. Jesus looked over his shoulder and said to them, "What are you after?" They said, "Rabbi" (which means "Teacher"), "where are you staying?" He replied, "Come along and see for yourself." They came, saw where he was living, and ended up staying with him for the day. It was late afternoon when this happened. Andrew, Simon Peter's brother, was one of the two who heard John's witness and followed Jesus. The first thing he did after finding where Jesus lived was find his own brother, Simon, telling him, "We've found the Messiah" (that is, "Christ"). He immediately led him to Jesus. (John 1:35-42, MSG)

In 1970, during 10th-grade gym class, I was introduced to Deborah Thompson. We instantly connected and remain close after all these years. Deborah gave her life to the Lord and immediately began sharing the Gospel with me. She probably didn't think of it as witnessing; she knew I had a fondness for well-spoken words, so she relayed what her pastor (and now mine) would preach during mid-week Bible study and the sermons on Sunday. In October 1988, she invited me to a concert at church. In November, she asked me to attend a choir performance at a local mall. In December, I woke up planning to go to brunch and ended up at church. I never left!

Today is Deborah's birthday. God knew her parents would give her life and that she would give that life to the Lord. In doing so, she was positioned to share the Gospel with others, including me. Like Andrew, she didn't keep the Good News to herself. I thank God she didn't.

"When we consider the blessings of God—the gifts that add beauty and joy to our lives, that enable us to keep going through stretches of boredom and even suffering—friendship is very near the top."
—Donald W. McCullough

INFLUENCE

You should know this, Timothy, that in the last days there will be very difficult times. For people will love only themselves and their money. They will be boastful and proud, scoffing at God, disobedient to their parents, and ungrateful. They will consider nothing sacred. They will be unloving and unforgiving; they will slander others and have no self-control. They will be cruel and hate what is good. They will betray their friends, be reckless, be puffed up with pride, and love pleasure rather than God. They will act religious, but they will reject the power that could make them godly. Stay away from people like that! (2 Timothy 3:1-5, NLT)

The quote "If we don't stand for something, we'll fall for anything" has been attributed to various people. Regardless of who coined the phrase, it's true, and it's why we must have standards we refuse to deviate from. We are either being influenced or influencing someone else, either overtly or covertly. It all comes down to influence.

Paul told Timothy that in the last days, people would change. Or perhaps, more likely, their true colors will be revealed. Since we usually adapt to our environment, we need to be careful about the company we keep. The reverse is also true; let's make sure our life reflects Jesus Christ so that those we influence will have a positive role model to follow.

Walk with the wise and become wise;
associate with fools and get in trouble.
(Proverbs 13:20, NLT)

YOU AIN'T SEEN NOTHIN' YET!

God can do anything, you know—far more than you could ever imagine or guess or request in your wildest dreams! He does it not by pushing us around but by working within us, his Spirit deeply and gently within us. (Ephesians 3:20, MSG)

You can look back over your life and see the accomplishments you've already achieved. Some of them may surprise you, because before you accomplished them you would not have believed it would be possible. Guess what? God has so much more to do with and through you. Are you ready?

The challenge is not to attempt to put God in a box. Don't think that God will replicate something He's already done. God is the creator of creativity. Give Him free reign. Ask Him to enlarge your territory. There is more inside you than you think or even believe. If you have the Spirit of God inside you, do you really believe you've peaked? Ask God to show you more, and then get ready for the adventure of your lifetime.

I can do everything God asks me to with the help of Christ
who gives me the strength and power.
(Philippians 4:13, TLB)

ASSUMPTIONS WILL GET YOU IN TROUBLE

But you, beloved, building yourselves up on your most holy faith, praying in the Holy Spirit, keep yourselves in the love of God, looking for the mercy of our Lord Jesus Christ unto eternal life. (Jude 20-21, NKJV)

We've probably all been guilty of making assumptions, whether consciously or not. We see a very tall man and assume he's a basketball player. We see an overweight woman and think she has unhealthy eating habits. We see people in business attire and believe they have a fantastic job. None of these assumptions are necessarily true. The tall man may be uncoordinated, the overweight woman may have already lost a tremendous amount of weight, and the professionally-attired people may be unemployed.

Assumptions can hurt us because based on what we think we know, we may not look any further than the surface.

My responsibility as a writer is to tell a story. It may take 100,000 words or 10,000, but when the story is done, I'm done. If you've never read the book of Jude, you may assume that because it doesn't have the length of some of the other books, it doesn't have much to say. You would be wrong! The book of Jude is one of the smallest books in the Bible with only 25 verses; the 35 words in today's Scripture are short and to the point—stay close to God and stay faithful. Since God's inspiration writes all Scripture, Jude knew it wouldn't take a lot of words to get the message across!

There is One Who can keep you from falling and can bring you before Himself free from all sin. He can give you great joy as you stand before Him in His shining-greatness. He is the only God. He is the One Who saves from the punishment of sin through Jesus Christ our Lord. May He have shining-greatness and honor and power and the right to do all things. He had this before the world began, He has it now, and He will have this forever. Let it be so. (Jude 24-25, NLV)

SAME PERSON, DIFFERENT NAME

And she shall bring forth a son, and thou shalt call his name JESUS: for he shall save his people from their sins. (Matthew 1:21, KJV)

My brother's birth name is Robert Dale Rogers. Throughout his life, I've heard him called Bob, Rob, and Robert. Whoever calls him will determine how he responds. One of my nieces calls him Rob. I call him Robert. I've heard others refer to him as Bob. Whether he's called Bob, Rob, or Robert, he's the same person.

Jesus is also one who is known by several names. Your need will determine what you call Him. Need someone to listen to you? He's the Wonderful Counselor. Need someone to help you in an impossible situation? He's the Mighty God. Need reassurance of someone's presence? He's the Everlasting Father. What about needing calm in the midst of a storm? He's the Prince of Peace.

It doesn't matter which name you call Him, He's going to answer you. Now, ain't that Good News?

For to us a child is born, to us a son is given, and the government will be on his shoulders. And he will be called Wonderful Counselor, Mighty God, Everlasting Father, Prince of Peace.
(Isaiah 9:6, NIV)

CAN YOU HANDLE IT?

Delight thyself also in the LORD: and he shall give thee the desires of thine heart. (Psalm 37:4, KJV)

One of my younger grandsons was excited because he thought he would start kindergarten last year, attending the same school as his sister who moved up to the first grade. He was disappointed because his parents decided he wasn't mature enough. He would only be four when school started; his birthday isn't until November. So, he'll go this year, better prepared to handle school.

We also get excited about things. We pray and believe that God will give them to us; we're disappointed when things don't happen. Perhaps like my son and daughter-in-law, God knows you're not mature enough to handle what you desire. His answer isn't necessarily no; it's more of a not yet. You have something to anticipate as you ask God to help you get ready.

One sign of maturity is handling delays and disappointments with God-like grace.

DIDN'T GOD BLOW YOUR MIND THIS TIME?

O Eternal One, You have explored my heart and know exactly who I am; You even know the small details like when I take a seat and when I stand up again. Even when I am far away, You know what I'm thinking. You observe my wanderings and my sleeping, my waking and my dreaming and You know everything I do in more detail than even I know. You know what I'm going to say long before I say it. It is true, Eternal One, that You know everything and everyone. You have surrounded me on every side behind me and before me, and You have placed Your hand gently on my shoulder. It is the most amazing feeling to know how deeply You know me, inside and out; the realization of it is so great that I cannot comprehend it. (Psalm 139:1-6, VOICE)

It is overwhelming to think that someone knows you better than you know yourself. We often think that once we reach a certain age, we know who we are, what we want, and how to achieve the goals we set for ourselves. And, to some extent, we're right; insight should come with chronological age. However, because the Master Creator conceives us, there are areas of our lives we haven't begun to touch upon because we are unable to wrap our minds around the idea that God knows our past, present, and future. It is mind-blowing.

When I ponder the intricacies of the relationship God wants to have with us, it's too much to comprehend. King David said, "Your works are wonderful" (Psalm 139:14), and I'm one of God's works. So, I've decided to enjoy the present, knowing that God has everything under control today and tomorrow and the day after.

How precious it is, Lord, to realize that you are thinking about me constantly! I can't even count how many times a day your thoughts turn toward me. (Psalm 139:17, TLB)

TURN IT UP!

He is your praise, and He is your God, who has done for you these great and fearsome things which your eyes have seen. (Deuteronomy 10:21, MEV)

Everybody has something to praise God for, even unbelievers. (If unbelievers have breath enough to deny Jesus, they have enough breath to praise God!) Turning up the volume on your praise doesn't mean increasing the noise level, although that may be an automatic response. It means to expand the intensity of your praise. Everything we experience contributes to our praise. Think about all you've been through the last few weeks and let your praise out! You'll feel better, I promise.

Praise the LORD!
Praise the LORD, O my soul!
While I live I will praise the LORD;
I will sing praises unto my God while I have my life.
(Psalm 146:1-2, MEV)

THE HITS JUST KEEP ON COMING

He gave the command, and a strong wind began to blow. The waves became higher and higher. The waves lifted them high into the sky and dropped them into the deep sea. The storm was so dangerous that the men lost their courage. They were stumbling and falling like someone who is drunk. Their skill as sailors was useless. They were in trouble, so they called to the LORD for help, and he saved them from their troubles. He stopped the storm and calmed the waves. The sailors were happy that the sea became calm, and he led them safely to where they wanted to go. (Psalm 107:25-30, ERV)

I have never been on a cruise because there is something very intimidating about looking around and seeing nothing but water. I'm sure that the fact I can't swim has a lot to do with my reluctance to participate in what has been relayed to me as an enjoyable experience.

I have, however, been on a roller-coaster and the above Scripture reminded me of that one-time experience. I was 18 and on a date. We went to the Ohio State Fair and my date suggested the roller-coaster. I had never been on one, but I agreed. It wasn't so bad going up but coming down was an entirely different thing. I was scared to death and there was nothing I could do about it other than to close my eyes and hold on for dear life. My date didn't seem to notice that I wasn't having a good time; in fact, once we got to the ground he wanted to go again. I declined and have never been on one since.

There are times when it's just one thing after another and we are caught in situations that are out of our control. It seems like we're being tossed around like a rag doll, staggering like a drunkard, and wishing that whatever the experience is will soon be over. The good news is that everything eventually comes to an end. The bad news is that sometimes we must endure unpleasant things until the end. But, the better news is that we have a God who is in control of every situation. He is an excellent navigator and all we can do is trust Him to bring us over, through and out.

Thank You, Lord, for never leaving or forsaking us,
regardless of the situation.

MY JOB

LORD our Lord, your name is the most wonderful in all the earth! It brings you praise everywhere in heaven. . . I look at the heavens you made with your hands. I see the moon and the stars you created. And I wonder, "Why are people so important to you? Why do you even think about them? Why do you care so much about humans? Why do you even notice them?" (Psalm 8:1, 3-4, ERV)

I love waking up in the morning. You may think, "Well, duh, so does everybody else!" and you're probably right. The reason I like waking up in the morning is that I sleep facing a bedroom window that has semi-sheer curtains. When I open my eyes, the first thing I say is "Thank You, Lord!" because He didn't have to make it so. I then notice the weather, and I say, "Thank You, Lord! It's going to be a great day." I don't care if it's snowing, raining, cloudy, or sunny, or if almost every joint in my body hurts; every day above ground is a good one!

    The fact that God allows me to wake up to see the new day is enough. The fact that God—who made the world and everything in it—enables me to enjoy His world is enough. The fact that God gives me the use of my faculties is more than enough to be grateful!

    Before this day is over, I may experience some unexpected challenges, and that's okay. I don't have to solve every problem; God does. I don't have to make every decision; God does. I don't have to answer every question; God does. All I am required to do is rejoice in the day that God has made; and I do!

The LORD liveth; and blessed be my rock;
and let the God of my salvation be exalted.
(Psalm 18:46, KJV)

WHAT GOES AROUND COMES AROUND

"If you give to others, you will be given a full amount in return. It will be packed down, shaken together, and spilling over into your lap. The way you treat others is the way you will be treated." (Luke 6:38, CEV)

We often think of this Scripture in terms of finances; however, I believe it's more. I surmise that the "it" in the second sentence is whatever you give. For example, if you smile at someone, they usually will smile back. If you say hello, you'll usually get a response. If you give out kindness and friendliness, you'll usually get it back. (Now, in this instance the return may not come from the person you extended the gesture to, but someone will extend the same "it" to you at some point.)

However, Jesus is talking about judging, condemnation, and forgiveness . . . which are big issues for most people, especially forgiveness: "Do not judge others, and you will not be judged. Do not condemn others, or it will all come back against you. Forgive others, and you will be forgiven" (Luke 6:37, NLT).

Forgiveness is one of those topics that sometimes makes people uncomfortable because they either need to forgive someone or are seeking forgiveness from someone. Needing to extend forgiveness challenges those who want to hold onto their bitterness, not realizing that they're being held in bondage also. Needing to seek forgiveness challenges those too prideful to say, "I'm sorry," which are two of the most beautiful words in the English language.

Forgiveness is a gift from God. Before we take our last breath, we're going to have to give and receive it. Please don't allow bitterness or pride to prevent you from experiencing all that God has for you.

"In prayer there is a connection between what God does and what you do. You can't get forgiveness from God, for instance, without also forgiving others. If you refuse to do your part, you cut yourself off from God's part."
(Matthew 6:14-15, MSG)

I LOVE TO TELL THE STORY

Therefore, if anyone is in Christ, he is a new creation; old things have passed away; behold, all things have become new. Now all things are of God, who has reconciled us to Himself through Jesus Christ, and has given us the ministry of reconciliation, that is, that God was in Christ reconciling the world to Himself, not imputing their trespasses to them, and has committed to us the word of reconciliation. Now then, we are ambassadors for Christ, as though God were pleading through us: we implore you on Christ's behalf, be reconciled to God. For He made Him who knew no sin to be sin for us, that we might become the righteousness of God in Him. (2 Corinthians 5:17-21, NKJV)

Do you know people who as soon as they start talking you know what they're going to say? They repeat the same story over and over. You've heard it so often that you can quote it verbatim. When my youngest brother, Ivan, passed away in 2010, I got tired of repeating the story of what happened. I found myself customizing the details depending on who I was talking with; some people got the longer version; others the condensed one. However, there is something to be said for rehashing the same story. Familiarity may help us remember extra details. Or, the more we tell it, the smoother the delivery becomes.

We often love to quote the "a" clause of 2 Corinthians 5:17, but what about the rest of today's Scripture? We have been given the ministry of reconciliation and told we are ambassadors for Christ. Doesn't that mean we're supposed to share our faith? When was the last time you told your salvation story to someone outside of your circle? There's a world on the way to Hell and they need some Good News!

Then He said to His disciples, "The harvest truly is plentiful,
but the laborers are few."
(Matthew 9:37, NKJV)

PLEASE RELEASE ME. . .

Then Naomi heard in Moab that the LORD had blessed his people in Judah by giving them good crops again. So Naomi and her daughters-in-law got ready to leave Moab to return to her homeland. With her two daughters-in-law she set out from the place where she had been living, and they took the road that would lead them back to Judah. But on the way, Naomi said to her two daughters-in-law, "Go back to your mothers' homes. And may the LORD reward you for your kindness to your husbands and to me. May the LORD bless you with the security of another marriage." Then she kissed them good-bye, and they all broke down and wept. "No," they said. "We want to go with you to your people." . . . And again they wept together, and Orpah kissed her mother-in-law good-bye. (Ruth 1:4-10, 14, NLT)

Orpah's decision to leave Naomi and Ruth has been debated for years, especially when you talk of missed blessings or missed opportunities. A lot of people have maligned her character for not sticking with Naomi and Ruth. Consider that if she had stayed, the story as we know it may have ended differently.

Orpah teaches us a valuable lesson: You need to know when it's time to end something. You may have a knowing in your "knower" that this isn't what you're supposed to do. When you experience this feeling, you need to verify that it is of God and then do what God has said. It doesn't matter who doesn't agree or understand your decision. Orpah wasn't wrong for not going further; she did what she felt was right. She was in a situation where no matter what she did, somebody wasn't going to be happy.

We need to learn how to release people and things, regardless of how we feel about it. We might ask God what's going on, and He may choose to answer. But, even if He doesn't, it's not our place to hold onto people or things when God is clearly trying to take them or it from us.

> *"As the heavens are higher than the earth,*
> *so are my ways higher than your ways*
> *and my thoughts than your thoughts."* (Isaiah 55:9, NIV)

. . . AND LET ME GO

Then Naomi heard in Moab that the LORD had blessed his people in Judah by giving them good crops again. So Naomi and her daughters-in-law got ready to leave Moab to return to her homeland. With her two daughters-in-law she set out from the place where she had been living, and they took the road that would lead them back to Judah. But on the way, Naomi said to her two daughters-in-law, "Go back to your mothers' homes. And may the LORD reward you for your kindness to your husbands and to me. May the LORD bless you with the security of another marriage." Then she kissed them good-bye, and they all broke down and wept. "No," they said. "We want to go with you to your people." . . . And again they wept together, and Orpah kissed her mother-in-law good-bye. (Ruth 1:4-10, 14, NLT)

Yesterday, we looked at Orpah's decision to stay in Moab, rather than traveling to Bethlehem with Naomi and Ruth. Although we don't hear anything else about Orpah—justification for some that she didn't make the right choice—I choose to believe that God honored her decision, just like He's honored some of our decisions that may not have been His first choice for us. That is not to say that we should just do whatever we want and expect God to bless. (That's not going to happen because God doesn't bless mess!) But, it is to say that sometimes God looks at our heart and decides in His infinite wisdom and mercy to cover us. We don't know whether Orpah made the right decision or not; we do know that Naomi and Ruth's decision to keep going was the right one for them.

We need to keep moving forward in the direction God has said, even if we go alone.

Lord, please help us to move at Your command. Please provide us with strength for the journey and the boldness to stand alone when necessary.

RESTORATION IN PRAISE

Let everything alive give praises to the Lord! You praise him! Hallelujah! (Psalm 150:6, TLB)

Praise is one thing everyone can do, which is why the Bible commands us to do it. We don't need to be a singer or musician or liturgical dancer. We can have a voice that makes a frog's croak sound melodic, no musical talent whatsoever, and two left feet. It doesn't matter. God doesn't hear as we do; what sounds strange to others seems like a heavenly choir to Him. I don't know about you, but this knowledge makes me happy, joyful, and appreciative.

Praise is also one thing that will make any situation better. On those days when it seems like nothing is going right, praise God! The situation may not change, but you will feel uplifted. On the days when the dream you've been waiting to manifest appears to be dead, praise God! You do know that God is in the resurrection business, right? And even on the days when everything is going well, and there are no problems at either work or home, praise God! He loves it when we praise Him just because of who He is, and not for what He does.

Praise tugs on God's heart and causes Him to lean in our direction. There's **R**estoration **I**n **P**raise—our hearts are lighter, our outlook becomes clearer, and we feel closer to God.

Let them praises give Jehovah,
For His name alone is high,
And His glory is exalted,
And His glory is exalted,
And His glory is exalted,
Far above the earth and sky.
Hallelujah, Praise Jehovah. William James Kirkpatrick
(1838-1921)

THANK GOD FOR AGITATORS

With a prayer to the God of heaven, I replied, "If it please the king, and if you are pleased with me, your servant, send me to Judah to rebuild the city where my ancestors are buried." . . . When I came to the governors of the province west of the Euphrates River, I delivered the king's letters to them. The king, I should add, had sent along army officers and horsemen to protect me. But when Sanballat the Horonite and Tobiah the Ammonite official heard of my arrival, they were very displeased that someone had come to help the people of Israel. (Nehemiah 2:5-6, 9-10, NLT)

Nehemiah was the king's cupbearer and was granted a leave to rebuild the wall. As is frequently the case when we're trying to do something spectacular for the Lord, our enemies come out of the woodwork to distract and discourage us. Sanballat and Tobiah, along with Geshem, were regional governors serving under the king of Persia. These three took it upon themselves to antagonize the workers and used their best efforts to stop the process. Despite their attempts, Nehemiah and the workers continued to move forward on the project. The wall was finished in 52 days!

The entire book of Nehemiah is a motivating view of the strategy of a God-led man to complete a project for the Lord. We, too, can take a page from his blueprint by focusing only on what God has instructed us to do. There will always be unhappy people who want to rain on our parade. They don't want anything, and they don't want you to have anything either. It's a unique feeling to complete a project and look back to see how God's hand maneuvered you around the enemy's snares.

Then Ezra praised the LORD, the great God, and all the people chanted, "Amen! Amen!" as they lifted their hands.
Then they bowed down and worshiped the LORD with their faces to the ground. (Nehemiah 8:6, NLT)

BEST IF USED BY . . .

Then the children of Judah came to Joshua in Gilgal. And Caleb the son of Jephunneh the Kenizzite said to him. . ."I was forty years old when Moses the servant of the LORD sent me from Kadesh Barnea to spy out the land, and I brought back word to him as it was in my heart. Nevertheless my brethren who went up with me made the heart of the people melt, but I wholly followed the LORD my God. So Moses swore on that day, saying, 'Surely the land where your foot has trodden shall be your inheritance and your children's forever, because you have wholly followed the LORD my God.' And now, behold, the LORD has kept me alive, as He said, these forty-five years, ever since the LORD spoke this word to Moses while Israel wandered in the wilderness; and now, here I am this day, eighty-five years old. As yet I am as strong this day as on the day that Moses sent me; just as my strength was then, so now is my strength for war, both for going out and for coming in. Now therefore, give me this mountain of which the LORD spoke in that day. . ." (Joshua 14:6[a]-11, NKJV)

It is a horrible feeling to be used by someone who is only trying to get as much from you as they can. Once they've achieved their purpose, they discard you. Praise God, He isn't like that!

God wants to use us in unimaginable ways for our good and His glory. We need to make ourselves available to Him anytime and anywhere and any way He wants. The senior saints at my church are an inspiration for many of us because they are still active, alert, and in good health well into their 80s and 90s. They have also made themselves available for God's use. They have a spirit like Caleb, who at the age of 85 requested and received a mountain! As I'm in the middle of my sixth decade, there are some things I can't do as well, but my goal is to do the assignment God has for me to the best of my ability.

Got breath? God can use you!

THE COVENANT

Then God said to Noah and to his sons with him: "I now establish my covenant with you and with your descendants after you . . ." And God said, "I have set my rainbow in the clouds, and it will be the sign of the covenant between me and the earth. Whenever I bring clouds over the earth and the rainbow appears in the clouds, I will remember my covenant between me and you and all living creatures of every kind. Never again will the waters become a flood to destroy all life. Whenever the rainbow appears in the clouds, I will see it and remember the everlasting covenant between God and all living creatures of every kind on the earth." (Genesis 9:8-9[a], 13-16, NIV)

Last year on this date at approximately 6:20 p.m., I was coming home from work and saw a rainbow for the first time. I was so excited! I had seen pictures of them, of course, but I had never seen one in person. While the photos I'd seen were wonderful, they paled in comparison to the real thing. The colors were so vibrant—red, orange, purple, blue, yellow, and green. And, it wasn't just one, but two. . . A double rainbow . . . Wow! Thankfully, I was a passenger, so that I could admire God's handiwork all the way from the far west side to the far east side of Columbus. I couldn't understand why more cars weren't parked off to the side of the highway to admire something you don't see every day. Then, I thought, Lord, please don't ever let me take You or the things You do for granted. I thanked God for giving me a visual sign of the covenant He made with Noah for generations to come, including me.

Thank You, Lord, for looking through the portals of time to see me.

TODAY

Be careful then, dear brothers and sisters. Make sure that your own hearts are not evil and unbelieving, turning you away from the living God. You must warn each other every day, while it is still "today," so that none of you will be deceived by sin and hardened against God. For if we are faithful to the end, trusting God just as firmly as when we first believed, we will share in all that belongs to Christ. Remember what it says: "Today when you hear his voice, don't harden your hearts as Israel did when they rebelled." (Hebrews 3:12-15, NLT)

The above Scripture is often used by Christians when evangelizing because it holds an implied sense of urgency. However, I want us to examine it from a different angle in terms of obedience to what God has called us to do.

Sometimes God whispers His instructions to us and at other times He shouts. He may give us a nudge in a certain direction or a full-blown shove. Whichever way He chooses to communicate, the intent is to get our attention and, then, for us to follow His directions. *Today*—not tomorrow, next week, next month, or next year—when we hear His voice is when we are to act. God's timing is impeccable; when we hear Him speak, we are to move.

Lord God, today help me to remove the world's waxy build-up, so I can clearly hear Your voice. And, then, give me a sense of urgency to complete my assignments.

TOMORROW

No, dear brothers and sisters . . . I focus on this one thing: Forgetting the past and looking forward to what lies ahead. (Philippians 3:13, NLT)

As I write this, it is a beautiful fall day. The sky is an intense blue, the clouds are puffs of white cotton, the sun is shining in all its glory, and the trees are gently swaying to the beat of Heaven's drum.

God wants you to know that it doesn't matter what happens today. It will only last 24 hours, and then it will be over, never to be repeated. Tomorrow when you wake up, you will experience a brand-new day. God has great plans for you and wonderful things in store for you. Will you allow Him to shape and mold you into a vessel He can use? The choice is yours. You can continue the way things are, or you can be like Paul and forget those things that are behind—the good and the bad—and reach, with excitement and a sense of expectation, for those things that are ahead.

*Thank You, Lord, for the things You
have planned for me. I trust and believe
You know what is best for me.*

I WANT TO DO THAT, TOO

Show me Your ways, O LORD; Teach me Your paths. Lead me in Your truth and teach me, For You are the God of my salvation; On You I wait all the day. (Psalm 25:4-5, NKJV)

My fraternal grandmother, Viola Evans, made one of the best pound cakes in the world. She's been in Heaven a very long time; but, I still remember the taste. No matter how many times I watched her make it, even standing right beside her and following her directions, mine never taste like hers. Mine are good, just not great. Every time I eat a slice of pound cake (and I've had a lot of great cakes over the years), I find myself subconsciously looking for that specific "taste."

English writer Charles Caleb Colton (1780-1832) is credited with the saying, "Imitation is the sincerest form of flattery." My grandmother wanted me to be successful at duplicating her recipe; God desires the same. King David is recognized as the author of Psalm 25 and makes a simple request of God: Show me your ways. God honored his request. He'll do the same for you if you but ask.

Show me Your ways that I may walk with You.
Show me Your ways I put my hope in You.
The cry of my heart is to love You more,
to live with the touch of Your hand.
Stronger each day. Show me Your ways.
Show Me Your Ways. Russell John Fragar. 1996.

AIN'T HE ALRIGHT?

May God himself, the God who makes everything holy and whole, make you holy and whole, put you together—spirit, soul, and body—and keep you fit for the coming of our Master, Jesus Christ. The One who called you is completely dependable. If he said it, he'll do it! (1 Thessalonians 5:23-24, MSG)

Sometimes when preaching, my pastor (Bishop Timothy J. Clarke) will stop and enthusiastically ask, "Ain't He alright?" This usually occurs when he has just finished stating one of God's many praise-worthy attributes. In some ways, it's a rhetorical question. God is going to be *alright* whether you agree or not. But, on the other hand, it's an opportunity for you to respond because of the momentary reflection of what the question brings to mind. Of course, sometimes when that momentary reflection goes on too long, Bishop's sermon is in danger of being taken from him because the congregation becomes lost in the memories of exactly how alright God is!

> When I think of the goodness of Jesus,
> and all that He's done for me;
> My soul cries out hallelujah!
> I thank God for saving me.

When I Think of the Goodness of Jesus. Malcolm Speed. 1997.

WHAT? THIS WASN'T ENOUGH?

He answered, "Why are you looking for me? Is it because you saw miraculous signs? The truth is, you are looking for me because you ate the bread and were satisfied. But earthly food spoils and ruins. So don't work to get that kind of food. But work to get the food that stays good and gives you eternal life. The Son of Man will give you that food. He is the only one qualified by God the Father to give it to you." The people asked Jesus, "What does God want us to do?" Jesus answered, "The work God wants you to do is this: to believe in the one he sent." So the people asked, "What miraculous sign will you do for us? If we can see you do a miracle, then we will believe you. What will you do?" (John 6:26-30, ERV)

Do you know people who are never satisfied? The more you give, the more they want. The miracle of feeding a large amount of people with a small amount of food should have been enough to convince anyone that Jesus was the Messiah. But, it wasn't. These people had the audaciousness to ask for proof that Jesus was who He said He was!

Now, before we come down on them too hard, let's make sure we're not doing the same thing. God has already done more than enough—and doesn't need to do anything else—to prove His love for us. Yet, there are those who still seek something else. There is nothing else!

"Everyone who sees the Son and believes in him has eternal life.
I will raise them up on the last day.
This is what my Father wants."
(John 6:40, ERV)

WHAT MORE DO I NEED TO DO FOR YOU?

"I, the LORD, was ready to answer even those who were not asking and to be found by those who were not searching. To a nation that refused to worship me, I said, 'Here I am!' All day long I have reached out to stubborn and sinful people going their own way. They keep making me angry by sneering at me, while offering sacrifice to idols in gardens and burning incense to them on bricks. They spend their nights hiding in burial caves; they eat the meat of pigs, cooked in sauces made of stuff unfit to eat. And then they say to others, 'Don't come near us! We're dedicated to God.' Such people are like smoke, irritating my nose all day." (Isaiah 65:1-5, CEV)

Have you ever had a smell get in your nose that you can't get rid of? One of my co-workers had a lotion she put on every time she came out of the ladies' room. The lotion smelled good, but something in it really aggravated my nose. The discomfort only lasted a few minutes, but still I was almost to the point of replacing the lotion with a fragrance-free scent or asking her to wait until she got off work to go to the restroom (just kidding).

My point is that I'm sure that when God had the prophet Isaiah pen the words of today's Scripture, He had already looked down the portal of time to this year. He knows everything, but that doesn't mean He's pleased with what He knows. He's reached out to those who won't accept Him. He loves those who won't love Him. He's been good to those who won't be good to Him.

I'll ask the question for God: What more does He need to do for you to serve Him?

Let's make sure that our actions and attitudes don't offend God.
The last thing we want is to become a stench in His nostrils!

BUT, I DIDN'T EVEN DO NOTHING!

And the LORD spoke to Moses, saying, "Send men to spy out the land of Canaan, which I am giving to the children of Israel; from each tribe of their fathers you shall send a man, every one a leader among them . . .". Then they told him, and said: "We went to the land where you sent us. It truly flows with milk and honey, and this is its fruit. Nevertheless the people who dwell in the land are strong; the cities are fortified and very large; moreover we saw the descendants of Anak there. . .". Then Caleb quieted the people before Moses, and said, "Let us go up at once and take possession, for we are well able to overcome it." (Numbers 13:1-2, 27-28, 30, NKJV)

I grew up in a generation that believed in spanking. I also grew up in a household with a father who believed in everybody getting the same punishment if the guilty party didn't confess. Although 99% of the time my father knew which child did the deed, he didn't relent, despite our protests.

Joshua, Caleb, and the other ten spies were tasked with spying out Canaan. While Joshua and Caleb came back with an accurate report, the other spies voiced their protests louder. The children of Israel chose to believe that God wouldn't keep His Word to them of possessing the land and accepted the ten spies' negative report (Numbers 14:6-9). God wasn't pleased. Despite knowing and reporting the faithfulness of God, Joshua and Caleb had to endure the same punishment for the others' disbelief. "According to the number of the days in which you spied out the land, forty days, for each day you shall bear your guilt one year, namely forty years, and you shall know My rejection" (Numbers 14:34).

There may be times when we do the right thing and things still don't go our way, like the spankings I endured that weren't my fault. In the end, I survived; Joshua and Caleb did, too. And, so will you.

Lord, we don't like it when we feel punished for something we didn't do. However, if we believe that all things work together for good (Romans 8:28), then we must understand that somehow, some way, in the end, we'll be stronger for having endured and survived the test.

PART- TIME LOVER

Then Jesus said to his followers, "If any of you want to be my follower, you must stop thinking about yourself and what you want. You must be willing to carry the cross that is given to you for following me." (Matthew 16:24, ERV)

"I'm committed to you." "I'm committed to the process." "You have my full commitment." We hear these statements on a regular basis; yet, what some people really mean is, "I'm committed as long as this doesn't inconvenience me in any way."

When Elisha was called by Elijah, he willingly slaughtered one of his oxen and boiled it, using his own equipment to do so. He had no plans of returning to his former lifestyle (1 Kings: 19-21). When each disciple was called, they willingly chose to demonstrate their commitment to Jesus by walking away from their livelihood to follow Him (fisherman, tax collector, physician, etc.).

If your spouse told you that he or she would only be with you on Monday, Wednesday, and Friday, would that be acceptable? If you're single, do you give God every day or only particular ones that won't affect your schedule?

These may seem like extreme questions, but we do it to God every day. Just as you wouldn't want a part-time marriage, God doesn't want one either. We're God's bride and He expects and demands full-time marital privileges.

"Treat others (and God)
as you want them to treat you. . ."
(Matthew 7:12 [a], CEV, emphasis mine)

THE ORIGINAL

In the beginning God created the heaven and the earth. (Genesis 1:1, KJV)

Christiaan Barnard (1922-2001) was a South African cardiac surgeon who performed the first human-to-human heart transplant on December 3, 1967, in Cape Town, South Africa. The first patient survived only 18 days; his second transplant patient lived 19 months (www.nytimes.com). Can you imagine as a fellow cardiologist or potential medical student interested in cardiology being personally taught by a pioneer in the field? It would give you an advantage over anyone else because you received the information firsthand. You would be privy to Dr. Barnard's thoughts, ideas, and ways.

Now, think of how you feel when you hear a sermon that comes directly from God. Or, imagine yourself in the sandals of the disciples, sitting at Jesus' feet. It gives you a good feeling, doesn't it?

Most of us aren't cardiologists, so while Dr. Barnard's transplant innovations were remarkable, they don't necessarily affect us directly. And, none of us were around when Jesus walked the Earth. Yet, the amazing thing is we're still privy to His thoughts, ideas, and ways. We still have intimate access to Him as we engage in prayer and study His Word. Wow!

Thank You, Lord, for leaving us a way to always connect with You. We can pray, read, and study to know what You want and how You want things done. You left us a blueprint so that we can become more like You. That's incredible!

I'LL BE WITH YOU. . .FOREVER

You're blessed when you're content with just who you are—no more, no less. That's the moment you find yourselves proud owners of everything that can't be bought. (Matthew 5:5, MSG)

Today is my mother's birthday. Sadly, Ruby Ray Rogers is no longer here. She passed away 47 years ago, two weeks after I turned 18 and two months before I graduated from high school.

For years I convinced myself we had a good relationship—which we did—but it wasn't until one evening God confronted me that I realized just how mad I was that she left. See, my mother was the peaceful half of a two-parent household. My siblings and I often remark on how Mom never raised her voice. I saw firsthand people treating her unkindly; yet, she never retaliated. And, she displayed unconditional love for all of us. Mom "got" us and allowed us to be who we are.

Once I released the anger, I saw things differently. Don't get me wrong; it still hurts that my mother is not alive, even after all these years. However, she left me with the tools I needed to survive in this world. And, more importantly, she left me with memories of her. I believe my mother knew she was getting ready to leave this world and did her best to prepare me for what was to come. Of course, I didn't realize that then, but she'd often start a life-lesson with, "Now, I'm not always going to be here, so you need to . . . ." She wanted me to be successful and well-rounded.

When I reflect on my mother, I see a woman at total peace in her relationship with the Lord. How else could she endure the death of my older brother, a marriage with a person who wasn't always pleasant, six children with totally different personalities, and all the other myriad of events that occurred during her lifetime? She had the peace *of* God and peace *with* God, and that made all the difference. She visually demonstrated what a relationship with God looked like by her example. And that is the greatest legacy any parent can leave.

Such good people will never fall.
They will always be remembered. (Psalm 112:6, ERV)

BLESSED AND HIGHLY FAVORED

"But blessed are your eyes because they see, and your ears because they hear. For truly I tell you, many prophets and righteous people longed to see what you see but did not see it, and to hear what you hear but did not hear it." (Matthew 13:16-17, NIV)

When was the last time you thought of how privileged you are to be part of the Kingdom of God? Sometimes we become complacent as to just how big of a deal that is, as if we did God a favor.

God has been better than any of us deserve. He has opened and closed doors; provided and protected; saved and kept. Frankly, as far as I'm concerned God doesn't have to do another thing for me. My love for Him is secured; it's not going to fade out or fade away. I love Him today and I'll love Him tomorrow. More importantly, I know that I'm loved in return.

All my heart to Him I give, ever to Him I'll cling,
In His blessèd presence live, ever His praises sing,
Love so mighty and so true, merits my soul's best songs,
Faithful, loving service too, to Him belongs.
Love lifted me! Love lifted me!
When nothing else could help
Love lifted me!
Love Lifted Me.
James Rowe (lyrics)
Howard E. Smith (music). 1912.

EXCEPTIONAL

Before I made you in your mother's womb, I knew you. Before you were born, I chose you for a special work. (Jeremiah 1:5[a], ERV)

Please don't think I'm arrogant or conceited when I tell you I was born to be exceptional. And, in case you didn't know it, you were too. We are made in the image of Almighty God and there's nothing unexceptional about Him.

Our goal then should be to get into agreement with God, seek His face for our assignment, and get busy. God has something extraordinary for you to do and you're the only one who can do it. It may be teaching an elementary school class, giving students a foundation for life-long learning, as well as a visual of how a Christian looks and acts. It may be a father who demonstrates what his daughter should look for in men and how his sons should treat all women. It may be putting pen to paper and finishing that book, play, movie, or song you've always wanted to create.

When you embrace the exceptional in you and realize God put it there before you were even thought of, you can then appreciate fully what Paul wrote: "I *can* do all things through Christ who strengthens me" (Philippians 4:13, NKJV, emphasis mine). Tell God yes, step out of your comfort zone, buckle your seat belt, and get started on (or complete) what God has waiting for you. It may be scary, but it's also doable. Otherwise, God wouldn't have given it to you.

All road sign read destiny.
I'll follow where ever you lead.
Nothing can hinder me.
For the prize is all I see.
I will be what you called me to be.
I say yes, Lord, I agree.
My desire passionately
Is to be what you called me to be.
That's what I'll be.
Called to Be. Jonathan Nelson. 2010.

NOTHING AND NO ONE

So, what do you think? With God on our side like this, how can we lose? If God didn't hesitate to put everything on the line for us, embracing our condition and exposing himself to the worst by sending his own Son, is there anything else he wouldn't gladly and freely do for us? And who would dare tangle with God by messing with one of God's chosen? Who would dare even to point a finger? The One who died for us—who was raised to life for us!—is in the presence of God at this very moment sticking up for us. Do you think anyone is going to be able to drive a wedge between us and Christ's love for us? There is no way! Not trouble, not hard times, not hatred, not hunger, not homelessness, not bullying threats, not backstabbing, not even the worst sins listed in Scripture: They kill us in cold blood because they hate you. We're sitting ducks; they pick us off one by one. None of this fazes us because Jesus loves us. I'm absolutely convinced that nothing—nothing living or dead, angelic or demonic, today or tomorrow, high or low, thinkable or unthinkable—absolutely nothing can get between us and God's love because of the way that Jesus our Master has embraced us. (Romans 8:31-39, MSG)

I'll admit that out of the 66 books of the Bible there are quite a few passages I have problems understanding. Praise God, the passage for today isn't one of them.

I'll also admit that out of these same 66 books, some passages need no further explanation to understand what God is saying. Fortunately, the passage for today is one of those.

Whenever it seems like something or someone tries to detour us from our spiritual track, we need only remember what God has said: There's nothing (no thing) and no one who can change His mind about us! We're His, and that's the way it will remain until we either die or Jesus Christ comes back! That's a promise we can hold onto forever!

Be relaxed with what you have. Since God assured us, "I'll never let you down, never walk off and leave you," we can boldly quote, God is there, ready to help; I'm fearless no matter what. Who or what can get to me?
(Hebrews 13:5-6, MSG)

YEAH, WE LIED

Johanan, Jezaniah, the other army officers, and everyone else in the group, came to me and said, "Please pray to the LORD your God for us. Judah used to have many people, but as you can see, only a few of us are left. Ask the LORD to tell us where he wants us to go and what he wants us to do." "All right," I answered, "I will pray to the LORD your God, and I will tell you everything he says." They answered, "The LORD himself will be our witness that we promise to do whatever he says, even if it isn't what we want to do. We will obey the LORD so that all will go well for us." (Jeremiah 42:1-6, CEV)

The Israelites asked Jeremiah to seek the Lord on their behalf to determine whether they should go to Egypt. He accepted their petition and told them he would reveal the Lord's response (vv. 1-4). They knew Jeremiah to be one of God's prophets and had enough trust to approach him. Because they had seen the miracles God performed through Jeremiah, they were excited and anxious to hear what the Lord's response would be. I'm sure they thought they'd get a quick answer to their petition. But, no! The Bible says that the Lord didn't respond to Jeremiah until ten days after his request. We know that when waiting, ten days may seem like a lifetime. We also know that God is always on time and His answer is always correct (vv. 11-12).

The Israelites didn't like the Lord's response, which was for them to stay put. They accused Jeremiah of lying about what the Lord said and refused to obey God's Word, even though they had assured Jeremiah they would do everything God said. So, being stubborn as well as liars, they proceeded to leave Israel for Egypt. Everything that God promised would be waiting for them was there; they were punished (see Jeremiah 42:13-22).

God knows what's best for us, even when we don't want to hear it. He is always looking out for our good. We just need to be obedient.

TRANSITIONS

As for man, his days are as grass: as a flower of the field, so he flourisheth. For the wind passeth over it, and it is gone; and the place thereof shall know it no more. But the mercy of the LORD is from everlasting to everlasting upon them that fear him, and his righteousness unto children's children; To such as keep his covenant, and to those that remember his commandments to do them. (Psalm 103:15-18, KJV)

It would be wonderful if we could always do what we've done. You know, like when you were a child, skipping down the street without a care in the world. It wasn't your concern to find a place to live and sleep, to gather food to eat, or to wash your clothes. Alas, those days don't last. We grow up and learn to do things for ourselves. We make the transition to adulthood without a lot of fanfare or resistance.

As we grow older, we face another transition. This time it's a little more challenging. You've had years of doing things a certain way; now you have changed, sometimes seemingly in the blink of an eye. I thought about this as I looked around my church one Wednesday afternoon during Bible study. The people who were at my church when I arrived thirty years ago are now older. They're moving a little slower, still healthy, but the vibrancy has dimmed. But, one thing is evident: their faith in and love of God hasn't faltered. If anything, it's gotten stronger.

As I enter into the status of "senior," I want to emulate the senior saints at my church. It gives me peace to know that the older I get, the greater the love I have for Jesus.

Falling in love with Jesus was the best thing
I've ever, ever done.
Falling in Love With Jesus. Jonathan Butler. 2009.

SHARING IS CARING

What a wonderful God we have—he is the Father of our Lord Jesus Christ, the source of every mercy, and the one who so wonderfully comforts and strengthens us in our hardships and trials. And why does he do this? So that when others are troubled, needing our sympathy and encouragement, we can pass on to them this same help and comfort God has given us. (2 Corinthians 1:3-4, TLB)

Years ago, I was the leader of a single parenting group at my church. During one session, a mother was sharing the challenges she had raising a male child. The other participants offered suggestions and advice that she willingly accepted; however, I noticed that every comment I made was ignored. As the session continued, I mentioned something about my son; then her attitude changed. I believe she previously thought I was talking about something I didn't have personal experience in; boy, was she wrong!

The apostle Paul tells us that we're going to have trouble, that God will help us through the crisis, and then we're to pass the experience on when the opportunity arrives. He isn't saying that you tell everybody you meet all your business. What he is saying is that you can give insight into a specific situation because of your experience. There's theory, and then there's experience, and both have relevancy. When you combine the two, it gives more power to your statement. Sometimes we're too quick to escape things that are unpleasant. Perhaps we should consider that what we're going through isn't only for or about us; we all have something to impart into someone else's life.

Lord, help us to stand firm as we face life's challenges, knowing that
You're going to cause good to come
out of every situation, even when we can't see
or understand how that will happen.

IT DON'T TAKE ALL THAT!

David was dancing in front of the LORD. He was wearing a linen ephod
. . .Saul's daughter Michal was looking out the window. While the
LORD'S Holy Box was being carried into the city, David was jumping
and dancing before the LORD. Michal saw this, and she was upset at
David. . . "The king of Israel did not honor himself today! You took off
your clothes in front of your servants' girls. You were like a fool who
takes off his clothes without shame!" Then David said to Michal, "The
LORD chose me. . . So I will continue dancing and celebrating in front
of the LORD. I might do things that are even more embarrassing! Maybe
you will not respect me, but the girls you are talking about are proud of
me!" (2 Samuel 6:14, 16, 20-22, ERV)

The Bible is full of fascinating stories, and none more than the story of
David, Saul, and Michal. Saul gave his daughter in marriage to David as a
plot to kill him. Saul knew Michal loved David and planned to use it to
his advantage, but the plan backfired (1 Samuel 1:17-30). Saul continued
attempting to kill David, so he fled the area. He was gone a long time,
married other women, and Saul gave Michal in marriage to another man
(1 Samuel 25:42-43). When David replaced Saul as king, he demanded
Michal back and sent his men to get her, which made her unhappy (2
Samuel 3:12-16).

    David was excited because the ark was finally home. He
demonstrated his joy through dancing, and so did the people with him.
Unfortunately, when he went home, Michal attacked his behavior in an
area she thought would wound him—his vanity—when she pointed out
how the slave girls would interpret his actions. Michal had forgotten that
David had a relationship with God that went back to childhood. Praising
God was as natural to David as breathing and would never embarrass him.
It was sincere worship to the God he loved, and God honored his worship.
Michal should have left well enough alone and kept her opinion to herself.
If she had, perhaps she wouldn't have been barren, which in that culture
was truly an embarrassment (2 Samuel 6:23).

He is the one you should praise. He is your God. He has done great and amazing
things for you. You have seen them with your own eyes.
(Deuteronomy 10:21, ERV)

IT'S ABOUT TIME!

Is this not the carpenter's son? Is not His mother called Mary? And His brothers James, Joses, Simon, and Judas? (Matthew 13:55, NKJV)

Jude, a bondservant of Jesus Christ, and brother of James . . . (Jude 1, NKJV)

But I saw none of the other apostles except James, the Lord's brother. (Galatians 1:19, NKJV)

Whenever I watch the mini-series *The Temptations*—the story of the legendary R&B musical group whose music is just as popular today as it was when originally recorded—I often think of how wonderful to be at the beginning of something new and innovative.

I believe that Jesus' original disciples enjoyed that privilege. Yes, they were challenged with threats and disbelief; they were probably called insane, unbalanced, and just plain old crazy. However, their discomfort (except for Judas) was exonerated when Jesus rose from the dead. They had the privilege of seeing the Lord after His resurrection and watching Him ascend into heaven.

Unfortunately, the bad news is that Jesus' brothers couldn't share that experience because James and Jude didn't come to believe in Jesus until *after* His resurrection (John 7:5; Acts 1:14). Fortunately, the good news is that it's not about when you believe; it's only that you do come to belief in Jesus as Lord and Savior. I'm sure that James and Jude had regrets about not believing in their brother earlier. It's not right, but we can't hold it against them, just like we can't hold it against those who have yet to say yes to Jesus. Our prayer for them is that they will come to acceptance before it's too late, and then go on to proclaim the Good News, just like James and Jude.

Anytime is the right time to get saved

WON'T BE FOOLED AGAIN

Now for some time a man named Simon had practiced sorcery in the city and amazed all the people of Samaria. He boasted that he was someone great, and all the people, both high and low, gave him their attention and exclaimed, "This man is rightly called the Great Power of God." They followed him because he had amazed them for a long time with his sorcery. But when they believed Philip as he proclaimed the good news of the kingdom of God and the name of Jesus Christ, they were baptized, both men and women. Simon himself believed and was baptized. And he followed Philip everywhere, astonished by the great signs and miracles he saw. (Acts 8:9-13, NIV)

Perhaps this has been your experience. You meet someone who seems to be one way but the more you're around them, you realize that something isn't quite right. You "see" them clearly for the first time, or they "see" themselves as they really are.

That's what happened to Simon, the sorcerer. When he met the "real" Great Power of God after pretending for so long, he recognized that what he had been doing was wrong. . . so much so that he believed and was baptized. But, then, as sometimes happens with some of us former sinners, we revert to our former lifestyle. When Simon saw Peter and John laying hands on people to receive the Holy Spirit, he decided he needed to "buy" this gift. Peter rebuked him, set him straight, and then prayed for him (vv. 14-25).

Let's pray that God will show us people as they really are, and not as we think or want them to be. And, if you, like Simon, are playing a fake game of pretend, ask God for the boldness to put away childish things and become what He would have you to be.

"Fool me once, shame on you.
Fool me twice, shame on me"
—Author unknown.

THE LAST THING YOU'D EXPECT TO SEE

Have two goals: wisdom—that is, knowing and doing right—and common sense. Don't let them slip away, for they fill you with living energy and bring you honor and respect. They keep you safe from defeat and disaster and from stumbling off the trail. With them on guard you can sleep without fear; you need not be afraid of disaster or the plots of wicked men, for the Lord is with you; he protects you. (Proverbs 3:21-26, TLB)

Evidently Peter was one of those people who could fall asleep anywhere, even standing up. The guards were probably accustomed to prisoners begging for their life and trying to cut a deal for release. I'm sure they were wondering how Peter could be so calm since his days were literally numbered. Peter was scheduled to be executed after the Passover (Acts 12:1-4), but I believe he knew the church was praying for him and was confident that God was going to work things out.

Acts 12:6-7,9,11 (TLB) reads: "The night before he was to be executed, he was asleep, double-chained between two soldiers with others standing guard before the prison gate, when suddenly there was a light in the cell and an angel of the Lord stood beside Peter! The angel slapped him on the side to awaken him and said, "Quick! Get up!" And the chains fell off his wrists! . . .So, Peter left the cell, following the angel. All the time he thought it was a dream or vision and didn't believe it was really happening. . . Peter finally realized what had happened! "It's really true!" he said to himself. "The Lord has sent his angel and saved me from Herod and from what the Jews were hoping to do to me!"

I wonder what the guards thought the next morning when they were the only ones chained. Peter was nowhere to be found and only his shackles were left hanging. I'd love to have been privy to their explanations.

"Give your entire attention to what God is doing right now, and don't get worked up about what may or may not happen tomorrow. God will help you deal with whatever hard things come up when the time comes."
(Matthew 6:34, MSG)

IS YOU IS OR IS YOU AIN'T?

So roll up your sleeves, put your mind in gear, be totally ready to receive the gift that's coming when Jesus arrives. Don't lazily slip back into those old grooves of evil, doing just what you feel like doing. You didn't know any better then; you do now. As obedient children let yourselves be pulled into a way of life shaped by God's life, a life energetic and blazing with holiness. God said, "I am holy; you be holy." You call out to God for help and he helps—he's a good Father that way. (1 Peter 1:13-16, MSG)

I've discovered a lot of great music from watching the older cartoons. My grandsons and I were watching a *Tom and Jerry* cartoon and "Is You Is or Is You Ain't (My Baby)" started playing. Tom (the cat) was singing it to his girlfriend, who was being pursued by another cat. I don't know what Billy Austin and Louis Jordan had in mind when they wrote the lyrics and music to this song around 1944, but when I first heard it, I immediately thought of Christianity.

There are numerous people who are undecided as to whether they want to sell out for Christ or keep one foot in the world while in the Church. "I am holy; you be holy" isn't a suggestion! And God wants it settled once and for all: Are you or are you not going to follow me? In other words, "Is You Is or Is You Ain't" going to be a Christian? If you're going to follow God, then act like Him. If you're not going to follow God, then act like the one you are going to follow.

Living holy is challenging. You must embrace concepts of sacrifice, discipline, and self-denial. You must give up the right to be right. You must learn to love everybody, even the not so lovable. Yet, this is what God calls us to do, and He is willing to help us achieve and maintain a holiness lifestyle. Straddling the fence is hard work. Haven't you been doing it long enough?

You call out to God for help and he helps—he's a good Father that way. But don't forget, he's also a responsible Father, and won't let you get by with sloppy living. (1 Peter 1:17, MSG)

THE ANSWER TO THE QUESTION

Am I my brother's keeper? (Genesis 4:9[b], NKJV)

My daughter-in-law surprised my son with a three-day trip to Las Vegas to celebrate a significant birthday; the kids were staying with me. I love my grandkids, but I momentarily forgot there were five of them ranging in age from almost two to thirteen!

I had gotten up early to "try" to get a jump on the day. The 10-year-old got up first and hopped in the shower. The oldest one got up shortly after and just as he came out of the shower, the youngest three all woke up at the same time. I was trying to juggle showers, brushing teeth, and change a diaper—not quite that successfully, I might add. It had been a long time since I had been around that many little people at the same time.

Finally, in desperation, I asked the 10-year-old to stay with the baby while I got the toddlers together. Once finished, I went to relieve my grandson of his duties and stopped cold. See, what had happened was that my son—in their haste to bring the things necessary for that many children to be away from home—forgot to bring the base to the baby's playpen, which is where he was to sleep. So, they purchased a smaller one once they arrived in town. What stopped me was that the 10-year-old had gotten into the playpen with his brother! Once I got over the visual, I burst out laughing. "What are you doing?" I asked. His reply: "I'm playing with my brother. He was lonely!" Sometimes you need to think outside the box to have a successful outcome. My grandson didn't think about the fact the playpen was *not* designed for someone his age or size. His goal was to entertain his brother because he was left alone in the room, stuck in a playpen.

Isn't that what Jesus did for us who claim salvation? We were stuck in a playpen. Oh, we may not have called it that, but we were stuck in something. God saw a need and sent Jesus to keep us company.

Lord, thank You for thinking enough of us to send help when we need it.

CAN I GET A GOOD AMEN?

Give to the LORD the glory due His name; Bring an offering and come into His courts. Oh, worship the LORD in the beauty of holiness! Tremble before Him, all the earth. (Psalm 96:8-9, NKJV)

Beauty brings me a sense of awe. Flowers dressed in an assortment of colors. . . the height of a majestic mountain . . . a spectacular sunset captured on film for posterity. . . children laughing and playing. These are but a few of the things that inspire awe.

There is no one worthier of a sense of awe than God, the Creator and Sustainer of our soul. We have the privilege of appreciating His greatness anytime and anywhere, and there are no time restraints imposed. Let the Church agree and say Amen!

> O Lord my God, When I in awesome wonder
> Consider all the worlds Thy Hands have made;
> I see the stars, I hear the rolling thunder
> Thy power throughout the universe displayed.
> Then sings my soul, My Saviour God, to Thee
> How great Thou art, How great Thou art
> Then sings my soul, My Saviour God, to Thee
> How great Thou art, How great Thou art!
> *How Great Thou Art.*
> Carl Gustav Boberg (1859-1940)
> Translator: Stuart K. Hine (1949)

THE SUPPORTING ROLE

Tychicus, a beloved brother, faithful minister, and fellow servant in the Lord, will tell you all the news about me. I am sending him to you for this very purpose, that he may know your circumstances and comfort your hearts, with Onesimus, a faithful and beloved brother, who is one of you . . .Aristarchus my fellow prisoner greets you, with Mark the cousin of Barnabas (about whom you received instructions: if he comes to you, welcome him), and Jesus who is called Justus. These are my only fellow workers for the kingdom of God who are of the circumcision; they have proved to be a comfort to me. Epaphras, who is one of you, a bondservant of Christ, greets you. . .Luke the beloved physician and Demas greet you. Greet the brethren who are in Laodicea, and Nymphas and the church that is in his house. (Colossians 4:7-15, NKJV)

I overheard two women talking one day about a mutual friend. The one was irritated because the friend had been acknowledged for a project by name whereas the other woman wasn't mentioned.

I thought about their conversation when I read today's Scripture. The apostle Paul was usually quick to acknowledge those who helped him in ministry; yet, even with all the names he mentioned in his epistles, I'm sure he forgot one or two or more. Did they get upset when Paul's letters were read aloud, and they didn't hear their name? Did they stomp off in a huff and quit working? Or, did they accept that their job was to help Paul in whatever way necessary?

We can't all be out front, or nothing would ever get accomplished. Movies have supporting casts, employers have support staff, and the Church has members. When everyone does their part, success is guaranteed. We all want to be thanked for our labor, and it is nice when someone identifies us by name. It's even better when we understand that God knows not only our name but what we do. Isn't that more important?

Whatever you do, work at it with all your heart, as though you were working for the Lord and not for people. (Colossians 3:23, GNT)

NO DOUBT

Therefore say to them, "This is what the Sovereign LORD says: None of my words will be delayed any longer; whatever I say will be fulfilled, declares the Sovereign LORD." (Ezekiel 12:28, NIV)

When we experience a delay in a promise from God, we're sometimes tempted to begin doubting. Did I *really* hear from God, or was it my imagination? We know the Bible tells us that God doesn't lie, and we want to believe that with our whole heart, but, there's sometimes a small trickle of doubt that makes us feel bad for even thinking it.

I believe these moments of doubt are the enemy's way of keeping us in bondage. Oh, not the bondage of sin, but the bondage of not moving higher in the Lord. How? Through discouragement, dismay, and disappointment. The enemy will use anything to keep us stagnant in the Lord. God's desire is for us to grow in grace and love and move from baby's milk to meat.

The next time your mind allows doubt to raise its head, don't entertain the thought. After all, what has the enemy done for you lately that you would believe his lies over God's truth?

"Let your faith roar so loud
that you can't hear what doubt is saying."
—Anonymous

PRAISE YOUR WAY THROUGH

I will praise the Lord no matter what happens. I will constantly speak of his glories and grace. I will boast of all his kindness to me. Let all who are discouraged take heart. Let us praise the Lord together and exalt his name. (Psalm 34:1-3, TLB)

Praising our way through the challenges of life does not mean we wear blinders. This isn't a *que sera, sera* moment, where whatever will be, will be. Nor, do we have a Pollyanna mentality, where everything is sweetness and light. It's okay to say, "God, I don't understand what's going on, but I'm going to trust You, regardless." It's nearly impossible to praise and complain at the same time.

"God, help me with my attitude" is the request we should make. Asking God to show us what to do with life events keeps us focused on Him with laser-like sharpness. Adverse life experiences can be a stumbling block or a stepping stone, and only we can determine which one we'll follow. With God's help, we can turn everything into a stepping stone, bringing us closer to God.

I praise the LORD because he is good.
I praise the name of the LORD Most High.
(Psalm 7:17, ERV)

DOES IT GET ANY BETTER THAN THIS?

No, you have come to Mount Zion, to the city of the living God, the heavenly Jerusalem, and to countless thousands of angels in a joyful gathering. You have come to the assembly of God's firstborn children, whose names are written in heaven. You have come to God himself, who is the judge over all things. You have come to the spirits of the righteous ones in heaven who have now been made perfect. You have come to Jesus, the one who mediates the new covenant between God and people, and to the sprinkled blood, which speaks of forgiveness instead of crying out for vengeance like the blood of Abel. (Hebrews 12:22-24, NLT)

During my tenure with the city of Columbus, I worked in City Hall at one time, where the Mayor's office is located. Although I was in the same building, I didn't have the privilege of walking into his private office whenever I wanted to talk about whatever was on my mind. There would have been numerous obstacles to overcome, including an armed guard, before I'd even get close to him. Fortunately, I never felt anything was so pressing that I needed to risk my life to talk with the Mayor.

As powerful as our government and elected officials may be, access to them is often denied. But, Praise God, we have access to the most influential person in the Universe when we open our mouths. It really is that simple. We no longer have the Old Testament method of the High Priest entering the chamber of the Holy of Holies once a year to place our petitions before the Lord. Jesus made the way for us to access God for ourselves, and the amazing thing is that He's waiting to hear from us! We can commune by standing or kneeling, whispering or shouting, crying and sighing, or even moaning! No matter the method, God is listening for us.

So, the answer to the question in the title is, no, it doesn't get any better! One of the paramount privileges we have is to talk with Jesus whenever we want. I don't know about you, but that's one of the best benefits of salvation.

Along with the gift of salvation came the gift of communication.
Are you taking advantage of the gift?

ALL I DO IS SIT AND WAIT

The LORD is good to those who wait for him, to the soul who seeks him. (Lamentations 3:25, NKJV)

It seems that I spend a significant amount of time waiting, which reminds me of the opening to Nikki Giovanni's poem: "all i gotta do is sit and wait, sit and wait, and it's gonna find me. all i gotta do is sit and wait, if I can learn how." ("All I Gotta Do," from *The Women and the Men*, 1975).

Whoever said patience is a virtue needs to be smacked! Okay, not really. But, sometimes when I've waited a long time for something to happen, I tend to get annoyed, although I am aware there is no better way to learn how to wait than to wait! I try not to get frustrated since there's not a lot I can do about it. Getting upset is a waste of energy because when I'm finished fussing, I'm still waiting.

One way I get past the frustration is to remind myself that I'm not the only one waiting for something or someone. There are people all around me who are in similar situations. There are also witnesses in the Bible who show us how to wait with the right attitude. Joseph waited 13 years for the dreams and visions he was given as a child to begin to come true. David waited almost 15 years between the anointing and the appointment to become king. Sarah waited almost 20 years to hold her own child.

If people promise you something, you might want to take it with a grain of salt. They're human, so they may not be able to do what they said. However, if God has promised you anything, remember that His Word is solid. If He said it will happen, consider it done. We only have to sit and wait.

"The times we find ourselves having to wait on others may be the perfect opportunities to train ourselves to wait on the Lord."
—Joni Eareckson Tada

"Patience is also a form of action." —Auguste Rodin

WORTH THE WAIT

"Do not let your hearts be troubled. You believe in God; believe also in me. My Father's house has many rooms; if that were not so, would I have told you that I am going there to prepare a place for you? And if I go and prepare a place for you, I will come back and take you to be with me that you also may be where I am." (John 14:1-3, NIV)

I have another thought about waiting. People (me included) often say, "I can't wait for . . ." but we will wait because we have no choice. No matter how we (or the stores) want to rush Christmas, it occurs on the 25th of December every year. What about Girl Scout cookies, which I love? We complain about the price increasing and the contents decreasing, but every year when it's Girl Scout cookie time, we're gleefully placing our orders while telling ourselves we'll put some in the freezer for a later time.

Okay, admit it. You don't like to wait any more than I do. Why is it so difficult to wait? Is it the excitement and anticipation of what's to come? Or, is it our wanting something to be over? Or, is it the not knowing if what you're waiting for is going to happen?

Jesus *is* coming back. No one knows when, but it is going to happen. And, when we are united with Jesus, we'll admit that He was well worth the wait.

Lord, help us to patiently wait for Your return. In the meantime, help us to finish our assignments so we can hear You say, "Well done, good and faithful servant! You have been faithful with a few things; I will put you in charge of many things. Come and share your master's happiness!"
(Matthew 25:21, NIV)

WHAT ARE YOU WAITING ON?

"Call to Me, and I will answer you. And I will show you great and wonderful things which you do not know." (Jeremiah 33:3, NLV)

If someone gave you a blank check and told you that regardless of whatever amount you fill in, the check could be cashed, what would you do? Would you hold on to it? Would you fill in an exorbitant amount to see what would happen? Would you sit down and calculate how much you need before filling out the check? Would you throw it away, thinking it was a hoax?

God has given us something better than a blank check with unlimited financial resources. He's given us the promise of answering us when we ask for anything and everything we need. That's better than money that, if not handled properly, will soon be gone. So, what are you waiting on? You have an open line to God, and He's waiting on your call.

"If ye abide in me, and my words abide in you, ye shall ask what ye will, and it shall be done unto you."
(John 15:7, KJV)

YOU CAN'T MAKE ME!

"Today I am giving you a choice of two ways. And I ask heaven and earth to be witnesses of your choice. You can choose life or death. The first choice will bring a blessing. The other choice will bring a curse. So choose life!" (Deuteronomy 30:19, ERV)

As you watch children play or listen to them talk, you might hear one child say to another, "You can't make me!" implying that the child they are talking to doesn't have what it takes to make them do anything. Sometimes the taunt results in a fight; other times both parties walk away laughing.

God made us in His image and a little lower than the angels (Genesis 1:27, Psalm 8:5); yet, at no time does He *make* us choose Him.

- Just as you wouldn't want someone to be with you because you make them, God doesn't force us to come to Him.
- Just as you wouldn't want someone to be with you because of what you could do for them, God's mercy is unwavering.
- Just as you wouldn't want someone to be with you because it's politically correct to do so, God's faithfulness is everlasting.

God doesn't make us do anything. He created us with free will— the ability to choose and make decisions. When we consider all that God has done, is doing, and will do, the choice to me is obvious.

> *But maybe you don't want to serve the LORD.*
> *You must choose for yourselves today.*
> *Today you must decide who you will serve.*
> (Joshua 24:15[a], ERV)

TODAY COULD BE THE DAY

In those days Hezekiah was sick and near death. And Isaiah the prophet, the son of Amoz, went to him and said to him, "Thus says the LORD: 'Set your house in order, for you shall die and not live.'" (Isaiah 38:1, NKJV)

I praise God that I have yet to receive a diagnosis so severe that I was told I would die. However, I know numerous people who have. The surprising thing about their reaction is that it falls into two categories—they either accept the diagnosis and give up, or they make up their mind that God has the final say, not the physicians.

Hezekiah was the son of Ahaz, one of the worst kings in Judah's history. He was also the great-grandson of Uzziah, the king who died while Isaiah was in service to him. This is who he chose to pattern his life after. When Hezekiah received the message from Isaiah, he immediately went into prayer; God relented and added 15 years to his life (Isaiah 38:2-8).

None of us know when we'll take our last breath, which is why it's important to live each day as if it's our last. Stop putting things off, whether it's taking a much-needed vacation or seeking forgiveness from someone you may have hurt. Today is all you have; tomorrow isn't promised, and there's nothing you can do about yesterday.

"Yesterday is history, tomorrow is a mystery,
today is a gift from God, which is why we call it present."
—Bill Keane

WHAT'S YOUR NEED?

Two other men, both criminals, were also led out with him to be executed. When they came to the place called the Skull, they crucified him there, along with the criminals—one on his right, the other on his left. Jesus said, "Father, forgive them, for they do not know what they are doing." And they divided up his clothes by casting lots. . . . One of the criminals who hung there hurled insults at him: "Aren't you the Messiah? Save yourself and us!" But the other criminal rebuked him. "Don't you fear God," he said, "since you are under the same sentence? We are punished justly, for we are getting what our deeds deserve. But this man has done nothing wrong." Then he said, "Jesus, remember me when you come into your kingdom." Jesus answered him, "Truly I tell you, today you will be with me in paradise." (Luke 23:32-34, 39-43, NIV)

Sometimes God makes us recognize we have a need and that He is the only One who can fulfill it. That's what happened with the thief on the cross. God knew that Jesus would be crucified between two thieves and that one would accept the gift of salvation. The thief didn't realize his true condition until he recognized he was in the presence of royalty. Most career thieves would tell you that stealing is not their desired occupation. I'm not condoning their behavior because it's flat out wrong, but we don't always know the circumstances that lead to a person choosing a specific path. If thieves are like most people, their friends are of a like mind; thus, it's difficult to break out of a conditioned environment.

Isn't that what happened on the cross? The one thief was doing what he had probably always done . . . reflecting his negative behavior onto someone else. The other thief might have remembered a time when he wasn't influenced by his friends. Maybe he *could* have a better life. He knew he was going to die that day, but at some point, hanging beside Jesus on the cross, he remembered fragments of comments he heard about Jesus and thought, "I've got nothing to lose." He asked Jesus for a place in the Kingdom. To his utter amazement, Jesus said "Yes." The thief was able to die in peace knowing he was forgiven.

No matter what you've done, the Good News is that God is willing and able to forgive you.

DON'T BACK DOWN

Now Pilate wrote a title and put it on the cross. And the writing was: JESUS OF NAZARETH, THE KING OF THE JEWS. Then many of the Jews read this title, for the place where Jesus was crucified was near the city; and it was written in Hebrew, Greek, and Latin. (John 19:19-20, NKJV)

Have you ever noticed how God will use anything, and anybody, to get His point across? He used a donkey to get Balaam's attention (Numbers 22). He used an angel to convince Gideon that he was, in fact, a mighty man of valor (Judges 6). And, he used Pilate to confirm in writing that Jesus is the King of the Jews.

During the trial of Jesus, Pilate had the opportunity to stand up to the crowd. He could have denied their request to exchange Barabbas for Jesus, but he didn't. He knew in his heart that Jesus was innocent; yet, he didn't have enough fortitude to stand up for what he believed (John 18:28-40; 19:1-16). Then, he and Herod joined forces to create an unholy alliance against Jesus (Luke 23:12). And even his wife told him to wash his hands of the entire incident because of what she saw in a dream (Matthew 27:19). Pilate, however, turned a deaf ear to his wife's warning and proceeded to exchange Jesus for Barabbas. It was only after the crucifixion that Pilate found his backbone. He had a sign posted to the cross in the languages of the area—Hebrew, Greek, and Latin—JESUS OF NAZARETH, THE KING OF THE JEWS (John 19:19). When the chief priests told him to change it, he finally stood his ground by responding, "What I have written, I have written. It stays exactly as it is" (John 19:21-22, NLT).

Lord, please help me to do the right thing immediately, regardless of what others may think or say. Help me stay so close to You that Yours is the only voice I hear.

I'VE GOT THIS!

"After all, it is I, the Eternal One your God, who has hold of your right hand, who whispers in your ear, 'Don't be afraid. I will help you.'" (Isaiah 41:13, VOICE)

Over the years I've learned through a few unpleasant experiences that I can only count on myself. Don't get me wrong. I don't have a problem asking for help. My issue stems from those who say they'll help, and when the time comes, the help isn't around. I understand there are unexpected situations that may cause a person not to fulfill their obligation. Those are not the people I'm talking about; I'm referring to those who knew when they committed that they weren't going to keep their word. Thus, asking for help becomes more challenging. We are not God; but we can be god-like when we keep our commitments.

Today's Scripture reminds us that God keeps His Word, and I am forever grateful that He does! The thought of someone holding your hand through a situation is heart-warming. Hand-holding is one of life's greatest pleasures; combine that with God's assurance of help adds another layer of comfort. When God says, "I've got this!" we can be assured of gaining all the support we'll ever need.

God is not a man—He doesn't lie.
God isn't the son of a man to want to take back what He's said,
or say something and not follow through,
or speak and not act on it.
(Numbers 23:19, VOICE)

STEPPING INTO TOMORROW

Then Joshua told the leaders of the people, "Go among the tents and tell the people, 'Gather together the things you will need. For within three days you will cross this Jordan to go in to take the land the Lord your God is giving you for your own.'" (Joshua 1:10-11, NLV)

When we are the recipient of a promise from God, we need to be careful to do what the promise requires. In the case of the children of Israel, they had to cross over the Jordan River, resting in the promise that God would bring them to the other side. Scary? Absolutely! Amazing? Yes! But, this is an explicit example of faith in action, especially since they weren't quite sure who (or what) was waiting on the other side.

Has God ever allowed you to do something that was so awe-inspiring that even while you were doing it, your mouth was hanging open in amazement? That's what the children of Israel experienced. Can you even imagine walking on dry land in the middle of a river? Most of the people with Joshua weren't around for the crossing of the Red Sea—because of disobedience, the ones who started out with Moses weren't there at the finish—so they only had Joshua, Caleb, and some of the women to tell them what happened. Still, even hearing about it would be totally different from doing it. This is something they would have to personally experience to fully appreciate. And, even when they told future generations about it, it would be hard to believe.

And the priests that bare the ark of the covenant of the LORD stood firm on dry ground in the midst of Jordan, and all the Israelites passed over on dry ground, until all the people were passed clean over Jordan.
(Joshua 3:17, KJV)

HANDLING DISAPPOINTMENT

Now a man named Lazarus was sick. He was from Bethany, the village of Mary and her sister Martha. . . So the sisters sent word to Jesus, "Lord, the one you love is sick." When he heard this, Jesus said, "This sickness will not end in death. No, it is for God's glory so that God's Son may be glorified through it." Now Jesus loved Martha and her sister and Lazarus. So when he heard that Lazarus was sick, he stayed where he was two more days. . . (John 11:1, 3-6, NIV)

A friend of Jesus had died, and the sisters of His friend couldn't understand why He hadn't come to see them. They believed that if He had been there, Lazarus wouldn't have died. The Scripture tells us the way the two sisters approached Jesus when He finally got there: one with straight talk—"If you had been here, this wouldn't have happened"—resulting in a theological discussion about the resurrection; the other with the same words resulting in worship (John 11:17-32).

It's human nature to experience disappointment. Someone may not do what they promised. Something may not happen the way we want. Something may not work the way it should. The challenge comes when we determine how we'll handle it. It is then that we can follow Mary and Martha's example:

Admit you're disappointed. There's no reason to pretend that everything is okay, because it's not.

Reflect on who exactly Jesus is. When we remind ourselves that He is sovereign, it puts things in correct perspective.

Accept His sovereignty and worship Him. There's the saying that when praises go up, blessings come down. We often think in terms of material things, but sometimes the blessing that comes down is peace to accept whatever situation we're in.

When Lazarus died, Mary and Martha assumed that was the end of the story. We do the same thing when faced with disappointment.

Lord, I believe; help my unbelief! (Mark 9:24, NKJV)

DONE!

Turn to the LORD for help in everything you do, and you will be successful. (Proverbs 16:3, ERV)

The clock was ticking down.
The deadline was fast approaching.
Deadlines had been set, missed, re-set, and re-missed.
I tried not to get anxious because the Bible says don't.
I tried to stay focused and confident.
I had so many conversations with myself; I was beginning to think I was crazy.
I had quoted all the positive affirmations I knew, and some I just made up on the spur of the moment, and they weren't working.
But, then, I remembered what I had already done.
I prayed, fasted, and sought God's permission before saying yes to this monumental task.
I set aside time to handle those last-minute things that always happen.
I made sure I'd backed up everything on the computer just in case.
I surrounded myself with people I knew were praying for me.
I spent more time with God as we delved into this project.
And, then, something else happened. One morning during my devotional period when I was specifically praying for this book, God said, "Done!" And you know what, I stopped worrying about it.

Our Lord and God! You are worthy to receive glory and honor and power. You made all things. Everything existed and was made because you wanted it. (Revelation 4:11, ERV)

I KNOW I WAS CLEAR

The Word of the Lord came to Jonah the son of Amittai, saying, "Get up and go to the large city of Nineveh, and preach against it. For their sin has come up before Me." But Jonah ran away from the Lord going toward Tarshish. He went down to Joppa and found a ship which was going to Tarshish. Jonah paid money, and got on the ship to go with them, to get away from the Lord. (Jonah 1:1-3, NLV)

Okay, true confession time. Have you ever thought that you knew how to handle a situation better than God? If you answered yes, you're in good company. Most of us at one time or another have been guilty of doing this. The thing is that God is always clear and concise when He tells us what to do. "I want you to do this, this, and this." Instead, because we're hardheaded and rebellious at times, we decide He didn't mean it the way He said it.

In Jonah's case, he didn't want to see Nineveh saved— as if it were his decision—so he went in the opposite direction, only to discover that he was going to end up in Nineveh anyway doing exactly what God told him to do. As the saying goes, you can either do it the hard way or the easy way, but you *are* going to do it!

How much time have you wasted doing everything *but* what God has said? It's not too late to become obedient. We should be grateful that God is a God of another chance.

The Word of the Lord came to Jonah a second time, saying, "Get up
and go to the large city of Nineveh, and tell the people there the news
which I am going to tell you." So Jonah got up and
went to Nineveh, as the Lord had told him.
(Jonah 3:1-3[a], NLV)

YOU'VE GOTTA GO!

Then the Lord sent a powerful wind upon the sea, and there was such a big storm that the ship was about to break up. . . .So they picked up Jonah and threw him into the sea, and the storm stopped. (Jonah 1:4, 15, NLV)

Sometimes circumstances beyond our control place us in perilous situations. We find ourselves caught in the middle of something that is not of our choosing. The sailors had no idea when they allowed Jonah to hitch a ride that he was going to cause them to lose cargo and have their lives placed in danger. And isn't it typical that the person causing the problem has the nerve to be unaffected? Jonah was asleep while the sailors were fighting for their lives and livelihood. The captain's question, "How can you sleep?" could be interpreted as: "You're not on a cruise ship! We're in trouble here! Get up and do something!" (vv. 5-6).

Despite determining that Jonah was the cause of the storm, the sailors were reluctant to do what was necessary (vv. 5, 11). Right before doing as Jonah requested and throwing him overboard (v. 12), the men were smart enough to cover themselves: "Then they called on the Lord and said, 'We beg You, O Lord, do not let us die for what this man has done. And do not let us become guilty for killing someone who is not to blame. For You, O Lord, have done as You have pleased" (v.14).

After tossing Jonah overboard, the storm ceased immediately. I'm sure they had to clean up the mess the storm had made, and they may have even had some cuts, bumps, and bruises to attend to because of the severity of the storm. But, in the end, they had peace, and isn't that what you want when you're in a storm?

God, please don't let us be the cause of someone else's problems by our disobedience. Help us to do what You say the first time for our good and Your glory.

THIS ISN'T WORKING FOR ME

The word of the LORD came to Jonah the son of Amittai, "Arise, go to Nineveh, that great city, and cry out against it; for their wickedness has come up before Me." . . . But Jonah went down to Joppa, and found a ship going to Tarshish . . . But the LORD sent out a great wind on the sea, and there was a mighty tempest on the sea, so that the ship was about to be broken up. . . Then they said to him, "Please tell us! For whose cause is this trouble upon us?" So he said to them, "I am a Hebrew; and I fear the LORD, the God of heaven, who made the sea and the dry land." Then they said to him, "What shall we do to you that the sea may be calm for us?" And he said to them, "Pick me up and throw me into the sea; then the sea will become calm for you. For I know that this great tempest is because of me." . . . So they picked up Jonah and threw him into the sea, and the sea ceased from its raging. (Jonah 1:1-4, 8-12, 15-16, NKJV)

Sometimes the problems we encounter are because of our connection to someone else. The captain of the ship thought he was doing Jonah a favor, but giving him a ride without knowing the "baggage" that came with the offer was a problem. Once Jonah admitted his role in the disaster, the situation changed. Although reluctant to do so, they nevertheless kicked Jonah off the boat. None of them knew God had prepared a fish; they only knew that Jonah was the cause of their problem.

There may be people in your life that you, too, need to throw overboard so that your life will once again become calm. It doesn't necessarily mean they're bad people; it means they're not good for you now. God may allow you to reconnect later. Like Jonah and the fish, you don't know what God has in store; you only need to believe that right now they're not beneficial to you.

Lord, help us to be wise enough to hear Your voice,
strong enough to release whoever it is, and
patient enough to wait on the outcome.

WOW! THAT'S A REALLY BIG FISH

The Lord sent a big fish to swallow Jonah, and he was in the stomach of the fish for three days and three nights. (Jonah 1:17, NLV)

God often puts us in limbo to give us time to think about what we're doing or what we're about to do. Of course, chances are good that He's not going to have a large fish to swallow you whole. However, our "fish" could be a text message that doesn't go through because it would cause more harm than good. Or, a computer crash while viewing inappropriate material. Or, not having any cell phone service when attempting to call the wrong person. These events happen to allow us time to come to our senses.

When frustrating things happen, don't get upset. Do what Jonah did—"Then Jonah prayed to the Lord his God while in the stomach of the fish" (Jonah 2:1, NLV)—only do it first instead of spending three days floating in fish guts!

Then the Lord spoke to the fish, and it spit Jonah out onto the dry land. (Jonah 2:10, NLV)

I KNEW THIS WOULD HAPPEN

Then the people of Nineveh believed in God. They called for a time when no food was to be eaten. And all the people, from the greatest to the least, put on clothes made from hair. . . When God saw what they did, and that they turned from their sinful way, He changed His mind about the trouble He said He would bring upon them, and He did not destroy Nineveh. . . But Jonah was not pleased at all, and he became angry. He prayed to the Lord and said, "O Lord, is this not what I said You would do while still in my own country? That is why I ran away to Tarshish. For I knew that You are a kind and loving God Who shows pity. I knew that You are slow to anger and are filled with loving-kindness, always ready to change Your mind and not punish." (Jonah 3:5, 10; 4:1-2, NLV)

There are some people who—when they're wrong—will try to convince you that it's your fault that they did whatever they did. They must be related to Jonah!

He was wrong for not doing what God told him to do, and even when God gave him the message the second time, the inference is that he still had an attitude even while delivering God's Word. Then, when God relents from destroying Nineveh, Jonah gets mad! He tried to justify his rebellion by second- guessing God and tried to make his negative attitude God's fault: "If you weren't so good, I wouldn't have gone to Tarshish!" Jonah had a bad case of amnesia since it wasn't that long ago that he was inside a fish. If it weren't for God's gracious nature, he would have been nothing but a memory!

Let's be careful that we don't care more for possessions than people. Both have their place; just don't get your priorities mixed up.

Dear friends, since God loved us this much, we must love each other.
(1 John 4:11, CEV)

DO YOU EVEN KNOW WHY YOU'RE MAD?

But Jonah was not pleased at all, and he became angry. . . Then God said to Jonah, "Do you have a good reason to be angry about the plant?" And Jonah said, "I have a good reason to be angry, angry enough to die." (Jonah 4:1, 9, NLV)

Do you know people who are just mad all the time? They don't like anything or anybody, and all they do is complain, moan, and groan. When you see these people coming, you go in the opposite direction; or when you see their phone number on your caller ID, you choose not to answer. They may not be bad people; they just have issues.

That's one of the reasons I love the honesty of the Bible and the people reflected in it. Their transparency helps me walk this Christian journey, knowing that what is happening to me has already been experienced by someone else. Their humanness is relatable. Jonah was told to go right but insisted on going left, only to discover he was going to go right anyway.

God questioned Jonah to get to the real issue behind his rebellion, which was selfishness. Jonah wanted all of God's goodness for himself. He wanted to tell God who to bless and not bless. We do the same thing. We say we want everybody to know the goodness and blessing of being in a relationship with God; then, we turn our nose up at certain people who get converted. We're not sure they're sincere or worthy, but who are we to question? Didn't God save us, too?

Everybody ought to know who Jesus is.
He's the lily of the valley
He's the brightest morning star
He's the fairest of ten thousand
Everybody ought to know.
Everybody Ought to Know. Dennis Leonard (lyrics). 2004.

PRAY!

The wrath of God is being revealed from heaven against all the godlessness and wickedness of people, who suppress the truth by their wickedness, since what may be known about God is plain to them, because God has made it plain to them. For since the creation of the world God's invisible qualities—his eternal power and divine nature—have been clearly seen, being understood from what has been made, so that people are without excuse. For although they knew God, they neither glorified him as God nor gave thanks to him, but their thinking became futile and their foolish hearts were darkened. Although they claimed to be wise, they became fools and exchanged the glory of the immortal God for images made to look like a mortal human being and birds and animals and reptiles. Therefore, God gave them over in the sinful desires of their hearts to sexual impurity for the degrading of their bodies with one another. They exchanged the truth about God for a lie and worshiped and served created things rather than the Creator—who is forever praised. Amen. (Romans 1:18-25, NIV)

We all know someone who needs to know Jesus. The moral atmosphere of the world today is not a good time to be outside the arc of safety. These lost souls need to come into the fold. The only way that happens is if they hear the Word of God spoken or see it lived out in our lives. It is our responsibility to bring as many people as we can into the Kingdom before it's too late. Jesus *is* coming back for His Church, and those outside the arc are at risk. Hell will not be a pleasant experience.

The Lord is not slow in keeping his promise, as some understand slowness. Instead he is patient with you, not wanting anyone to perish, but everyone to come to repentance. But the day of the Lord will come like a thief. The heavens will disappear with a roar;
the elements will be destroyed by fire, and the earth and everything done in it will be laid bare. (2 Peter 3:9-10, NIV)

I'M TELLING YOU WHAT I KNOW
TO BE TRUE

The LORD directs the steps of the godly. He delights in every detail of their lives. Though they stumble, they will never fall, for the LORD holds them by the hand. (Psalm 37:23-24, NLT)

Have you ever had someone try to explain something to you based on theory and not experience? It can be somewhat frustrating because they have no actual proof to back up what they're saying. When David wrote Psalm 37, he was both transparent and autobiographical. He was telling us what he knew to be true because he had personally experienced the events mentioned. He had seen evil doers punished (v. 1); he had seen the Lord give him the desires of his heart (v. 3); he knew the importance of commitment and trust (v. 5); and he had seen the Lord vindicate him (v. 6). But, even better than this, David knew the faithfulness of God!

Today's Scripture is one of those bad news/good news readings. The bad news is that because we are not perfect, we are going to mess up. That doesn't mean we take advantage of God's mercy. Things happen that are sometimes out of our control. The good news is that when that happens, we can be assured the failure isn't the end. God is holding us in the palm of His hand, and we will survive! If we haven't experienced this yet, we only need to believe someone who has: King David.

God, thank You that despite warts and all, You still love us!

ENOUGH, ALREADY!

And the Lord said to me, "You have traveled around this mountain long enough." (Deuteronomy 2:3, NLV)

Consistently, men and women do doctor-recommended self-examinations on various body parts. Countless people are alive today because of early detection. But, I wonder how many of us do spiritual self-examinations to determine if where we are, is where God wants us to be?

The children of Israel walked around in circles for years before God said, "Enough!" I believe He is saying that to some of us today. Is there an area where you're stuck, going in circles, making yourself and everyone around you dizzy? The only way you'll know is if you ask God. Trust me, He will answer! You might not like His response, but then that's not a requirement. You only need to be obedient to whatever He says.

Speak, Lord, for your servant is listening.
(1 Samuel 3:10, NLV)

ROOMMATE WANTED

Then Christ will make his home in your hearts as you trust in him. (Ephesians 3:17[a], NLT)

You see signs all the time advertising for roommates. It's interesting to me that people would willingly live with a total stranger; however, I understand that sometimes circumstances dictate doing things outside the norm.

Jesus wants to be a permanent roommate in your heart. You won't have to worry about Him making a mess for you to clean up, eating your share of the food, or failing to pull His weight financially.

Trust me, He'll bring much more than He'll ever take. Just extend the invitation; He's packed and ready to move in.

"I came so they can have real and eternal life,
more and better life than they ever dreamed of."
(John 10:10[b], MSG)

PLEASE CALL ME BACK!

Now the boy Samuel ministered to the LORD before Eli. And the word of the LORD was rare in those days; there was no widespread revelation. And it came to pass at that time, while Eli was lying down in his place. . .that the LORD called Samuel. And he answered, "Here I am!" So he ran to Eli and said, "Here I am, for you called me." And he said, "I did not call; lie down again." And he went and lay down. . . Then Eli perceived that the LORD had called the boy. Therefore Eli said to Samuel, "Go, lie down; and it shall be, if He calls you, that you must say, 'Speak, LORD, for Your servant hears.'" So Samuel went and lay down in his place. (1 Samuel 3:1-5, 8-9, NKJV)

I have both a landline and a cell phone, and both have voicemail capabilities. I never intentionally ignore the phone, but there are times when it's inconvenient to answer. When that happens, I can retrieve a message, or I can scroll to see the number of the last incoming call. Years before we had any of the modern telephonic tools we have today, a missed call meant you had to wait for the person to call you back.

When Samuel was a child, God called him. It's understandable that Samuel may not have known the voice of God, so he did what most children would have done. He went to an older person to determine what they wanted. Eli hadn't called Samuel but gave him instruction on what to do if God called again.

There are times when we, too, have missed the first few calls of God. If you think back to your pre-salvation days, there were probably times you felt "something" but didn't know what it was. In hindsight, you recognize it as the call of God. God doesn't have a problem with us missing a call because of lack of understanding; He has a problem with us ignoring His call altogether. That's a dangerous place and a terrible way to live.

The next time you feel "something," go ahead and respond. God is waiting for you to say, "Speak, Lord, for Your servant hears."

BIONIC HEARING

"Because he has set his love upon Me, therefore I will deliver him; I will set him on high, because he has known My name. He shall call upon Me, and I will answer him; I will be with him in trouble; I will deliver him and honor him. With long life I will satisfy him, And show him My salvation." (Psalm 91:14-16, NKJV)

You often hear jokes about people who allegedly can't hear what you're saying until it's something they want to hear. You know, the ones who can hear a pin drop but can't hear you calling them to help with something around the house.

Aren't you glad God doesn't treat us like that? Whether we whisper or holler, God has promised that He will answer every time we call. That's a promise you can count on.

"Give all your cares to the Lord and He will give you strength.
He will never let those who are right with Him be shaken."
(Psalm 55:22, NLV)

I'M AVAILABLE

O lord, thou hast searched me, and known me. Thou knowest my downsitting and mine uprising, thou understandest my thought afar off. Thou compassest my path and my lying down, and art acquainted with all my ways. (Psalm 139:1-3, KJV)

I have always been able to relate to Peter because we have a similar disease—foot in mouth—and our good intentions aren't always manifested correctly. And, like Peter, Jesus looks far beyond my faults and uses me anyway.

Once fully surrendered to God and restored by Jesus, Peter went on to do what he was anointed and appointed to do. God used his basic personality traits—loud, rough, bold—to minister to His people. How humble Peter must have felt to know that the same mouth he used to open and insert his foot would be the one God would use to speak healing, wholeness, salvation, and restoration. The same hand used to lift a sword to cut off an ear would be used to lay hands on people and heal them. The feet that took him away from Jesus on that fateful night would lead others to Jesus. The eyes that shed tears of disappointment would see miracles and wonders performed through the Holy Spirit.

Peter reminds us that God can use anything and anybody, in any way. We only need to make ourselves available.

Lord, Your vision is perfect. You see
what others either can't or won't, and despite that,
You use me anyway. Thank You!

WHEN TOMORROW COMES

Elisha said, "Listen to the message from the LORD! The LORD says, 'About this time tomorrow, there will be plenty of food, and it will be cheap again. A person will be able to buy a basket of fine flour or two baskets of barley for only one shekel in the marketplace by the city gates of Samaria.'" Then the officer who was close to the king answered the man of God. The officer said, "Even if the LORD made windows in heaven, this could not happen." Elisha said, "You will see it with your own eyes, but you will not eat any of that food." (2 Kings 7:1-7, ERV)

It is challenging to keep the faith when you've experienced something devastating, even if it's only a fleeting moment of doubt. The good news is that because of our humanity, God understands that moment. The better news is that God has a set time for the devastation to end.

Samaria had been in a drought when Elisha gave them a message from God that things were about to change. It was hard to believe the news. Some of the people needed to see it with their own eyes first. Aren't we the same way sometimes? We need to work harder at believing without seeing, knowing that if God said it, it's already done. The challenge comes when what has been promised doesn't happen when we expect. It is those times that we need to stand firm and trust in God's Word.

Patience is a difficult concept to embrace,
but with God's help, it can be achieved.

BACK TO THE FUTURE

Then it came to pass, at the end of two full years, that Pharaoh had a dream; and behold, he stood by the river. Suddenly there came up out of the river seven cows, fine looking and fat; and they fed in the meadow. Then behold, seven other cows came up after them out of the river, ugly and gaunt, and stood by the other cows on the bank of the river. And the ugly and gaunt cows ate up the seven fine looking and fat cows. So Pharaoh awoke. (Genesis 41:1-4, NKJV)

When you're in the season of a feast, do you think about famine? When you're in a season of famine, do you think about the feast? Feast and famine are not necessarily always about food. It can be anything such as money, health, relationships, and so forth. My question is, do we plan for the lean times or do they catch us by surprise because we're unprepared?

Periods of feast and famine also occur in our spiritual lives. It is during these times that we discover what we're made of and what we "think" we can handle. I stress the word *think* because unless we have the mindset of Christ, our thinking is going to be distorted. If we're in a feast season, we may believe the bad times are over; if we're in a famine season, we may think the good times will never return. Neither mindset is correct because God uses seasons to mold and shape us into the people He wants us to be.

The next time you're in either season, prepare for the next one. God has already planned your life; you're only living it out day by day. Ask God to show you what to do to successfully endure whichever season you're going through.

It's an unavoidable fact of life that things are going to change.
Lord, please help us stay faithful and true,
regardless of what season we're experiencing.

THE PITMASTER

And God remembered Rachel, and God hearkened to her, and opened her womb. And she conceived, and bare a son; and said, God hath taken away my reproach: And she called his name Joseph; and said, The LORD shall add to me another son. (Genesis 30:22-24, KJV)

And when they saw him afar off, even before he came near unto them, they conspired against him to slay him. And they said one to another, "Behold, this dreamer cometh. Come now therefore, and let us slay him, and cast him into some pit, and we will say, 'Some evil beast hath devoured him' and we shall see what will become of his dreams." (Genesis 37:18-20, KJV)

God *is* in the middle of all problems. The challenge is to resist our flesh's inclination to handle the situation, which usually makes things worse.

Joseph was thrown into a pit by his brothers. He was then sold into slavery, put in charge of Potiphar's household, lied on by Potiphar's wife, thrown into jail, and eventually released after interpreting Pharaoh's dream (Genesis chapters 37-41).

Joseph's journey to the pit led him to becoming governor of Egypt. Shadrach, Meshach, and Abednego's trip to the fiery furnace (their pit) caused Nebuchadnezzar to bless the name of God (Daniel 3:28-29). Daniel's journey to the pit, called the lion's den, allowed Darius to recognize God as *the* Living God, above all others (Daniel 6:25-27).

The pit is unpleasant but necessary. Hopefully, our journey isn't as extreme as that of Joseph, Shadrach, Meshach, Abednego, or Daniel. When we find ourselves facing the pit, we should follow these biblical examples and trust our care to God. God *will* get us out of the pit, perhaps not as soon as we'd like, but as soon as He has prepared our next step. God must *take* us through to *bring* us through to the other side.

For our light affliction, which is but for a moment, worketh for us a far more exceeding and eternal weight of glory. (2 Corinthians 4:17, KJV)

I DON'T NEED TO KNOW EVERYTHING

LORD, my heart is not proud; my eyes are not haughty. I don't concern myself with matters too great or too awesome for me to grasp. Instead, I have calmed and quieted myself, like a weaned child who no longer cries for its mother's milk. Yes, like a weaned child is my soul within me. (Psalm 131:1-2, NLT)

Although I am one of those people who typically likes to know how things work, I've accepted the fact that there are some things out of my realm of understanding. Better said, there are some things I no longer try to figure out.

Take airplanes, for example. I understand the principle of lift and thrust; yet, when I look out an airplane window and see nothing but clouds and sky, I can't help but believe that something other than mechanical engineering is keeping us in the air! I'll never comprehend how a brown cow can eat green grass and produce white milk! I understand about digestion and elimination; yet, to some extent, there is no viable explanation. I understand that John 3:16 tells us that God loved us enough to allow His Son to die; yet, that level of love is beyond my comprehension, although I'm grateful for it!

What I do understand and accept is that God, Jesus, and the Holy Spirit are all I need to survive. Like David, I'm satisfied with what I know, and it's enough. What about you?

I'm satisfied with Jesus, whatever He may do,
And this same satisfaction is waiting now for you;
I'm satisfied with Jesus, wherever I may be,
And, while I now obey Him, He's satisfied with me.
Satisfied With Jesus. E. G. Masters. 1897.
Public Domain.

A RECIPE FOR SUCCESS

Be full of joy all the time. Never stop praying. In everything give thanks. This is what God wants you to do because of Christ Jesus. (1 Thessalonians 5:16-18, NLV)

Making a cake from scratch requires that specific steps be done in order. You cream the butter and sugar, then add eggs, and alternate (depending on the recipe) between the dry and liquid ingredients. Mixed in the wrong order, you'll have a mess; mixed correctly, it will produce a delicious product.

On the first day of culinary school, we were instructed that if we did not follow the recipes exactly as written, we would receive an "F" for the day. The chef didn't care if we liked more salt or sugar, larger fries, or chunkier coleslaw. We followed the recipe to ensure that the finished product was consistently the same.

Today's Scripture is but one recipe for success God has provided in His Word. Like my culinary professor, God is telling us that if we want success, we must follow the three steps exactly. Our personal preference is irrelevant.

Be full of joy doesn't mean happy. Joy comes from the inside; happiness is external. When we allow God to fill the empty spaces of our lives, joy is one of the byproducts.

When I was newly saved, I thought the phrase *"always pray"* meant praying out loud continuously. I couldn't understand how someone was supposed to do that and sleep, eat, work, and the like. Maturity always brings understanding. I discovered this means being in an attitude of prayer. Prayer, as we know, can be done aloud or silently, with a lot of words or a brief "Jesus!"

In everything give thanks takes time to develop. Once you achieve it, you'll be thankful for the traffic jam that may be preventing your involvement in something devastating, or the promotion to the dream job you've envisioned since you were a child. You want to be thanked for what you do; God is no different, and He's done a lot more than you ever will.

My mother passed down a lot of recipes that I still use.
Thank You, God, for providing several of Your own.
Help me to use them daily.

THE BALANCE OF CONTENTMENT

I am not saying this because I am in need, for I have learned to be content whatever the circumstances. I know what it is to be in need, and I know what it is to have plenty. I have learned the secret of being content in any and every situation, whether well fed or hungry, whether living in plenty or in want. (Philippians 4:11-12, NIV)

One day my culinary instructor started talking about "Mise en place" and I eagerly took out paper and pen. Once he started explaining what it is, I stopped writing. Mise en place is simply a cooking term for having all your ingredients in place before you start. That's something my mother taught me when I was eight years old, although she never used the French term! Still, I was glad to discover that I was already doing something right.

I felt the same way the first time I read today's Scripture. For as long as I can remember, I've always been satisfied with what I had. For me, the challenge with contentment comes from finding the balance between wanting more and being satisfied with where you are. I think one of the key factors to this balance is appreciation. My first house was barely big enough for my son and me, but it was ours and we were happy. The house I live in now is considerably larger and it's still mine (and the bank's!) and I'm still happy.

It's okay to want more, be more, do more. We should always be striving for better. Just don't neglect the present while seeking the future.

"Do not spoil what you have by desiring what you have not;
remember that what you now have was once
among the things you only hoped for." —Epicurus

IMAGINE THIS

Now I saw a new heaven and a new earth, for the first heaven and the first earth had passed away. Also there was no more sea. Then I, John, saw the holy city, New Jerusalem, coming down out of heaven from God, prepared as a bride adorned for her husband. And I heard a loud voice from heaven saying, "Behold, the tabernacle of God *is* with men, and He will dwell with them, and they shall be His people. God Himself will be with them *and be* their God. And God will wipe away every tear from their eyes; there shall be no more death, nor sorrow, nor crying. There shall be no more pain, for the former things have passed away." Then He who sat on the throne said, "Behold, I make all things new." And He said to me, "Write, for these words are true and faithful." (Revelation 21:1-5, NKJV)

I have a vivid imagination. As a writer, it comes in handy. But, even in my wildest imagining, I cannot come close to grasping the concept of Heaven. I can't imagine a time with no more pain, sickness, or disease; no more sadness, discouragement, distress; no more hatred, mistrust, deceit—but I want to see for myself. No, I'm not rushing death, but the thought of Heaven gives me something to look forward to when life becomes just a little too challenging. I'm ready to embrace the moment when the weary will cease from troubling, and the world will be at peace. Until then, I'll keep trusting, believing, and reaching toward the prize.

But as the Scriptures say, "No one has ever seen,
no one has ever heard, no one has ever imagined
what God has prepared for those who love him."
(1 Corinthians 2:9, ERV)

NEXT!

"I am the LORD, that is My name; and My glory I will not give to another, nor My praise to carved images. Behold, the former things have come to pass, and new things I declare; Before they spring forth I tell you of them. Sing to the LORD a new song, and His praise from the ends of the earth, you who go down to the sea, and all that is in it, you coastlands and you inhabitants of them!" (Isaiah 42:8-10, NKJV)

Around this time every year I begin to look back in astonishment at all that has occurred over the past year. Some things were wonderful; other things, not as wonderful. I realize now that as these experiences were occurring, I sometimes thought the day would never come to an end. If it was a good day, I wanted to savor the moment like a good piece of cake and have it linger a little while longer. If it was a not so good day, I wanted to rush through the mess to get to the other side. Regardless of whether a day was good or bad, I tried to always remember to give thanks to God for allowing me to see it, because He didn't have to let it be so.

As this year winds down, what are you going to do differently next year? What results are you hoping to achieve? It's okay to plan and dream so long as you realize things may not turn out the way you hoped. God alone knows the beginning from the end so all we can do, really, is fasten our seat belt and go along for the ride. I'm ready for a new adventure. How about you?

The mind of a man plans his way, but the Lord shows him what to do.
(Proverbs 16:9, NLV)

LET THERE BE PEACE ON EARTH

If it is possible, as much as depends on you, live peaceably with all men. (Romans 12:18, NKJV)

I ran into this Scripture early in my salvific walk. I'll admit I haven't always adhered to it, but, I'm better at it than I once was. Sometimes I just want to give people a piece of my mind. Then, I remember two things: (1) I may need that "piece" later, and (2) I was bought with a price—the precious Blood of Jesus.

What do you think would happen if everyone strove to be peaceful? If everyone took the high road? If everyone gave up the right to be right?

I challenge you for the rest of this year to try living peaceably and see what happens. This just might be the greatest Christmas present you will ever give or receive.

Therefore let us pursue the things which
make for peace and the things by which one
may edify another. (Romans 14:19, NKJV)

GO SOMEWHERE AND SIT DOWN

It will not be necessary for you to fight in this conflict. Take your positions, stand, and observe the deliverance of the LORD for you, O Judah and Jerusalem. Do not fear or be filled with terror. Tomorrow, go out before them, and the LORD will be with you. (2 Chronicles 20:17, MEV)

If your parents were like mine, at some point in your life you heard them say, "Go somewhere and sit down." This was usually voiced when you had gotten in the way or were bugging them about something they weren't ready to do. The phrase was usually spoken in such a way that you knew they weren't playing, and if you continued harassing them, the punishment was going to be severe.

I have often been asked if there's an age I'd like to go back to and my answer is always no. I am appreciative of the age I am. Certainly, there are things I'd like to do over. I have regrets about some decisions and actions that occurred when I was both chronologically and spiritually younger. However, for the most part, I wouldn't trade this journey for anything, especially when I've heeded God's advice to go somewhere and sit down. When I've allowed God to fight my battles, I've seen Him perform incredible miracles on my behalf. He only had to do it once for me to get the message: He can handle things a lot better than I can! Every battle is not my fight.

> Jesus, You brought me all the way.
> You carried my burdens every day.
> You're such a wonderful Savior.
> I've never known You to fail me yet.
> You brought, thank God, all the way.
> *Jesus, You Brought Me All the Way.*
> Kenneth W. Louis. 1997.

THE INVITATION

"Come to Me, all you who labor and are heavy laden, and I will give you rest. Take My yoke upon you and learn from Me, for I am gentle and lowly in heart, and you will find rest for your souls. For My yoke is easy and My burden is light." (Matthew 11:28-30, NKJV)

I have friends who can't understand why I am reluctant to accept every invitation extended to me. I am an introvert; I don't like being around a lot of people, which is ironic since the church I attend has multiple thousands of members. I would be hesitant to join a church the size of mine, but when I arrived 30 years ago, there were approximately 150 members. We grew up together.

The invitation in today's Scripture is one I gladly embrace on a regular basis. See, I'm one of those people who could quickly become overwhelmed with life's issues. It's good to know that I have Someone willing and able to "perfect the things that concern me" (Psalm 138:8). You do, too, if you'll accept God's help.

Give it to me, I'll bear it. Give it to me, I'll share it.
If there's a need in your life, I will take it,
if you only give it to me.
Give it to Me. James Cleveland. 1976.

WHO YOU GONNA CALL?

Then you called out to GOD in your desperate condition; he got you out in the nick of time. (Psalm 107:28, MSG)

There are times when you don't have time for long, drawn-out prayers or to get reacquainted with the Lord. When the trouble you're in is severe enough, you'll summon the only One who can help you, and that's Jesus! This primarily works if you have a relationship with the One you're calling on for help. I say "primarily" because we know that God hears the prayers of sinners or none of us would be saved. However, there are certain privileges reserved for those who have yielded their lives to the Lord.

It is never too late to get right with God. Why not do it now instead of during times of desperation? You'll be glad you did! Your life will be so much better and brighter knowing that without a doubt, there is Someone who can handle every situation, including the ones you think are impossible.

God wants to call you His friend!
Will you accept His invitation?

DID YOU REALLY THINK
THIS WAS YOUR IDEA?

"The Father loves me because I give my life. I give my life so that I can get it back again. No one takes my life away from me. I give my own life freely. I have the right to give my life, and I have the right to get it back again. This is what the Father told me." (John 10:17-18, ERV)

Years ago, I had a boss who only thought an idea was great if it came from him. He would listen to the suggestion without responding; a few days later he would present the suggestion as if it were his own and would take all the credit. It wasn't an honorable way to do business, but people do things like this every day around the world. And, it's not even an original idea!

When the Pharisees plotted and planned Jesus' death, they thought it was their idea. God knew from the foundation of the world that Jesus would have to die for the salvation of people—"And I will put enmity between you and the woman, and between your seed and her Seed; He shall bruise your head, and you shall bruise His heel" (Genesis 3:15, NKJV)—and God knew all the players (including Judas) who would participate in the drama.

As the Pharisees and Jesus' other haters rubbed their hands together and patted each other on the back for getting rid of the troublemaker, their bubble burst three days after the crucifixion when Jesus not only rose from the grave but walked around Jerusalem. His actions confirmed once and for all that no human could have pulled this off. Jesus was who He said He was, and He did what He said He would do. And, it was His idea!

"Greater love has no one than this, than to lay down one's
life for his friends. You are My friends if you do whatever
I command you. No longer do I call you servants, for
a servant does not know what his master is doing;
but I have called you friends, for all things that
I heard from My Father I have made known to you."
(John 15:13-15, NKJV)

COME ON IN; THE WATER'S FINE

Naaman the captain of the army of the king of Syria was an important man to his king. He was much respected, because by him the Lord had made Syria win in battle. Naaman was a strong man of war, but he had a bad skin disease. . . . So Naaman came with his horses and his war-wagons, and stood at the door of Elisha's house. Elisha sent a man to him, saying, "Go and wash in the Jordan seven times. And your flesh will be made well and you will be clean." . . . So Naaman went down into the Jordan River seven times, as the man of God had told him. And his flesh was made as well as the flesh of a little child. He was clean. (2 Kings 5:1, 9-10, 14, NLV)

Naaman's dipping seven times in the Jordan River is a well-known story. I've often wondered what was left after each dip. For example, did each plunge signify a release of anger, arrogance, pride, self-centeredness? It's possible, since Naaman inhabited those traits, just like some of us. But, I also believe that each dip brought something to Naaman, as well. Things like healing, understanding, faith, trust.

Each of the seven dips was important to Naaman's restoration. As one dip wasn't enough to fulfill God's wish for him, one infilling of the Holy Spirit isn't enough for us, either. We daily need power from on high to navigate our place in the Earth.

"The Spirit-filled life is not a special, deluxe edition of Christianity. It is part and parcel of the total plan of God for His people."
—A. W. Tozer (1897-1963)

DON'T FORGET YESTERDAY

"When you reap your harvest in your field, and forget a sheaf in the field, you shall not go back to get it; it shall be for the stranger, the fatherless, and the widow, that the LORD your God may bless you in all the work of your hands. When you beat your olive trees, you shall not go over the boughs again; it shall be for the stranger, the fatherless, and the widow. When you gather the grapes of your vineyard, you shall not glean *it* afterward; it shall be for the stranger, the fatherless, and the widow. And you shall remember that you were a slave in the land of Egypt; therefore I command you to do this thing." (Deuteronomy 24:19-22, NKJV)

Few things irritate me more than people who act as if they were born with everything they need. Their attitude is such that you would think they never had any lack or struggle from the time they took their first breath. Because of their absence of empathy, they are unable to see the people around them in need.

Today's Scripture reminds us not to forget that we, too, were once slaves. Perhaps you were never purchased with money and turned over to the hand of someone else, but you were a slave to sin. And, unless you've turned your life over to the Lord Jesus Christ, you're still in sin, whether you live in a mansion or a worn-out cardboard box in a homeless camp.

Typically, we're told not to dwell on the past; what's done is done. But, Deuteronomy 24:19-22 encourages us to remember the past only in terms that someone once helped us. Therefore, it is our responsibility to be willing to help others who may be less fortunate.

"Then the righteous will answer Him, saying, 'Lord, when did we see You hungry and feed You, or thirsty and give You drink? When did we see You a stranger and take You in, or naked and clothe You? Or when did we see You sick, or in prison, and come to You?' And the King will answer and say to them, 'Assuredly, I say to you, inasmuch as you did it to one of the least of these My brethren, you did it to Me.'" (Matthew 25:37-40, NKJV)

I HAVE PRAYED FOR YOU

"Simon, Simon, how Satan has pursued you, that he might make you part of his harvest. But I have prayed for you. I have prayed that your faith will hold firm and that you will recover from your failure and become a source of strength for your brothers here." (Luke 22-31-32, VOICE)

People sometimes say to me, "I'm praying for you," and I always respond with, "Thank you." I appreciate the fact that someone thinks enough of me to call my name before the Lord. There are also times when I've asked a specific person to pray for me because I need them to join their faith with mine. Then, there are times someone is praying for me who I don't even know because they've taken it upon themselves to intercede on behalf of the Church, of which I am a part.

Simon (Peter) didn't ask Jesus to pray for him; instead, Jesus knew that Peter would need assurance that his imminent failure wasn't permanent. Jesus' prayer was twofold. He knew that humans tend to stay stuck when they make a mistake, and Jesus needed Peter to be able to move past what he had *done* to embrace what he would *do* effectively. Jesus also knew that humans tend to avoid sharing their mistakes, and He needed Peter to be able to unfailingly testify to how God restores us back into the fold when we sincerely repent.

I'm glad Jesus prayed for Peter because that means He prayed for me, too.

"Prayer is where the action is."
—John Wesley

DON'T JUDGE A BOOK BY THE COVER

God doesn't look at what people see. People judge by what is on the outside, but the LORD looks at the heart. (1 Samuel 16:7[b], ERV)

As a published author, I am aware of the importance of an attractive book cover. It is the first thing people notice, even before the title or the author's name. Usually what happens is a person picks up the book because of the cover, turns it over to read a synopsis of the contents from the back jacket, and then flips through the pages to get an idea of what the book is about (because the back jacket isn't always as informative as needed). Once they go through this process, they decide whether to purchase the book. There have been numerous times when I've gone through the above process only to return the book back to the shelf, usually because the contents weren't of interest. However, that doesn't negate the fact that the cover was intriguing.

God does the same thing with us. He's not impressed with our outward adornment, but He is very much concerned with our content. When He sees His character being emulated, He's pleased. When He doesn't, He returns us to the shelf and gives us more time to mature into His likeness. If you've been sitting on the shelf for a while, you might want to ask God what you need to repair in your life or what you're doing that is not reflective of Him. (Of course, there is the possibility that He has you in a holding pattern and you haven't done anything wrong. But, you won't know that until you check with Him.)

We spend a lot of time, energy, and money making sure the external looks good. Let's invest that same amount of effort in working on the internal.

So God created humans in his own image. He created them to be like himself. He created them male and female. (Genesis 1:27, ERV)

A NECESSARY EXCHANGE

"The Spirit of the Sovereign LORD is on me, because the LORD has anointed me to. . . bind up the brokenhearted, to comfort all who mourn, and provide for those who grieve in Zion—to bestow on them a crown of beauty instead of ashes, the oil of joy instead of mourning. . ." (Isaiah 61:1[a], 3[a], NIV)

Before we take our last breath, we will all experience pain, disappointment, and sorrow. That's the bad news of living in a fallen world. However, the good news is found in our Scripture for today.

God knows all about sorrow. He willingly allowed Jesus to come to Earth: "It's what GOD had in mind all along, to crush him with pain. The plan was that he gave himself as an offering for sin so that he'd see life come from it—life, life, and more life. And GOD's plan will deeply prosper through him" (Isaiah 53:10, MSG).

There is always a purpose for what we go through, even when it hurts. Romans 8:28 (TLB)—a familiar passage—reads: "And we know that all that happens to us is working for our good if we love God and are fitting into his plans." Isaiah 61 doesn't tell us how or when or even where God will make the exchange; just that it will be done. Sometimes that assurance is all we need to survive.

He will wipe away all tears from their eyes, and there shall be no more
death, nor sorrow, nor crying, nor pain. All of that has gone forever.
(Revelation 21:4, TLB)

TURN UP THE LIGHT

"Let your light so shine before men, that they may see your good works and glorify your Father in heaven." (Matthew 5:16, NKJV)

I have energy-saving incandescent light bulbs throughout my house. These bulbs last several years before they need to be replaced. When I first began using them, I thought I had defective bulbs because the lights took a while to get bright. Upon research, I found they emit light by heating the filament in the bulb. It only takes a couple of minutes for the light to reach full brightness. They start out dim and get stronger or brighter the longer they're on.

Isn't that the way of Christians? God wants our light to shine before men, but sometimes it takes a moment for our light to reach full brightness. I don't believe we'll ever reach full brightness until we get to Heaven because we're continually growing in the Lord.

In the case of my incandescent bulbs, it wasn't that the light wasn't on; I only needed to wait a few moments for the light to get stronger. That's what the world is waiting to see. It's not that your light isn't shining; it just needs to be stronger.

God, please let our light shine so strong and bright that people
need sunglasses to be around us.

NEVER NEVERLAND

Since God assured us, "I'll never let you down, never walk off and leave you," we can boldly quote, God is there, ready to help; I'm fearless no matter what. Who or what can get to me? (Hebrews 13:5-6, MSG)

According to Merriam-Webster's online dictionary, the word *never* means at no time; not in any degree; not under any condition. In other words, sometimes the word has a negative connotation and what you're wanting, hoping, wishing for is impossible.

I submit there is only one place where "never" doesn't mean impossible, but possible. That's in today's Scripture. In the *Jamieson-Fausset-Brown Commentary* (public domain) we're told that God will never leave us (withdraw His presence) or forsake us (withdraw His help). So, this means that whatever you're experiencing, God is with you.

That's good news, especially in a day and time when people are so fickle. Today they love you; tomorrow they turn their back on you as if you never existed. You don't have to worry about that happening with God. The writer of Hebrews wanted us to ingrain this in our psyche, so he added verse 8: "For Jesus doesn't change—yesterday, today, tomorrow, he's always totally himself." With the assurance of God's help and Jesus' consistency, is there anything you can't accomplish?

Lord, we thank You for the blessed assurance of
Your presence, help, and consistency. When
humans disappoint, we can always stand on Your promises.

THANK YOU!

Then he showed me Joshua the high priest standing before the Angel of the LORD, and Satan standing at his right hand to oppose him. And the LORD said to Satan, "The LORD rebuke you, Satan! The LORD who has chosen Jerusalem rebuke you! Is this not a brand plucked from the fire?" Now Joshua was clothed with filthy garments and was standing before the Angel. Then He answered and spoke to those who stood before Him, saying, "Take away the filthy garments from him." And to him He said, "See, I have removed your iniquity from you, and I will clothe you with rich robes." And I said, "Let them put a clean turban on his head." So they put a clean turban on his head, and they put the clothes on him. And the Angel of the LORD stood by. (Zechariah 3:1-5, NKJV)

Gift-*givers* fall into two categories—those who give solely for the pleasure of giving, and those who give wanting or expecting something in return. Likewise, gift-*receivers* fall into two categories—those who can joyfully accept a gift, and those who don't feel worthy.

Our Scripture demonstrates the need for, and the importance of, both groups. God saw a need for us to be "accepted in the beloved" and sent His Son, Jesus Christ, to save us. Joshua (not to be confused with Moses' successor) represents Israel and us. We could easily replace Joshua's name with ours. We were filthy and in need of cleansing. The change of clothing symbolizes the cleansing that Jesus' Blood does in our life. More importantly, it signifies restoration and the opportunity to build a relationship with Him.

I don't know about you, but I'm glad that when God decides on a gift, we don't have to worry about it being the right size or color. It is tailor-made, specific to our proportions!

Thank You, Lord, for being willing to invite us into
Your realm. Help us to accept the gift
and share it with others willingly.

GOD ALWAYS KEEPS HIS WORD

Now go and call together all the elders of Israel. . . "The elders of Israel will accept your message. Then you and the elders must go to the king of Egypt and tell him, 'The LORD, the God of the Hebrews, has met with us. So please let us take a three-day journey into the wilderness to offer sacrifices to the LORD, our God.' But I know that the king of Egypt will not let you go unless a mighty hand forces him. So I will raise my hand and strike the Egyptians, performing all kinds of miracles among them. Then at last he will let you go. And I will cause the Egyptians to look favorably on you. They will give you gifts when you go so you will not leave empty-handed." (Exodus 3:16[a]-21, NLT)

When God gave Moses instructions for the release of the Israelites from Egyptian bondage, at no point did He say it would be an easy task. Wouldn't it be nice if He had? God doesn't always explain everything to us because He wants us to trust that He always has our best in mind.

I'm sure that when Moses reflected back on His initial conversation with God, he realized that everything happened just as God said it would: Moses engaged the elders in the plan (vv. 16-18); they went to the king who denied the Israelites' petition (vv. 18-19); the king needed to be persuaded (v. 20); and the Israelites didn't leave empty-handed (vv. 21-22).

This is a good reminder for all of us who have received a promise from the Lord. We may have to work to make it happen, and the work may not be easy. We may have to wait an indefinite period before we see the manifestation of the promise. However, if God has said it will happen, then it's a done deal.

You may not be able to trust the word of humans, but you can always trust the Word of God!

WHEN, NOT IF

"Do not fear, for I have redeemed you; I have summoned you by name; you are mine. When you pass through the waters, I will be with you; and when you pass through the rivers, they will not sweep over you. When you walk through the fire, you will not be burned; the flames will not set you ablaze. For I am the LORD your God, the Holy One of Israel, your Savior. . ." (Isaiah 43:1[b]-3, NIV)

My pastor often says we need to insert ourselves into the biblical stories we read. Yes, the events recorded in the Bible occurred way before we were born, so it's easy to think the stories portrayed don't apply to us. However, that's not necessarily true. The Bible is the inspired Word of God recorded for the benefit of all who read it, whenever they read it.

Today's Scripture is one of those we might not want to insert ourselves in because it doesn't sound pleasant. Yet, these situations are necessary for our growth. Notice that Isaiah doesn't record "if" you pass through or "if" you walk through. No, the word "when" is used, meaning it is going to happen.

God doesn't say our challenges will be easy, but they will be doable. And, when we come through to the other side, we'll be better for the experience. It may not seem like it when problems, troubles, and difficulties are occurring, but if you hang in there, before you know it, those problems, troubles, and difficulties will be nothing but a memory of the goodness of God.

Weeping may endure for a night.
Keep the faith it will be alright, right.
Troubles don't last always.
No, no, no, it won't last always.
Troubles Don't Last Always. Timothy Wright. 1991.

WHO'D HAVE THUNK IT?

And the special gift of ministry you received when I laid hands on you and prayed—keep that ablaze! God doesn't want us to be shy with his gifts, but bold and loving and sensible. (2 Timothy 1:6-7, MSG)

We have many hidden talents waiting for us to tap into. God has already put everything inside of us to be successful at what He has called us to do. Let Him stir it up; He already knows what's going to come out.

I remember when God gave me my first novel to write; I told a friend of mine that I was nervous because I had never written dialogue. She reminded me that I had never written a book either; yet, I already had one published. I embraced her words of encouragement, and now, I'm a whiz at putting words in a character's mouth! I've learned that something new is only hard the first time you try it. I didn't know I could write until I wrote. I didn't know I could teach until I taught. I didn't know I could speak in public until I spoke.

A lot of times we put ourselves into a box, but God has called us to use a sledgehammer to knock down the walls surrounding us. Walls can be used for protection or confinement. We need to have healthy boundaries; we don't need walls stifling what the Kingdom needs.

Ask the Lord to give you new territories to conquer. He is so creative, and I know you will be amazed to discover what is inside of you, just waiting to be loosed.

"No one's ever seen or heard anything like this. Never so much as imagined anything quite like it—what God has arranged for those who love him. But you've seen and heard it because God by his spirit has brought it all out into the open before you."
(1 Corinthians 2:9-10, MSG)

WHEN JESUS STANDS UP

But when Christ had offered for all time a single sacrifice for sins, he sat down at the right hand of God, waiting from that time until his enemies should be made a footstool for his feet. (Hebrews 10:12-13, ESV)

But he, full of the Holy Spirit, gazed into heaven and saw the glory of God, and Jesus standing at the right hand of God. And he said, "Behold, I see the heavens opened, and the Son of Man standing at the right hand of God." (Acts 7:55-56, ESV)

Theologians, scholars, and preachers love to debate the Scriptures as to their meaning and purpose. I believe Acts 7:55-56 falls into the category of controversial issues. Some scholars think Stephen's utterances have no significant meaning other than verifying that Jesus had returned to Heaven. Others believe it showed respect for the faith of one of God's chosen.

I think it was a matter of love. No parent can see their child mistreated and not display some emotion. Stephen was stoned for relaying the history of mistrust and pain hurled on our Lord and Savior (Acts 7:1-53). He eloquently and passionately provided this lesson after being accused of blasphemy (Acts 6:8-15). As is often the case, sometimes the truth hurts. "When they [the Synagogue of the Freedmen] heard these things, they were cut to the heart, and they gnashed at him with their teeth" (Acts 7:54). That's when Stephen saw Jesus standing up. God always leans toward us when He sees faith in action.

The nonbelievers threw Stephen out of the city and stoned him. Before he took his last breath, he paraphrased the words Jesus said hanging from the cross: "Lord Jesus, receive my spirit" and "Lord, do not charge them with this sin" (vv. 59-60).

Tests, trials, and tribulations come to increase our faith.
Is your faith worthy of Jesus standing?

NOT AGAIN

Praise the Lord, O my soul. And all that is within me, praise His holy name. Praise the Lord, O my soul. And forget none of His acts of kindness. He forgives all my sins. He heals all my diseases. He saves my life from the grave. He crowns me with loving-kindness and pity. He fills my years with good things and I am made young again like the eagle. . . He has taken our sins from us as far as the east is from the west. The Lord has loving-pity on those who fear Him, as a father has loving-pity on his children. For He knows what we are made of. He remembers that we are dust. (Psalm 103:1-5, 12-14, NLV)

There is a scene in the movie *The Bodyguard,* where Kevin Costner's character has a confrontation in the kitchen with an employee of Whitney Houston's character. The event takes place without any spoken words, until Costner's character says at the end of a successful confrontation, "I don't want to talk about this again."

I believe that God feels the same way when we keep bringing things up to Him that He has forgotten. I would imagine He says, "What! Are you kidding me? Do you want to spend your precious time with me talking about this *again*? You said you'd praise me and never forget the things I do for you, so why are you digging something up that clearly is dead and buried?"

Part of our reluctance to accept God's forgiveness is that we're putting Him on the same level as humans, which is a humongous mistake. People say they forgive you, and then bring the issue up the first time you do or say something they don't like. God isn't like that, and we all should be incredibly grateful that He isn't! When God forgives, He also forgets.

Let's stop harassing God about things that He has forgotten
and move forward in His love and forgiveness.
Your life will be better when you do!

BUSTED!

Then James and John, the sons of Zebedee, came to Him, saying, "Teacher, we want You to do for us whatever we ask." And He said to them, "What do you want Me to do for you?" They said to Him, "Grant us that we may sit, one on Your right hand and the other on Your left, in Your glory." But Jesus said to them, "You do not know what you ask . . . And when the ten heard it, they began to be greatly displeased with James and John. (Mark 10:35-38, 41, NKJV)

One of the reasons I love reading the Bible is the reality of the people whose stories are told, which makes the Bible even more relatable to our situations.

Two brothers who were part of Jesus' inner circle decided to seek positions of power. They boldly asked for what they wanted after assuring themselves that Jesus would give them what they asked. However, they didn't really listen to Jesus' response. He never said He would grant their desire; He simply asked, "What do you want Me to do for you?" knowing what they were going to say before they uttered a word. It's amazing how you can be around a person and still not know a person. They had seen Jesus perform miracle after miracle; why didn't they realize He was already prepared for their question and would use His response as a teachable moment for all the disciples?

Like me giving the car keys to my three-year-old grandson who can't drive or even reach the pedals, James and John asked for something they weren't equipped to handle. They had no idea what they were asking for, so Jesus took the time to explain to them the importance of serving others and sufficiently diffused the anger the other disciples were feeling toward James and John. God doesn't have a problem with our asking for things; He just wants to make sure our motives are pure.

Lord, help us to always search our heart to ensure we're doing, saying, asking for the things that are pleasing to You.

WHAT'S THAT SMELL?

But thanks be to God, who always leads us as captives in Christ's triumphal procession and uses us to spread the aroma of the knowledge of him everywhere. For we are to God the pleasing aroma of Christ among those who are being saved and those who are perishing. To the one we are an aroma that brings death; to the other, an aroma that brings life. And who is equal to such a task? (2 Corinthians 2:14-16, NIV)

Occasionally I ride past a large sewage treatment plant which, as you can imagine, isn't the most pleasant-smelling place; you never have to question the cause of the smell. Even with the windows closed, the odor manages to permeate inside the vehicle. Fortunately, it doesn't last long. On the flip side, there are times someone walks by with such an intoxicating fragrance that you want to run up and ask them what they're wearing because it smells just that good.

Christians are to be that type of fragrance to the world. Unlike the trash plant that can't help the way it smells because of the contents, we can. All we need do is make sure we layer our fragrance to last. We shower in prayer, lotion up with the Word, and spritz on the Eau de Parfum of the Holy Spirit.

We can take over the world
with the overpowering scent of Jesus!

NO COMPARISON

Blessed are you, GOD of Israel, our father from of old and forever. To you, O GOD, belong the greatness and the might, the glory, the victory, the majesty, the splendor; Yes! Everything in heaven, everything on earth; the kingdom all yours! You've raised yourself high over all. Riches and glory come from you, you are ruler over all; You hold strength and power in the palm of your hand to build up and strengthen all. And here we are, O God, our God, giving thanks to you, praising your splendid Name. (1 Chronicles 29:10-13, MSG)

In today's world, with so much access to a steady stream of information, there are a lot of things that try to capture our attention and cause us to lose focus on God and all He does for us. Whenever you're tempted to engage in distraction, remember today's Scripture. As the saying goes, "If that don't ring your bell, your clapper must be broke!"

Then I remember something that fills me with hope. The LORD's
kindness never fails! If he had not been merciful, we would have been
destroyed.
The LORD can always be trusted to show
mercy each morning. Deep in my heart I say,
"The LORD is all I need; I can depend on him!"
(Lamentations 3:21-24, CEV)

BEEN THERE, DONE THAT, WROTE THE BOOK

While they were there, the time came for the baby to be born, and she gave birth to her firstborn, a son. (Luke 2:6-7[a], NIV)

Then Jesus was led by the Spirit into the wilderness to be tempted by the devil. (Matthew 4:1, NIV)

But he was pierced for our transgressions, he was crushed for our iniquities; the punishment that brought us peace was on him, and by his wounds we are healed. (Isaiah 53:5, NIV)

For we do not have a high priest who is unable to empathize with our weaknesses, but we have one who has been tempted in every way, just as we are—yet he did not sin. (Hebrews 4:15, NIV)

"I have come that they may have life and have it to the full." (John 10:10[b], NIV)

Armchair theologians have often debated why Jesus didn't come to Earth fully grown. That isn't anything I ever question because I wouldn't be able to relate to a Savior who couldn't relate to me. If Jesus had not come as a baby, he would not have been able to help me make it through life.

No, I don't debate why Jesus didn't come as an adult. I need someone who can relate to everything I'm going through from birth to death. That's why He was born of a virgin. That's why He willingly died for me. That's why He rose again. And, that's why He's the Savior of the world!

> Living, he loved me; dying, he saved me;
> Buried, he carried my sins far away;
> Rising, he justified freely, for ever:
> One day he's coming—O, glorious day!
> *One Day*. J. Wilbur Chapman (lyrics); Charles H. Marsh (music).
> 1911. Public Domain.

GIFT IT UP

He said to them, "Go into all the world and preach the gospel to all creation. Whoever believes and is baptized will be saved, but whoever does not believe will be condemned." (Mark 16:15-16, NIV)

I remember giving a gift to someone who turned around and allowed their children to destroy it. I had taken the time to find the right gift for their personality and the occasion and even had it professionally wrapped; so, I confess, I was upset.

Later I came to realize that once a gift is released, you no longer have control over it. Some people give things with strings attached as if to say, "If you do this, *then* I'll do that." Or, they want to continually remind you of something they did for you, as if you should genuflect each time you see them. (Actually, we should but only as it pertains to Jesus Christ!) Or, they give something to you but are constantly borrowing it back.

God reminded me that we humans don't always appreciate the Gift He's given us. The gift of Jesus Christ was freely given, but it was by no means free. He gave up a lot so that we may have a better life, not just on earth but also in heaven. One way we show our appreciation for the Gift is to go into the highways and byways and "gossip" the Good News.

Tell them, even if they don't believe you.
Tell them, even if they don't receive you.
Oh, tell them for me, tell them for me.
Please, tell them for me, that I love them.
And I came to let them know.
Tell Them. Andrae Crouch. 1993.

CAN I GET A WITNESS?

Jesus told them, "Go back to John and tell him what you have heard and seen—the blind see, the lame walk, those with leprosy are cured, the deaf hear, the dead are raised to life, and the Good News is being preached to the poor." (Matthew 11:4-5, NLT)

One of my all-time favorite TV shows is *Perry Mason*. It was a well-written television show from the 1950s with fully evolved characters: Perry, Della Street, Paul Drake, and Hamilton Burger. (I always thought that having the name "hamburger," if shortened, was clever.) The main characters were friendly until they were in court. Then, Perry and Hamilton were respectful adversaries.

Usually, at some point during the courtroom scenes, Hamilton would ask a question that Perry would challenge as hearsay. The judge would sustain the objection and Hamilton would sarcastically say, "I'll rephrase." He would then ask the witness, "Do you know for a fact what such and such did on the night in question?" He wanted the witness to share the story as observed firsthand.

If you were on the witness stand, what would you be able to say about Jesus that you know for a fact? Could you tell how He brought you out of darkness, changed your life, or healed your body? Could you tell how He made the crooked places in your life straight, put you on the right path, or put you in your right mind? Could you tell how He willingly took your place on the cross, died on Good Friday, and rose on Resurrection Sunday? The only person who can give firsthand testimony of what God has done in your life is you!

"But you will receive power when the Holy Spirit comes upon you. And you will be my witnesses, telling people about me everywhere—in Jerusalem, throughout Judea, in Samaria, and to the ends of the earth." (Acts 1:8, NLT)

YOU'RE THE ONLY ONE

The angel replied, "The Holy Spirit shall come upon you, and the power of God shall overshadow you; so the baby born to you will be utterly holy—the Son of God." (Luke 1:35, TLB)

There are several words to describe Jesus that can apply to humans. Words such as awesome, great, wonderful, amazing, beautiful, powerful, excellent, and so on. We use them as adjectives to describe how we feel about people, places, and things. However, there is one word that belongs to Jesus Christ alone—Holy.

You are holy, Lord of glory.
Filled with splendor and majesty.
All creation bows before you.
We acknowledge your sovereignty.
It's you, Lord, it's You.
We worship. Worship.
It's You, Lord, it's You.
We praise.
You Are Holy. Mark Harris, Michael W. Smith,
and Carolyn Arends. 2015

STILL

Jesus Christ is the same yesterday, today, and forever. (Hebrews 13:8, ERV)

It is refreshing to have Someone to depend on who is trustworthy and consistent. Because of that, I'm going to praise God . . .

> When there's more month than money. . .
> When nothing seems to be going right. . .
> When the temptation to disown family is strong. . .
> When it feels like every one of the 206 bones in my body hurts. . .
> When I don't think I have a tear left, and smiling is a thing of the past . . .

Still, I will praise God because of who He is and what He means to me.

> So many doors you've opened,
> So many ways you've made,
> So many times you've healed me,
> You've been better than good to me.
> *Lord, You Are Good.* Todd O'Neal Galberth. 2017.

REMEMBER WHEN

And Moses summoned all Israel and said to them: "You have seen all that the LORD did before your eyes in the land of Egypt, to Pharaoh and to all his servants and to all his land, the great trials that your eyes saw, the signs, and those great wonders. But to this day the LORD has not given you a heart to understand or eyes to see or ears to hear. I have led you forty years in the wilderness. Your clothes have not worn out on you, and your sandals have not worn off your feet. You have not eaten bread, and you have not drunk wine or strong drink, that you may know that I am the LORD your God. . . . Therefore keep the words of this covenant and do them, that you may prosper in all that you do." (Deuteronomy 29:2-6, 9, ESV)

Sometimes when you're around someone who has known you for a long time, they'll start a sentence with "Remember when" and repeat an incident from the past. God did the same thing with the children of Israel. He didn't want them to be confused about Who brought them out of Egypt, or how He took care of them during their tenure in the desert.

Today's Scripture is an excellent reminder for us, as well. Sometimes we forget from whence we came. We need to remember so we can share with someone else. They need to know what God can do for them, too.

Great is the LORD, and greatly to be praised, and his greatness is unsearchable. One generation shall commend your works to another and shall declare your mighty acts.
(Psalm 145:3-4, ESV)

ANYWAY

Figs might not grow on the fig trees, and grapes might not grow on the vines. Olives might not grow on the olive trees, and food might not grow in the fields. There might not be any sheep in the pens or cattle in the barns. But I will still be glad in the LORD and rejoice in God my Savior. The Lord GOD gives me my strength. He helps me run fast like a deer. He leads me safely on the mountains. To the music director. On my stringed instruments. (Habakkuk 3:17-19, ERV)

Life happens so fast that we can barely keep up, or so it seems at times. This is when we need an anchor to help us stay grounded. Despite what may be going on, we know that God is in control. So, why not praise Him anyway?

Be not dismayed whate'er betide, God will take care of you!
Beneath His wings of love abide, God will take care of you!
Through days of toil when heart doth fail,
God will take care of you!
When dangers fierce your path assail, God will take care of you!
All you may need He will provide, God will take care of you!
Trust Him, and you will be satisfied, God will take care of you!
Lonely and sad, from friends apart, God will take care of you!
He will give peace to your aching heart,
God will take care of you!
No matter what may be the test, God will take care of you!
Lean, weary one, upon His breast, God will take care of you!
God will take care of you, Through every day, o'er all the way;
He will take care of you; God will take care of you!
Be Not Dismayed.
Lyrics: Civilla Durfee Martin (1866-1948)
Music: Walter Stillman Martin (1862-1935)

HOW'S THE VIEW UP THERE?

Raise your eyes and look from where you are to the north and south and east and west. (Genesis 13:14, NLV)

If you were to see any of my elementary school pictures, you'd notice I was one of the two tallest people in the class. It was irritating to hear the photographer say, "You're so tall, stand in the back." The comment usually resulted in snickers from the other students. There was nothing I could do about my height. It came from my mother, who was almost 6 feet tall, and my father, who was around 6′3″.

There is an advantage to being tall; it offers you a different view of what's around you. Among the noticeable anatomical differences between an ant and a giraffe is the giraffe's ability to see further than almost any other creature. A broader view gives you a better understanding of what's ahead of you.

Regardless of your physical stature, you can have a more magnificent view. All you have to do is ask God to increase your vision.

God, please open our eyes, so we see what You see.
And, then, help us to keep walking toward the vision.

NOW OR NEVER

Now a woman, having a flow of blood for twelve years, who had spent all her livelihood on physicians and could not be healed by any, came from behind and touched the border of His garment. And immediately her flow of blood stopped. And Jesus said, "Who touched Me?" When all denied it, Peter and those with him said, "Master, the multitudes throng and press You, and You say, 'Who touched Me?'" But Jesus said, "Somebody touched Me, for I perceived power going out from Me." Now when the woman saw that she was not hidden, she came trembling; and falling down before Him, she declared to Him in the presence of all the people the reason she had touched Him and how she was healed immediately. And He said to her, "Daughter, be of good cheer; your faith has made you well. Go in peace." (Luke 8:43-48, NKJV)

Have you ever encountered someone who could help you? The help wasn't necessarily monetary; perhaps they knew someone who had the answer to your need. When that happens, we have two choices. We can either: (1) let pride prevent us from seeking help; or (2) take a breath and go for it.

Most of us are familiar with the story of this nameless woman in today's Scripture. I'm sure she never imagined her predicament, subsequent boldness, and demonstration of faith would reverberate down through the ages, but I'm sure glad it does. She shows us what happens when we take a leap of faith. Is there anything in your life requiring a now or never moment?

Reach out and touch the Lord, as He's passing by.
You'll find He's not too busy to hear your heart's cry.
He is passing by this moment, your needs He'll supply.
Reach out and touch the Lord, as He's passing by.
Reach Out and Touch the Lord.
Bill Harmon. 1958, 1986.

A TIME FOR REFLECTION

Remember my suffering and my aimless wandering, the wormwood and poison. My soul continues to remember these things and is so discouraged. The reason I can still find hope is that I keep this one thing in mind: The LORD's mercy. We were not completely wiped out. His compassion is never limited. It is new every morning. His faithfulness is great. My soul can say, "The LORD is my lot in life. That is why I find hope in him." The LORD is good to those who wait for him, to anyone who seeks help from him. (Lamentations 3:19-25, GWT)

As the old year hovers on the brink of extinction, we often take time to reflect on the events of the past year. It would be wonderful if everything happened the way we wanted, but that's not realistic. The year brought pain and sorrow, sunshine and rain, joy and happiness, and somehow it all worked for our good, even if we didn't necessarily enjoy it.

The hope we have is that God is ever-present. We're never alone or abandoned, despite our feelings or circumstances. We have Someone who loves and cares for us, even when it appears no one else does.

As this year closes, let's realize that everything we experienced—the good, the bad, and the ugly—happened to bring us closer to God.

Lord, we thank You for allowing us to live to see this day. We ran the gamut of emotions this past year, but the one that supersedes all is our love for You! Help us to always remember to bless and praise You!

Books by Obieray Rogers

The Heaven on Earth Fiction Trilogy:
A Hug From Daddy
The Wonder of Love
Kiss Yesterday Goodbye

The Men of Standards Fiction Trilogy:
An Unexpected Love
An Unexpected Blessing (December 2018)
An Unexpected Gift (December 2019)

Non-Fiction
Waiting for Boaz: Encouragement for Women Desiring Marriage God's Way
On the Other Side of Yes: Understanding the Power of Agreement
Victory Through Humiliation: Experiencing Triumph After Tragedy

Inspirational
Walking With God: 365 Daily Devotionals
But As For Me: 365 Daily Devotionals

Made in the USA
Columbia, SC
14 December 2018